YO-DUX-806

Asheville-Buncombe
Technical Community College
Learning Resources Center
340 Victoria Rd.
Asheville, NC 28801

GANDHI'S RELIGION

Gandhi's Religion

A Homespun Shawl

J. T. F. Jordens

First published in Great Britain 1998 by
MACMILLAN PRESS LTD
Houndmills, Basingstoke, Hampshire RG21 6XS and London
Companies and representatives throughout the world

A catalogue record for this book is available from the British Library.

ISBN 0–333–72071–7

First published in the United States of America 1998 by
ST. MARTIN'S PRESS, INC.,
Scholarly and Reference Division,
175 Fifth Avenue, New York, N.Y. 10010

ISBN 0–312–21240–2

Library of Congress Cataloging-in-Publication Data
Jordens, J. T. F.
Gandhi's religion : a homespun shawl / J.T.F. Jordens.
p.   cm.
Includes bibliographical references and index.
ISBN 0–312–21240–2 (cloth)
1. Gandhi, Mahatma, 1869–1948—Religion.   2. Gandhi, Mahatma,
1869–1948—Views on Hinduism.   3. Hinduism.   I. Title.
DS481.G3J7184 1997
294.5'092—dc21   97–41964
                                                                          CIP

© J. T. F. Jordens 1998

This book is printed on paper suitable for recycling and made from fully managed and sustained forest sources.

10   9   8   7   6   5   4   3   2
07   06   05   04   03   02   01   00   99

Printed and bound in Great Britain by
Antony Rowe Ltd, Chippenham, Wiltshire

To my grandchildren Ruby, Rosalee, Clare and Joshua,
who were all born during the gestation of this work

Contents

Acknowledgements

First of all I wish to express my thanks to the Australian National University (ANU), which made it possible for me to pursue the research necessary for writing this work. In 1989–90 I was given several months' sabbatical to complete my research in India. I was also given a grant to employ a research assistant to help in my analysis of the *Collected Works of Mahatma Gandhi*. The ANU allowed me to continue my work after my retirement by granting me a Visiting Fellowship for five years. I also thank the staff of the ANU Library for their cheerful and competent assistance over the years.

A number of people have helped me in various ways, and I thank them all. I want to especially thank Dr Michael Comans, whose assistance in my study of the *Collected Works* was extremely valuable. I was fortunate to be able to spend a week at Santa Barbara with Professor Stephen Hay, who has a very special interest in the early years of Mahatma Gandhi. I am grateful for his stimulating conversations, and for the many rare materials he generously passed on to me.

Last, but not least, I owe a very special debt of gratitude to my wife, Ann-Mari. She not only gave me her advice as an historian and stylist, but also typed my manuscript onto disk. She has all my loving thanks for her invaluable support and help.

Introduction

When Gandhi fell under the assassin's bullets, his final words were 'He Ram!' A few months earlier he had told his grand-niece Manu, 'If I die taking God's name with my last breath, it will be a sign that I was what I strove for and claimed to be.' Why did Gandhi need a sign to prove the validity of his claim? Because, although Gandhi was, in Nehru's words, 'a Hindu to the depths of his innermost being', many Hindus, especially the most orthodox, decried him as unorthodox. In fact, the bullets that killed him were fired by a Hindu fanatic.[1]

As early as 1924 Gandhi had stated: 'It has been whispered that by being so much with Mussulman friends, I make myself unfit to know the Hindu mind. The Hindu mind is myself.' It was precisely because his Hinduness was repeatedly doubted that Gandhi again and again proclaimed that he was '*sanatani* Hindu', an 'eternal Hindu', rooted in the ancient tradition:

> I claim to be a sanatani Hindu. People may laugh and say that to call myself a sanatani Hindu when I eat and drink from the hands of Mussulmans and Christians, keep an untouchable girl in my house as my daughter and do not even hesitate to quote the Bible, is nothing short of doing violence to language. But I would still adhere to my claim, for I have faith in me which tells me that a day would come – maybe most probably after I am dead . . . – , when my critics would recognise their error and admit the justness of my claim.[2]

The invocation of Ram on his lips as he breathed his last, was the ultimate sign of the justness of his claim.

This incapacity, or unwillingness, of many contemporary Hindus to understand Gandhi's approach to Hinduism shows, among other things, the very complexity and dynamism of that conception. Gandhi's long, rich life was stacked with activities most people could not accommodate in two lives. His varied and voluminous writings were scattered in scores of different journals and archives, and did not lend themselves to easy analysis and understanding. It was extremely difficult to find all of

1

these writings and then to unravel their sequence and chronology. Many studies of Gandhi consequently tended to omit the careful analysis of the development of his ideas, and tended to make sweeping statements about his religious conceptions. The recent completion of the publication of the *Collected Works of Mahatma Gandhi* was a great boon to the student of Gandhi. It has now become possible, and relatively more easy, to study Gandhi's ideas in a strictly chronological fashion. This study has taken full advantage of that possibility by systematically searching through the ninety volumes in order to discover not only the religious world of the Mahatma, but also its development.

The choice of topics treated has been strongly influenced by the repeated assertion of Gandhi himself that religion was not primarily about theological, mythological, or ritual structures, but about action and ethics.

> There is nothing apart from conduct which can be defined as religion . . . I am convinced that God asks us now, not what we label ourselves but what we are, i.e. what we do. With Him *deed* is everything, belief without deed is nothing. With Him doing is believing . . . I have felt that the Gita teaches that what cannot be followed out in day-to-day practice cannot be called religion.[3]

This powerful stress on action does not mean that Gandhi had no interest in the thought structures which formed the foundation of his religious edifice. The great confusion about religion which he experienced during his first year in South Africa was caused by the fact that he did not have a basic frame of reference into which he could fit the many religious ideas assailing him. He needed to get his ideas clear, and he needed the fundamental principles organised so that he could distinguish the essential from the peripheral.

That attempt at clarification was Gandhi's first serious sustained religious effort, and it took a lot of reading and thinking during his first two years in South Africa. Chapter 2 analyses that process in detail. The practical side of Gandhi's religious striving took off very slowly, and accelerated to a fast pace from the mid-point of his stay in South Africa. Chapter 1 describes this process that totally transformed a callow, naive youth into a religious personality deserving the title 'Mahatma', great soul. When Gandhi said farewell to South Africa for ever he had built up a strong and logical frame of reference about the essence of religion in general, not just of Hinduism. But he had also become a renouncer, an ashram-dweller, a servant of the people, for whom the political fight for freedom was a sacred duty. This political service of the people was also conceived by Gandhi as a method of realising the highest goal of Hindu religion: *moksha*, liberation from the cycle of transmigration. The study of Gandhi's religion during the Indian period 1914–48 presents great difficulties because of the immensity of the materials assembled in the 75 volumes of the *Collected Works*. This forbidding mass of material is compounded by the enormous complexity of the various ways Gandhi's religion expressed itself. Religion was for him not just a vague ideological background and a routine of occasional rituals. Religion was a way of life that penetrated all aspects of his private, public, and political activity. Moreover, his religious conceptions were challenged again and again by the formidable forces of Hindu orthodoxy, who did not accept Gandhi's religious authority. I decided that a chronological development of the totality of all aspects combined over the 35 years would be very difficult to handle and tend to be rather confusing. I decided, therefore, to divide the world of Gandhi's religion into a number of sections, which would each be followed in detail throughout the period.

To begin with, I distinguish two aspects of Gandhi's religion: the first has primarily to do with the ideas about religion and the positions Gandhi took in religious matters. This became Part II, 'Convictions and Attitudes'. In this section I look at Gandhi's basic conceptions about Hinduism as a whole in Chapter 4, and his judgement about the most important ritual, social, and sectarian realities of Hinduism in Chapter 5. Chapter 6 studies the development of Gandhi's basic Advaitic creed, and Chapter 7 looks at his changing understanding of religious authority. The final chapter of this section studies the development of Gandhi's conception of religious pluralism: what the place of Hinduism is in the commonwealth of religions, and how it relates to the universal religion that transcends Hinduism.

In Part III, 'Religion in Action', I focus on the main practical ways in which Gandhi's religion of action expressed itself. Six chapters successively look at the development during the Indian period of the following activities: ashram attendance, prayers and vows, sexual control, fasting, non-violence, and the duty of service. By studying these practices separately and in detail, it was possible to draw important conclusions about both the nature and the development of Gandhi's religion.

From the beginning of my research I decided that my work would be totally grounded in Gandhi's pronouncements. The 90 volumes of the *Collected Works* were carefully studied in order to extract all the materials that related to religion. The footnotes show the extensive use that was made of those materials. All conclusions of importance refer to many sources, and never depend on the single clever quotation. I have allowed Gandhi to speak for himself, and the footnotes often refer to additional texts supporting the same view. I hope that this will help those wanting to do research in some aspect of Gandhi's religion. The first slice of Gandhi's life, infancy and youth, naturally predates his writings. My preamble does not claim any new research findings; it puts together what is known about that period in the matter of religion on the basis of the works of the excellent scholars who researched it.

Preamble:
Infancy and Youth – Carding
the Home-grown Wool

Gandhi himself acknowledged the great importance of the childhood years for the development of the adult: 'the child never learns in after life what it does in its first five years . . . after birth the child imitates the parents and for a considerable number of years entirely depends on them for this growth.'[1]

Mohandas Gandhi was born into a very devout, traditional Hindu family belonging to the Vaishya caste. The daily household worship was strictly adhered to, and the great Hindu celebrations were observed. Moreover, visits to local temples were part of the daily routine of his parents and other members of the large household. There was regular hymn-singing, and during his father's illness Tulsidas' *Ramcharitmanas* was chanted daily. Mohandas' father did not let his heavy State duties interfere with his daily temple-worship, and he took great pleasure in discussing religion with visitors of many faiths. Towards the end of his life, he started the regular reading of the *Bhagavadgita*. His mother, Putlibai, was equally devoted to temple-worship and home ritual. She added to these regular religious duties her frequent fasts for her own self-purification, and the well-being of her family. By stringent vows she committed herself to heavy fasts, which she would not break, even when she had the perfectly good excuse of illness.

Notwithstanding the strong ritual leanings of his parents' devotions, Mohandas very early developed a very negative attitude to temple ritual and idol worship, as he recalled in his autobiography. 'Being born in the Vaishnava faith, I had often to go to the Haveli. But it never appealed to me. I did not like its glitter and pomp. Also I heard rumours of immorality being practised there, and lost all interest in it.'[2]

During adolescence, he read the *Manusmriti*, which did not impress him, but made him 'inclined somewhat towards atheism'.[3] Some devotions in the household, however, made an indelible impression on his young mind; the chanting of bhajans, the reading of Tulsidas' *Ramcharit-manas,* and the fasting vows of his mother. Another religious practice that influenced him was the recitation of the name of Rama, the practice of *Ramanama,* which was recommended to him by his nurse Rambha to cure him of his fear of ghosts and spirits.

Gandhi wrote in his autobiography that one conviction took deep root in him, 'the conviction that morality is the basis of things, and that truth is the substance of all morality'.[4] This statement must be taken with a grain of salt, because it is an interpretation of his early convictions as seen through the mirror of his own life. However, a close look at the life of the family he grew up in makes Gandhi's later judgement eminently plausible. His parents were not only strict Hindus committed to ritual duties. They lived in fact a life of very high moral standard.

First of all, they constituted the very centre of a household that normally consisted of some 20 to 25 people.[5] Service of the large family totally dominated Mohandas' mother's life. But she never neglected her extensive ritual duties, and her private fasts. Joseph Doke, Gandhi's first biographer, recalls that Gandhi told him about his mother 'if there were sickness in the home she would sit up night after night discharging the duties of nurse. If anyone nearby was in need, Brahmin or Shudra, she was the one to render help.'[6] This total service of his mother kindled in Mohandas' heart the desire to serve her: 'there was nothing dearer to my heart than her service'.[7]

Gandhi's father's life was similarly dominated by service. His wife's niece described him as follows:

> He gave up his sleep and his leisure to see to the happiness of the people under his protection. Even though earning more than any of his relatives, he spent almost nothing on himself, and saw that his remaining money went to buy food and clothing for those in the Gandhi clan earning the least; he was constantly looking for ways to help them to get ahead in life.[8]

Besides his service for his extended family, Kaba Gandhi's work as Divan, Chief Minister of the State, was one that was an example of 'public service'. When Kaba Gandhi became ill, Gandhi took up the task of nursing him.

> My parents had surrendered themselves to my love. My father would never ask any of the servants to do anything for him, but he would insist on my doing it. If it was water that he wanted, or a shampoo of

his legs, there was sure to be a call for me. He simply doted on me. It is hard to find a father so loving as he.[9]

Two plays strongly reinforced in Gandhi's young mind the high ideal of service. He remembered their impact in his autobiography. The topic of both plays, *Shravana* and *Harischandra*, was heroic parental devotion to the point of suffering all and sacrificing one's life. Their influence on young Gandhi was so great that even at the time of writing his autobiography, he stated that they were still 'living realities' for him.[10]

Another indication of the religious and moral leanings of Mohandas can be found in his description of the sins of his childhood. A very close school-friend, healthy and fearlessly daring, convinced the slight, unathletic and rather fearful Mohandas that it was the consumption of meat that made the difference. So Mohandas came to the decision that if he wanted to be strong to defeat the British in the fight for freedom, he had to eat meat. He did it in secret with his friend for about a year, and painfully conquered his distaste for meat. The most interesting aspect of this episode is, that the reason Mohandas gave up eating meat was not his belief in non-violence. It was the fact that deceiving his parents became unbearable to him:

> Therefore, I said to myself, though it is essential to eat meat, and also essential to take up food reform in the country, yet deceiving and lying to one's father and mother is worse than not eating meat. In their lifetime, therefore, meat-eating must be out of question. When they are no more and I have found my freedom, I will eat meat openly . . . [11]

During his school years he also became attached to smoking in secret with a relative. In order to be able to get the cigarettes, they stole coppers from the servants' pocket money. But the deception of his parents became too much to bear, which led to a rather infantile and half-hearted attempt at suicide, which brought an end to that episode. Later – he was about fifteen then – he got involved in more serious theft. His brother had run up a debt of about 25 rupees. Gandhi removed a bit of his brother's solid golden armlet, sold it, and cleared the debt. But again, it was the thought of having deceived his father, that led him to confess in writing, asking for forgiveness and punishment. His father, who was ill at the time, did not explode in anger, but wept silently. Gandhi recalled, 'these pearl-drops of love cleansed my heart and washed my sin away'.[12]

Thus Gandhi considered that the most serious sinfulness of the lapses of his youth arose from the fact that they constituted betrayals of his parents' love for him and shortcomings in his love for them. The same was true of his greatest lapse, to which he referred as his 'double shame' which he described at length in his autobiography. At age thirteen he had been married to Kasturbai in what he later called 'a preposterously early marriage.'[13] His father had been ill for a long time, and Mohandas was his principal nurse. That evening he left his father's bedside to join his pregnant wife in their conjugal bed. Minutes later he was called urgently – his father had died. 'The shame to which I have referred in a foregoing chapter, was this shame of my carnal desire even at the critical hour of my father's death, which demanded wakeful service.' The shame was that of not having served well enough, of letting lust prevent total service.[14]

There can be no doubt that his parents exercised enormous influence on young Mohandas. What influenced him most was not their adherence to ritual duties, but their total dedication to the overriding moral imperative of service. From very tender years he strove to return that service to them, and he saw his major moral lapses essentially as betrayals of his duty of parental love and service. It is important also to indicate that in both parents this service was not confined to the large family, but spilled over into the public sphere. His father was the ideal servant of his large family, and also the servant of the State he was Divan of. Service for him ruled in both realms.

There is another important characteristic of the religious atmosphere of the Gandhi household, its spirit of religious tolerance. Whereas Mohandas' father belonged to the famous Vaishnavite sect of the Vallabhacharyas, his mother was an adherent of the Pranami sect, an eclectic, non-idolatrous sect that sought to combine the best of Hinduism and Islam. Moreover, the house was frequently visited by Jain monks, who provided religious counselling, and by Muslim and Zoroastrian friends. Mohan's father enjoyed their company and their conversation on religious subjects. Thus Mohandas grew up in an atmosphere of religious pluralism and tolerance. There was, however, one exception to this attitude: the proselytising methods of the local Christian missionaries, who tended to vilify Hinduism, filled the young boy with a deep revulsion for Christianity.[15]

THE LONDON EXPERIENCE

What, then, was the young Gandhi like when on 4 September 1888 he set sail for England in order to obtain a law degree? Before his death his father had named him as his successor to take charge of the family. So, a great responsibility to succeed rested on his young shoulders. When he was asked why he went over to England, his answer was clear, 'In a word, ambition.' But besides this ambition, another anticipation fired his imagination: 'if I go to England not only shall I become a barrister . . . but I shall be able to see England, the land of philosophers and poets, the very centre of civilization.'[16] His mother had reluctantly given him permission to go, provided he took the triple vow of not touching wine, meat, and women during his absence. This vow was recommended and administered by a Jain monk, who was a family adviser.[17] Although his Rajkot caste fellows did not object to his going overseas, the caste hierarchy in Bombay tried to prevent it because of the gross pollution he would incur. When Gandhi resisted their urging and stuck to his resolve, he was declared an outcaste in a public meeting.[18]

What kind of religious baggage did Gandhi carry on his journey to England? His knowledge of Hinduism was very poor; the only Hindu text he had tried to read was the *Manusmriti*, and he had been repulsed by it. What experience he had of ritual had made him feel very indifferent and negative towards it. The three practices he had appreciated and enjoyed were bhajan singing, the reading of the *Ramcharitmanas*, and some recitation of *Ramanama*. These had several things in common; they were essentially practices belonging to the stream of *bhakti*, loving devotion to God, and they were not part of the rituals of high Hinduism, but popular practices, essentially communal and vernacular. They were not practices he could take with him, and they were left behind as he set foot on the ship.

His most important baggage were the three vows, to which he would remain true, despite all difficulties. They were the spiritual link to his mother. With them he carried that deep sense of moral responsibility of which his parents had been shining examples. At the centre of this moral sense was the duty of service. But in England he was far from all his family and the question of service could scarcely arise in a hectic student life driven by ambition in a foreign land.

His first reaction to London was one of wonder and admiration for that largest city in the world, six times larger even than Bombay. His intoxication made him want to undertake 'the all too impossible task of becoming an English gentleman'. He bought himself the most elegant clothing, and took lessons in dancing, violin, and French. However, all this did not last long for the simple reason that he could not afford it. That was the fundamental reason why he started to reduce his expenses and to look for a simpler life.[19]

In matters religious, Gandhi's London experience consisted of his interaction with three groups of people he came into contact with – the Vegetarians, the Theosophists, and Christian church people. Of the three his acquaintance with Christianity was the least important. A friend, whom Gandhi told of his negative experience with the missionaries in Rajkot, advised Gandhi to read the Bible. Gandhi bought one, but found the Old Testament excruciatingly boring. Nevertheless he plodded through it, 'just for the sake of being able to say that I had read it.' The New Testament interested him much more, and the Sermon on the Mount 'went straight to his heart'.

The verses 'but I say unto you, that ye resist not evil; but whosoever shall smite thee on thy right cheek, turn to him the other. And if any man take away thy coat let him have thy cloak too', delighted me beyond measure and put me in mind of Shamal Bhatt's 'For a bowl of water give me a goodly meal' etc.[20]

Gandhi told his first biographer Doke how he visited various churches in order to listen to famous preachers of the day. He was especially impressed by the popular Reverend Joseph Parker, but it is impossible to determine whether it was the oratory or the ideas that impressed the young man. Many of the ardent vegetarians Gandhi met were also dedicated Christians, but there is no indication that they exerted any pressure on Gandhi to convert to Christianity.[21]

Gandhi's contact with Theosophists was more influential. Two Theosophist brothers told Gandhi that they were reading the translation of the *Bhagavadgita* by Sir Edwin Arnold, and asked him to read it with them in Sanskrit. He confessed that he had never read the text, and that his knowledge of Sanskrit was minimal, but he nevertheless agreed to join them. The impact of the *Gita* was instantaneous, and it would later occupy a commanding position in his spiritual life. The brothers also recommended he read Sir Edwin's *The Light of Asia*, which presented the life and teachings of Gautama Buddha. He devoured it with great interest. The brothers took him along to the Blavatsky Lodge where he met Madame Blavatsky and her newest recruit, Annie Besant. This contact stimulated in him 'the desire to read books on Hinduism, and disabused him of the notion fostered by the missionaries that Hinduism was rife with superstition.'[22] Gandhi was also very impressed by Annie Besant's insistence that 'truth' was at the very centre of her religious conception.[23]

Gandhi recalled that he read Annie Besant's *Why I Became a Theoso-*

phist and Madame Blavatsky's *The Key to Theosophy*. To the young law
student not used to reading theoretical and philosophical writings, much
of these texts must have been rather abstruse, obscure, and forgettable.
However, some of the themes must have been stimulating new revela-
tions to him. Both authors repeatedly attacked the Christian concept of
the personal creator God, preferring the idea of a Universal Spirit which
is the root of Nature, and of which man is just a spark.[24] Probably
Gandhi did not know enough about Hinduism to recognise the similarity
with Advaita Vedanta. Both authors also fully accepted the Hindu
doctrines of transmigration of souls and *karma*, which were in total
opposition to Christian concepts.[25] Moreover, throughout their writings
they approvingly referred to a number of aspects of Hinduism, some of
which Gandhi barely knew about: the richness of old Brahmanical
philosophies, the concept of *atma* and the three bodies that surround it,
the practice of Yoga leading to the trance of *samadhi*, the *mantra*,
rhythmic chanted prayers of the *Veda*, the days and nights of Brahma,
periodic evolutions and involutions of the cosmos.[26] One wonders if
Gandhi registered Madame Blavatsky's conviction that all religions were
based on the same truths, and that ethics were the most important aspect
of religion, not ritual and dogma.[27] No wonder that his meeting with
Theosophists gave Gandhi confidence in the value of Hinduism, and the
desire to learn more about it. However, he could not follow it up
because there was no free time left in his busy life. It also fostered the
idea that various religions had lots of basic concepts in common, and that
the central importance of 'truth' was one of them. However, he did not
join the society, mainly because of 'its secret side – its occultism. It has
never appealed to me.'[28]

But for Gandhi the most important encounter during the London years
was that with the Vegetarians. After rather miserable and unsuccessful
attempts to satisfy his hunger by the non-meat foodstuffs that came on
the table, Gandhi discovered a vegetarian restaurant. This satisfactorily
solved his dietary difficulties. While he was there he also bought a
pamphlet for sale in the restaurant, Henry Salt's *A Plea for Vegetarianism*. The booklet impressed him greatly. Thus far he had been a vegetarian because of his solemn vow, now he became a vegetarian by choice,
by conviction, convinced as he was by an Englishman's plea for kindness
to animals. 'I was thus like a convert to a new religion,' he reminisced
later.[29] But it was only afterwards, during his final year in London, that
his vegetarian ideals brought him into close contact with some leading
eccentric, idealistic thinkers of that period.

He started reading the *Vegetarian*, organ of the London Vegetarian

Society, became a member of the Society, and in September 1890 he was elected to the Executive Committee. In his contact with the leading members of the Society and in his perusal of the *Vegetarian,* the young student came under the influence of some of the finest ethical idealists of London. Stephen Hay has written a masterful analysis of the ideology of the *Vegetarian* and of the leading vegetarians Gandhi had close contact with. The following paragraphs simply present the most important aspects of that exposé as they relate to Gandhi's religious development.[30]

Arnold F. Hills, founder and owner of the *Vegetarian,* was chairman of the Executive Committee during Gandhi's tenure. He was an enthusiastic missionary for a vegetarian ideal which encompassed a whole way of life: simple living, sexual purity, harmony between workers and employers, universal love, and a high ideal of truth. In his debate with Dr Allinson, who advocated artificial birth control, he supported self-control. Josiah Oldfield, who was an employee of Hills, became Gandhi's closest friend during his last year in London. In these final months, after he had finished his exams, the young man actually shared rooms with Oldfield, and spent much time with him in the advocacy of the ideals of vegetarianism. Oldfield believed in the existence of a Universal Law, of which all transgressions carry an inevitable punishment, and he was a lover of Truth above all. He had an ideal political vision based on the highest ethics:

> But when the inspiration of the diviner love has burnt into the national life – once the laws of men are made harmonious with the laws of God – then the new Jerusalem, perfect in its political purity, lovely in its moral strength, will descend as a bride adorned for her husband. There will be no bitterness or division then. . . . This is the last chord of Christian civilization. It begins with the individual and ends with the Commonweal.[31]

Although most of the writers for the *Vegetarian* were ardent Christians, none called for conversions; instead they insisted that the main goal was a constant progress towards moral and spiritual perfection.

Gandhi became aware of Henry Salt's works, who with his friend, Edward Carpenter, joined the Fellowship of the New Life. They lived a simple life in a rural setting with a humane diet, rational dress and manual labour. Gandhi admired them both and he probably met Carpenter in the weekly discussion teas at a vegetarian restaurant. The Humanitarian League they belonged to had goals very similar to those of Hills and Oldfield.

The Humanitarian League has been established in the belief that the promulgation of a high and positive system of morality in the conduct of life, in all its aspects, is one of the greatest needs of the time. It will assert, as the basis of that system, an intelligent and consistent principle of Humaneness, viz.: that it is iniquitous to inflict suffering directly or indirectly, on any sentient being, except when self-defence or absolute necessity can be pleaded.[32]

There was a strong convergence of ideas and ideals of those personalities who surrounded Gandhi during those decisive years in London. They were all enthusiastic idealists. Their ideals were of personal moral and spiritual perfection to be achieved by a life of simplicity, purity, truthfulness, and love of all humanity. Those who were fervent Christians were not interested in conversion, but only in the promotion of their ethical ideas for the well-being of all society. They were idealists who kept their feet firmly on the ground, and they did their best to put into practice what they preached.

The young man Gandhi who boarded his ship to India in June 1891 was very different from the raw-recruit student who arrived in England three years earlier. His superficial contact with Christians and his relations with Theosophists had two main effects. Whereas on arrival in London his knowledge and attachment to Hinduism had been very weak, now he knew more of Hinduism through his readings, especially of the *Bhagavadgita,* and he desired to increase that knowledge, because he thought much more positively of his native religion now. Secondly, his contact with Christians and Theosophists had sown in his mind the idea that various religions had very fundamental things in common.

When he arrived in London, he had been mainly driven by ambition, by the desire to go back to India as a 'civilised Englishman', and to earn position and riches on the basis of being a London-trained barrister. His contact with leading vegetarians, the reading of their writings and contemplation of their way of life, had presented him with a different ideal of life than that of ambition and accumulation of riches. Both the Christians and the non-Christians among them were inspired by an ideal of moral and spiritual perfection to be achieved by a life of simplicity, purity, truthfulness, and love of all humanity. One wonders if Gandhi ever pondered over the fact that his own parents were also inspired by those ideals. That was what he had most admired in them, much more than their devoted compliance with the ritual duties of Hinduism.

INTERREGNUM IN INDIA

The young barrister who arrived back in Bombay in July 1891 was full of ambition and high hopes, but he was in for some very rude shocks and disappointments. On arrival he was told that his mother had died recently. His grief was deep, but controlled. In accordance with her deathbed wish, he went through a purification ceremony at Nasik, which satisfied at least a section of his caste. His attempts at earning a living as a barrister were thwarted again and again. He soon left Rajkot because his ignorance of Indian law prevented him from getting any briefs. He moved to Bombay to work and study Indian law. At the hearing of his very first case he was paralysed by shyness, and unable to conduct a very simple interrogation. He then applied for a teaching post, but was rejected because he had no degree. He moved back to Rajkot, and found that he could manage to make a living by drafting applications and memorials. He tried to intercede on behalf of his brother with the Political Agent, but was rudely thrown out. His future as a barrister in the Princely State was as bleak as could be. At that stage he received an offer from Dada Abdulla and Co. to work for one year on a law suit in which they were engaged in South Africa. Gandhi, with all his ambitious hopes shattered, accepted readily. In April 1893 he sailed to South Africa. As for his religious development during these twenty months in India, Gandhi was so busy trying to fit into the barrister mode and to make a living, that religion was very much in the background. But immediately after his arrival in Bombay he had met a man who would have a profound influence on his religious development, Raj Chandra Mehta, mostly known as Raychand. Gandhi declared in 1928 in a speech on the centenary of the birth of Tolstoy that 'I would say that three men have had a very great influence on my life. Among them I give the first place to the poet Rajchandra, the second to Tolstoy, and the third to Ruskin.'[33]

Raychand was about Gandhi's age, a Kathiawari like him, and the son of a Vaishnava father and a Jain mother. He was a successful jeweller, and an excellent religious poet. Gandhi was enormously impressed from their very first meeting. He came to know him better during these two years, as he remained in close contact with him, and his admiration for him as a religious person of the highest order grew with the years. Raychand lived very simply, and was always in serene control of himself. He combined in his life high spirituality with an acute and successful business sense, and a total non-attachment to the things of this world. He was a believing Jain, but he had read many Hindu sacred books and did not despise other religions. Never before had Gandhi met an Indian of high religious quality, the only person in his whole life who somewhat approximated that impossible ideal of a guru he sometimes dreamt about. He was the only person he ever met who actually directed his life towards the acquisition of *moksha*, an ideal that for practically all Hindus was far too distant and speculative to become an actual goal.[34]

Part I
South Africa

1

The Making of the Mahatma

Gandhi spent twenty years in South Africa. He arrived there as a young man who had miserably failed in his attempts to be a barrister, and whose religious baggage was negligible: he knew very little about religion, which had practically no place in his life. When he left for India twenty years later he was a man of great political stature and fame, renowned for his deep religiosity. He was, however, not like most politicians: he had forged a union of his highest political aspirations and his deepest religious endeavours. Basically two great transformations took place in Gandhi as a man of religion. First, he learnt a great deal by study and reflection, and constructed for himself a firm theoretical framework about the essence of religion. Secondly, he transformed his basically secular life, by gradually infusing all aspects of it, private, familial, and public, with religion; later on this would earn him the title of Mahatma. Although the former of these processes chronologically came first, the latter was by far the most important, and also the most creatively original. That is why we decided to deal first with the making of the Mahatma.

In order to anticipate the magnitude of this transformation, it is helpful to contrast the Gandhi of the 1890s with the Mahatma who left South Africa in 1914. The early Gandhi dressed in a smart suit and tie, like an English barrister, lived in an upper-class house in a good suburb, and earned a very good living as a barrister employing up to four clerks. He had become the leader of the fight of the rich Indian merchants for their rights, threatened by new government regulations. These rich merchants constituted only about 6 per cent of the local Indian population. The other Indians were mostly indentured poor labourers; Gandhi was not involved with their lives. The Gandhi we encounter in 1914 was very different. He wore the simple dress of the Indian labourers, loincloth and kurta. This symbolised his new way of life. He had given up his law practice, and he had no longer a residence of his own, but had become an ashram-dweller. He had no personal assets any more and he had become the passionate representative of the poorest in their great Satyagraha struggle for human rights.

THE FIRST TEN YEARS:
TENTATIVE BEGINNINGS (1894-1904)

When Gandhi arrived in Pretoria in June 1893, he was warmly welcomed by Albert Weir Baker, attorney for the firm which was representing Gandhi's employers. Gandhi had just experienced two years of utter frustration in India, and during his journey from Durban to Pretoria, he had some dreadful encounters. He was bodily thrown out of the first-class train compartment, for which he had a ticket, and spent a long, cold night in the dark waiting room of Maritzburg. Next day on the stage-coach he was segregated and beaten, and that evening he was refused a room in a Johannesburg hotel. He felt like returning straight away to India. The warm reception by Baker and his friends was the nicest thing that had happened to him for a long time.

They were all fervent Evangelical Christians, and also exceptionally nice and friendly people,who desperately wanted to convert Gandhi to Christianity. This brought Gandhi into serious doubts and uncertainties. It led him to seek advice and do some serious reading. Within a year he cleared his doubts, and laid the theoretical foundation of his concept of religion. This process of doubt, study, and clarification will be considered in the second chapter.

Once Gandhi had settled that matter, and shown his legal competence, he took a leading role in the political endeavours of the merchant class. He now really settled down. He earned a very good living, and lived like an Englishman of the same social status. He admitted that much of that was 'solely for the sake of prestige'. His time was fully taken up by his legal and political work for the Indian merchant community. At the end of 1896 he brought out his wife Kasturbai and their two sons, and made them fit into his upper-class style of life.

The first changes in his daily life were changes towards simplification. He started washing his own clothes and taught Kasturbai that art because the washerman cost too much and proved unreliable. Gandhi also started cutting his own hair, with initially rather ludicrous effect. He decided to do this because he had been shown the door by a white barber. It is quite clear from Gandhi's own explanations that these first steps to simplification were not prompted by religious motives. He did later see in them the seeds of what was to become 'his passion for self-help and simplicity'. One cannot but remember here the important part that those two played in the spirituality of the Vegetarian Movement leaders he knew in London. But at this stage, his efforts were not religious, but mainly driven by a desire for economy and a resentment of racial discrimination.[1]

Around this time the idea of service started to interest him. He traced the actual beginning of it to the time when he took in a leper who came to the door, and nursed him. After that experience, he offered his daily services to a local small hospital. During his visit to India in 1896 to get his wife and children, he liberally gave his service to the State when there was a fear that the Bombay plague may threaten Rajkot. During that India visit he also nursed his brother-in-law until he died. This must have strongly reminded him of the time when he nursed his dying father.[2] Although his offer to organize an ambulance corps during the Boer War during the first two months of 1900 was primarily inspired by his sense of duty as a British subject, it involved him deeply in service and nursing. Gandhi saw this service as 'extra' service, which was done over and above one's normal duties. There is no evidence that he conceived his whole life as being a service at this stage.[3]

The idea of service led to his first public act of renunciation. On his departure for India at the end of 1901, at a farewell meeting at which he was presented with costly gifts in silver, gold, and diamonds (they included a gold necklace for Kasturbai worth some fifty guineas, a substantial sum at that time) Gandhi decided that he could not accept the gifts for two reasons. First, they were given to him for his service to the Indian community, and such a service should be given freely. Secondly, he felt that as he was simplifying his life, there was no place for such costly and useless ornaments in his home. He decided to put the gifts in a trust fund to be used for the community. He found it easy to get an agreement from his young children, but Kasturbai disagreed vehemently, as she felt that the funds would constitute some insurance for possible future family disasters. But Gandhi insisted, and, he wrote in his autobiography, 'I somehow succeeded in extorting a consent from her.'[4]

Service and simplicity, then, were the two ideas that started to influence Gandhi's way of life before he returned to India at the end of 1901. But the influence was quite mild. 'Basically,' wrote Pyarelal, 'he had not changed much'; he explained:

As yet a hearty eater, with a keen zest for sensual savours, he was eager to suck out all the marrow of life. Pretty much a man of the world, he was deeply attached to his children and his family to whom he wished to provide all the creature comforts and security for the future like any average householder. Financially, he was well off judged even by current standards of success at the Bar in South Africa. He thought he could very well settle down to a life of peace and domestic bliss combined with distinguished public service.[5]

Gandhi's stay in India from October 1901 to November 1902 was a mere interlude in his overall religious development. The seven years of frustrating political work in South Africa had borne little fruit, and back in India he set himself to build a new life in the public arena. First he wanted to learn about the Indian National Congress, and attended the 1901 Calcutta session. After that he did a tour of India by train to get to know the condition of his country. He travelled third class, experiencing directly the misery of the lower classes. The temples he visited disgusted him with their filth and their venality, and the ritual killings of goats at the Kali temple in Calcutta was 'a sight he had never forgotten'. After a successful trial as a lawyer in Rajkot, he went to Bombay, where his legal work soon picked up. But then came the SOS call from the Indian community in South Africa, a call he had promised to heed. So he promptly sailed back without his family.[6]

The two years 1903 and 1904 Gandhi spent in Africa without his family, turned out to be pivotal in the re-direction of his religious endeavour. This time he settled in Johannesburg in a simple single room next to his office, and he enthusiastically resumed his political and legal work. Being without his family, he had more leisure, and started spending a lot of time with local Theosophists. They looked upon him as a source for a better understanding of Hinduism. Gandhi realised his ignorance, and read Vivekananda's *Rajayoga*, and M. N. Dvivedi's book of the same title. More importantly, he started on a serious study of the *Bhagavadgita*. The idea of *aparigraha* (non-possession) and renunciation greatly impressed him, and as a consequence he allowed a life insurance, taken out two years earlier, to lapse.[7]

He now started to support vegetarianism in a tangible way: he financially assisted two short-lived vegetarian restaurants, losing a lot of money. *Return to Nature*, a book dealing with earth treatment, influenced him, and he moved away from prescribed medicines. Vegetarianism and simplicity started to move hand in hand in his life, as they had in the life of the leading vegetarians of London. The eruption of the plague in Johannesburg in early 1904 gave him another chance for service. Thus Gandhi's life was beginning to be influenced by religious aspirations. But, when Kasturbai and the children arrived in South Africa in early 1905, Gandhi was still a long distance away from deserving the title of Mahatma: he had only commenced the ascent.

A NEW WAY OF LIFE

In his second decade in South Africa the dramatic, total change in Gandhi's way of life occurred. There seem to have been four new circumstances which were absent in the first decade, which were, not directly and purposefully fabricated by Gandhi, but became instrumental in the acceleration of his religious efforts. As we will see, these changes were not peripheral or merely accidental; they constituted structural changes affecting his whole way of life.

The first two circumstances were connected in their effect. In 1904 Gandhi took charge of the publication of the weekly *Indian Opinion*. This was a major change that became permanent: from now on he would always produce a periodical most of which he wrote himself. His writing never was mere musing, information gathering, or diversion, but was always an integral part of his action; it was instruction, explanation, exhortation. This constant writing about his activities forced him to think regularly and carefully. Previously his life was so stacked with political, professional and family preoccupations, that there was not much time for deep analysis. His regular writing forced him into a new frame of mind of deeper thinking, and he was very much aware of it as he recalled in his autobiography.[8]

This 'thoughtfulness' was intensified by another new element that entered his life in 1908: the jail experience, which also would become a regular part of his life. Gandhi had four periods in jail between 1908 and 1914. During these periods he always read voraciously and reconsidered his life, his actions and his aims. It is no wonder that we find the change in Gandhi's religious endeavours accelerated during this period.

The third changed circumstance was in the area of political action. In the earlier period Gandhi's political concerns were those of the rich merchants he represented, whom he defended against the South African political forces. Swan has conclusively shown that he had very little awareness of, and no active concern for, the condition of the working class and indentured Indian community.[9] During the last ten years his concern widened and increasingly he took up the cause of the great majority of poor Indians and identified himself with them. Whereas during the first decade he had been primarily the lawyer who devoted some time to political work, in the second, his political work grew whereas the legal work shrank. This development ran parallel with the gradual change in the ideology of his movement, by which its religious aspect took on greater importance.

A last important change was that Gandhi abandoned his hold on

privacy, family intimacy, and attachment to his own house, and became
an ashram-dweller – living a communal life without a special place
reserved for himself and his immediate family. This was a slow process
of disentanglement, completed by 1912, when he not only lived at
Tolstoy Farm, but also renounced any proprietary rights by making it
into a Trust. This change too would remain a permanent feature of
Gandhi's life.

From the ethico-religious point of view, this period saw a systematic
growth in three closely related areas. The first is the area of renunciation: Gandhi renounced sex and divested himself gradually of all personal possessions. The second area is his concern for service, for public
service. Here we notice the growth of the idea that all his energy should
be directed towards freely given service of the community, which was
for him the road to total religious realisation. The third action-idea that
grew in importance in his programme and actions was that of 'soul
power'. These three were intimately related and would remain dominant
features of the Mahatma during the rest of his life.

RENUNCIATION OF SEX

The profession of the vow of total sexual abstinence in 1906 was his
very first radical step on the road to renunciation. He described his
reasons in detail in his autobiography, written more than twenty years
later. He acknowledged that he 'had not realised then how indispensable
it [brahmacharya] was for self-realisation.'[10] He was not at that time
aware of its mystic power, nor of its central function in the birth of
spiritual man. He took the decision to renounce sex during the long
marches in the Zulu Rebellion. The decision seems to have been primarily a practical one: if he wanted to continue and to expand his life of
public service, this would be made very difficult if he 'were engaged in
the pleasures of family life and in the propagation and rearing of children'.[11] Gandhi had lived without his family for over two years in
1903–4. During that time he had steady contact with Theosophist friends,
and looked after the victims of the plague. The return to the state of
pater familias on the arrival of Kasturbai, in a large house in Johannesburg, changed his life considerably. During the long marches of the Zulu
Rebellion his reflections made him conclude that his role as family head
had to be drastically reduced if he wanted to devote himself more to
public service. That meant no more children, and a less demanding
intimate family life.[12]

This pragmatic approach towards his vow of chastity, presented in his autobiography, is confirmed by contemporary evidence. In his Lectures on Hinduism of 1905, Gandhi did not even mention *brahmacharya*. In his translation and paraphrase of Salter's *Ethical Religion*, he only touched upon sexual mores by mentioning that profligacy is against morality. And after he established the Phoenix Settlement, Gandhi wanted his co-workers to settle down there and he encouraged them to get married. None of this indicates a negative attitude to marital cohabitation as being an evil or a drawback for man's spiritual well-being.[13]

But this had drastically changed by 1913, when he serialised 'health chapters' in *Indian Opinion*. The ninth chapter was entitled 'the secret chapter', and dealt exclusively with sexual abstinence. Right at the beginning Gandhi stated that among the many things that promote health, sexual abstinence was the most important; in fact, this chapter was the longest in the series. It is here that Gandhi presented for the first time his theory of the necessity of chastity not only for good health, but also for spiritual growth.[14]

He made it clear that *brahmacharya* did not only mean the abstinence from the sexual act, but also the eradication from the mind of the very thought of sex. Those who needed marriage should have intercourse only when they wished to produce a child. In order to eliminate temptation, they should avoid being alone together and sleep in separate rooms.[15]

What reason did he give for this totally negative attitude to sex? The human being has a store of *virya*, generative fluid, which is a 'secret power' bestowed by nature, and the main source of physical and mental well-being. This store is finite and all sexual activity diminishes it, and gradually leads to a decline in body and mind, and in old age to a total loss of intelligence. 'For a grain of pleasure we lose a maund of vitality.' Those who guard that treasure by strict chastity have incredible strength, 'the physical, mental and moral strength of one who has been able to observe unbroken brahmacharya must be seen to be believed; it cannot be described'.[16]

If chastity was the source of enormous physical and mental power, its violation was viewed as the cause of much evil.

In this world the violation of brahmacharya is the root cause and only source of evils such as a passion for pleasure, envy, ostentation, hypocrisy, anger, impatience and violent hatred. If one's mind is not under one's control . . . indulging oneself once every day or even more, what other crimes would one not commit, knowingly or unknowingly? What unforgivable sins would one stop short of?[17]

This is an hysterical indictment of all sexual activity, even within the bounds of marriage, as a prime cause of all kinds of evil.

What were the sources of this new strong trend of thought in Gandhi? The key idea around which all else revolved, was the conception of the finite treasure of generative fluid as a source of spiritual power which is squandered by every kind of sexual activity. This idea comes straight from the classical Hindu heritage, of which there is no handbook more authoritative than Patanjali's *Yoga Sutras*. Yoga Sutra II, 37 translates as follows, 'From the establishment of *brahmacharya* results the acquisition of power'. The word translated here as 'power' is *virya*, exactly the word Gandhi used in his Gujarati version, which variously means manhood, heroism, power, and semen.

We can accurately date the time when Gandhi came first into contact with these ideas. It was in 1903. At the end of 1902 he had come back from South Africa by himself, and in 1903 he became closely involved with local Theosophists in their study of Hinduism. That is when he read and studied the *Yoga Sutras,* and two commentaries on it by M. N. Dvivedi and Swami Vivekananda.[18] Vivekananda's commentary on Yoga Sutra II, 37 is as follows:

The chaste brain has tremendous energy and gigantic will power. Without chastity there can be no spiritual strength. Continence gives wonderful control over mankind. The spiritual leaders of men have been very continent, and this is what gave them the power.[19]

Elsewhere Vivekananda expounded more on that idea in connection with the tantric physiology of the chakras:

He [the Yogi] tries to take up all his sexual energy and convert it into Ojas [spiritual power]. It is only the chaste man or woman who can make the Ojas rise and store it in the brain; that is why chastity has always been considered the highest virtue. A man feels that if he is unchaste, spirituality goes away, he loses mental vigor and moral stamina.[20]

Vivekananda explained and reinforced the doctrine of the *Yoga Sutras* about the way chastity preserved and enhanced spiritual power. That certainly was part of Gandhi's thought as it appeared in his article on 'health'. We can safely assume that this idea came to Gandhi from the *Yoga Sutras,* and from the commentaries he read. However, there is an additional dominant theme that runs through Gandhi's 1913 article, namely his totally negative view of sex as the source of all kinds of evil. So far I have not succeeded in discovering a particular source of it in Gandhi's known reading in that period. We cannot detect the growth of it in his writings; it appears quite suddenly in his chapter in health. An indication that it was an idea that preoccupied him is found in Millie Polak's book. Often Gandhi discussed marriage and chastity, and Mrs Polak recollected that after such a discussion, Gandhi asked her:

Then, what are you quarreling with me about, and she answered 'Only that you are still making me feel that you think it to be a higher condition of life to be celibate than to be a parent, and I say that the condition may a difference of kind and not one of degree'. This question of 'to be or not to be' a parent was one frequently discussed. Mr Gandhi was reaching the point where he began to think that it would be better for the world, and probably for God, if mankind ceased to reproduce itself. There came a time when I felt if one were going to have a child it would seem as though it were 'conceived in sin and carried in wickedness'.[21]

Mrs Polack's suspicion was confirmed in the comment Gandhi wrote to Kashi Gandhi, on the birth of a daughter:

If I say that it is good, it would be a lie. If I express sorrow, it would be violence. According to my present ideas, I should remain indifferent . . . Meanwhile, I would only say and wish that you learn to control your senses in the right manner.[22]

In his *Hind Svaraj* he came back to the theme that chastity is necessary for firmness of mind, and that sexual indulgence caused loss of stamina and cowardice. He reiterated that sexual passion between married partners was 'prohibited animal indulgence, except for perpetuating the race'.[23]

RENUNCIATION OF PROPERTY

The second limb of Gandhi's programme of renunciation was non-possession, *aparigraha*. This idea also features in Patanjali's *Yoga Sutras*, but Gandhi clearly remembered when writing his autobiography, that it was the reading of the *Gita* with his Theosophist friends in 1903 that aroused his interest and enthusiasm for non-possession.[24] His first action in that direction was to cancel a life insurance policy which he had taken out a couple of years earlier, 'I had become convinced that God, who created my wife and children as well as myself, would take care of them.'[25]

Whereas in the case of chastity, Gandhi took an early radical decision for full implementation, followed by many years of thought for coming to a theoretical framework, in the case of non-possession the implementation was slow and gradual. At the beginning of 1905, when Kasturbai returned to South Africa, the style of living of the Gandhi household continued to be in accordance with Gandhi's status of prominent barrister, but he organised his own and his family's life along simpler lines. His reading of Ruskin's *Unto this Last* had impressed Gandhi with the value of manual labour, and thus helped to bring about his decision to establish the Phoenix Settlement from where *Indian Opinion* would be printed and published. Everyone would work on the farm and attend to the work for the press, and draw the same wage of three pounds. Accommodation was primitive, but Gandhi did not stay long as there was too much work for him in Johannesburg.[26]

Gandhi was trying to live as simply in Johannesburg as he would at the Phoenix Settlement. The family ground its own wheat early morning, made its own bread, and did its own cleaning and washing. Gandhi walked to and from work, a trip of one and a half hours. The frugal dinner at night was followed by religious reading and discussion. But at this time his law business was still turning over about three hundred pounds per month. When in mid-1906 he organised the Ambulance Corps in the Zulu Rebellion, he took his family to the Phoenix Settlement. On his return from the war, during which he took his vow of chastity, he left them there, and moved himself into a small house in a distant suburb of Johannesburg. It had only a minimum of furniture, bare floor boards, and a few blinds for privacy. He had no servants, and the Polaks shared the housework with him. He always walked the six miles home, even after an exhausting 15-hour workday.[27]

In an important letter to his brother Lakshmidas in April 1907, Gandhi tried to articulate for the first time the spiritual dimension of his progressive renunciation of possessions. Lakshmidas had written an angry letter to his younger brother in which he had demanded money, and strongly berated him for not properly fulfilling his family duties, a serious accusation indeed. Gandhi tackled the problem head on right at the beginning of this letter:

I am afraid our outlooks differ widely and I see no possibility, for the present, of their being reconciled. You seek peace and happiness through money. I don't depend on money for my peace, and for the moment at any rate my mind is quite calm and able to stand any amount of suffering.[28]

He accused his elder brother of greed, and told him that he had no money to send because all he earned was used first for the minimal needs of his family, and the rest 'for the benefit of the people'. Although he still had substantial income, he did not consider it as his own; 'I am not the master of my earnings since I have dedicated my all to the people. I do not suffer from the illusion that it is I who earn; I simply believe that God gives me the money for making good use of it.'[29] He acknowledged his duty to his elder brother, but he asserted that 'those who are more dependent on me have a greater claim', and recognised that 'family means something more than close blood relations . . . my family comprises all living beings'. He continued, 'I revere you as you are my elder brother. Our religion bids us treat our elders with veneration. I implicitly believe that injunction. But I have greater regard for truth. This too is taught by our religion.' This idea of the supremacy of truth will later assume the transcendence of divine reality.[30]

In early 1908 Gandhi did his first stint in jail. From then on most of his time would be occupied by the Satyagraha struggle and stretches in jail. When he stopped his legal practice in 1910, it was not a sudden decision, but rather the acknowledgement of the fact that recent years he had been so busy with his public work that he had practically no time for the law. But the renunciation of his profession was also the putting into practice of certain moral principles he had been developing. As we have seen, he held that work for the public good excluded personal earnings, but now he developed this idea even further. He expressed it most forcefully in his *Hind Svaraj* written on board ship returning from his visit to England in 1909.

Chapter 10 of *Hind Svaraj* treated the condition of India specifically as far as lawyers were concerned. At the beginning Gandhi put forward his thesis, 'my firm opinion is that the lawyers have enslaved India, have accentuated Hindu-Mahomedan dissensions and have confirmed English authority'. Although some lawyers had done some good, 'the profession teaches immorality', and the men who take it up do so 'not in order to help others . . . , but to enrich themselves'. He ended up by declaring, 'If pleaders were to abandon their profession, and consider it as degrading as prostitution, English rule would break up in a day.' Right at the end of the book, Gandhi made abundantly clear what a lawyer who really loved his country and wanted to dedicate himself to its freedom should do:

> If a lawyer, he will give up his profession and take up a handloom . . . He will devote his knowledge to enlightening both his people and the English . . . He will . . . give up the courts, and from his experience induce the people to do likewise . . . He will refuse to be a judge, as he will give up his profession.[31]

Shortly afterwards, in 1910, he terminated his practice. In September 1912, he gave away all he had, and made a Trust of the Phoenix Settlement. Thus he had divested himself completely of his professional income and all his possessions; his *aparigraha* ideal had been realised.[32]

THE ASHRAM-DWELLER

Another aspect of Gandhi's breaking his attachment to personal possessions was his becoming an ashram-dweller. This started with the communal living experiment of the Phoenix Settlement in 1904. The primary reason for this initiative was that *Indian Opinion* was running at a great loss and could no longer be financially sustained by Gandhi: something drastic needed to be done. The idea of a communal farm did have relation to Gandhi's reading of Ruskin's *Unto this Last*, which revealed to him that 'a lawyer's work had the same value as a barber's, and that a life of labour, the tilling of the soil, is the life worth living'.[33] These ideas were strengthened by Gandhi's visit to his cousins in Natal. Besides their store, they had an acre of fruit trees; their hired labour did a poor job, and Gandhi thought, 'Why could they not labour themselves and do it well?' His idea was also influenced by a successful rural commune, running a newspaper, that already existed at Phoenix. The decision was taken to establish a farm, where *Indian Opinion* would be produced by a group of people, who would be happy to receive the same meagre wage for whatever work they did, and till the soil for subsistence.[34]

The obvious conclusion is that the establishment of the Phoenix Settlement was not primarily inspired by religious motives. This is confirmed by the fact that Gandhi did not stay at the settlement because of his business and public commitments. It was not until two years after its inception, in 1906, that he sent his own family to Phoenix, at the time of the Zulu Rebellion. Another indication is that Gandhi encouraged his friends to get married before settling at Phoenix.[35] The main inspiration of the Phoenix Settlement was Gandhi's desire for a simple life free from the complications of western civilization, a life of frugality that would set one free for service. There was a common religious service for Hindus and Christians on Sundays, but one could not say that religion was central to the settlement. Prabhudas Gandhi remembered that when Kasturbai settled at the farm, Gandhi spend a few days there. 'During his stay there was a meeting at their house every evening. My mother would sing at those meetings. This was the beginning of what later became the daily prayer meetings.'[36] Looking back on it in 1930, Gandhi thought that 'it had a religious basis, but the visible object was purity of body and mind as well as economic equality . . . I did not then consider *brahmacharya* to be essential'.[37] Prabhudas recalled how in the first years of settling down in Phoenix they still ate well and that Gandhi 'relished good food'. It was only in later years that the movement towards austerity started.[38]

In the middle of 1910 the passive resisters who courted jail could not look after their families. Their upkeep was maintained by a system of monthly cash allowances, but this became an impossible financial burden to the movement. A solution had to be found. Gandhi's friend Kallenbach purchased a large farm and the satyagrahi families settled there; it was called Tolstoy Farm. Basic buildings were erected, men's quarters and women's quarters. All had to work in the garden, the kitchen, or the small sandal and carpentry industries. A school was arranged for the children. Food and clothing were basic and simple. The new initiative, like the Phoenix Settlement, originated from urgent financial constraints, and the need to care for the satyagrahi's families. Gandhi formulated it differently in his History written much later, he called it 'an ashram where the satyagraha families could live and lead a religious life'. He even called it 'a centre of spiritual purification and penance for the final campaign'.[39]

Admittedly, there were sometimes evening bhajans and a weekly religious service catering for Hindus and Christians, but it is difficult to look on Tolstoy Farm as a religious institution. Although a common kitchen was provided which some joined, others had private kitchens of their own.[40] There was also a clandestine night time when a group of young people gathered with their tuck boxes full of 'forbidden' goodies and spicy dishes. Gandhi never came to know about that.[41] Gandhi and Kallenbach jointly experimented with diet, sometimes joined by others. More important were Gandhi's experiments in fasting. Whereas earlier he sometimes fasted for health reasons, he now commenced fasting 'as a means of self-restraint'. Here too Kallenbach was his main companion, but he extended his experiment by asking others to join the Muslims in their long fast of Ramadan. Gandhi wrote in his autobiography that 'the result of these experiments was that all were convinced of the value of fasting, and a splendid *esprit de corps* grew up among them'.[42]

From the religious point of view, the most important experiment as far as the future was concerned was Gandhi's fast at the Phoenix Settlement towards the end of his stay in South Africa. He described it under the heading *Fasting as Penance*. In Johannesburg he 'received tidings of the moral fall of two of the inmates of the Ashram.' He decided that the heaviest responsibility was his own, and 'The only way the guilty parties could be made to realise my distress and the depth of their own fall will be for me to do some penance. So I imposed upon myself a fast for seven days and a vow to have only one meal a day for four months and a half.' This was the first of a number of public penitential fasts. Gandhi felt it was successful, 'My penance pained everybody but it cleared the atmosphere. Everyone came to realise what a terrible thing it was to be sinful, and the bond that bound me to the boys and girls became stronger and truer.'[43]

One of the most striking conclusions from this survey of the growth of Gandhi's religious practice is that it mostly happened within the context of a community: his large family that always included friends and collaborators, or the communal family of the Phoenix Settlement and Tolstoy Farm. Besides this there was the wider context of politico-social work for the larger Indian community. This 'public service' was totally dedicated to that community, and towards the middle of the period evolved into the Satyagraha, which would later become the main weapon in the armoury of the freedom fighter.

A LIFE OF SERVICE

The theme of service consistently pervaded the development of Gandhi's religious endeavour. The main argument for taking the vow of chastity was service, and this theme also figured strongly in the progressive simplification of life, and the shedding of personal property. This service was a binding duty, which should not be paid. Consequently, the earnings from his legal work had to be devoted to the community until his practice withered away. From the South African period on, this duty of service was fulfilled at two levels. There was the macro level of the whole Indian community of South Africa, and there was the increasingly intense micro level of the ashram family. The idea of service also became increasingly inspired and motivated by intense religious feelings. In his autobiography Gandhi suggested that the reason for his service was from early days his 'desire for self-realisation'. 'I had made the religion of service my own, and felt that God could be realised only through service.' This clearly is a later interpretation, because the first time Gandhi ever explicitly made the connection between service and *moksha* was in November 1910 in a letter to Maganlal Gandhi written from Tolstoy Farm, 'True public service can be rendered only if fearlessness can be achieved as regards [the loss of] prestige, money, caste, wife, family and even life. Then only will *moksha*, the ultimate end of life be attained.'[44]

For a Hindu, the highest honour that can be bestowed on human activity, is to maintain that it will produce *moksha*. For the follower of the Patanjali *Yoga Sutras*, it is the meditation-concentration activity that triggers the trance which produces *moksha*. It is no wonder that the *sannyasi* who devotes himself to pursue that aim, is freed from all ritual and social duties, so that he can devote all his energy to that search. To the follower of *bhakti* it is the emotional surrender to the Lord that will lead to *moksha*; that emotional surrender consequently becomes the prime duty of the *bhakta*. When Gandhi declared that service was the activity that leads to the realisation of *moksha*, he made a statement nowhere to be found in the Hindu tradition. Hinduism does include in its basic moral imperatives the duty of non-violence, which encompasses mercy and kindness. The practice of these duties is part of the preparation of the serious seeker after *moksha* in the different schools. But no school or sect did ever elevate the activity of service itself into one that caused the realisation of *moksha*.

The question therefore arises, how Gandhi towards the end of his South African period arrived at the conclusion that service was the activity that led to *moksha*. Although we referred above to one single statement, it would be regularly reiterated, and became a central idea that remained firm in Gandhi's mind until the end of his life. Since the idea is not part of the great systems of Hinduism, the question how Gandhi arrived at it is vital for understanding the growth of his personal religion. The proposition that *moksha* is achieved by service can be divided into two parts, '*moksha* is achieved by the moral activity of man', and 'the essence of that activity is service'. The first of these statements was very strongly supported by much of the reading material Gandhi studied in his early stay in Pretoria. The letters of Raychand emphatically put the task of realising *moksha* in the hands of the aspirant, and so did the readings Raychand recommended, and Maitland's *The Perfect Way*. All supported the concept of a pure spirit contaminated by matter, a spirit that has the innate power by its own activity to cleanse itself and thus realise *moksha*, its total liberation from matter. All these texts recommended the destruction of egotism by renunciation and asceticism, and the acquisition of wisdom, as the prime means of purification. However, none of them even mentioned service.[45]

Gandhi himself later pointed to the third chapter of the *Bhagavadgita* as the 'gospel of service', and he did read the work a lot in South Africa. However, this is an interpretation Gandhi put on the text later on. While it glorifies action in the form of caste duty and selfless duty, it never even mentions the word 'service'. In other words, Gandhi's glorification of service was not caused by his reading of that text, but after having developed his ideas, he then read them into his favourite text. The same argument can be used for showing that the Gospel's 'Beatitudes' were not the source of Gandhi's idea of service.[46]

There are only two texts which Gandhi read in South Africa that explicitly gave great prominence to the idea of service. They are Tolstoy's works, and Salter's *Ethical Religion*. Tolstoy's *The Kingdom of God is Within You* has the following as its concluding paragraph, 'The only meaning of man's life consists in serving the world by co-operating in the establishment of the kingdom of God . . . '[47] Throughout the volume that theme of service being the highest duty of man is repeated: 'only with the recognition of the equality of all men, with their mutual service, is possible the realisation of the greatest good which is accessible to men . . . '[48] It appears again throughout Tolstoy's other work read by Gandhi, *The Gospel in Brief*, 'My teaching is, that life is given to man not that others may serve him, but that he should give his whole life to service of others.'[49] Clearly, Tolstoy firmly held, within the context of his idiosyncratic conception of Christianity, that love and total service were the supreme duty and aim of human existence, and the primary means of establishing the Kingdom of God.

William Mackintire Salter gave a similar prominence to service in the context of his rationalistic *Ethical Religion*, which Gandhi paraphrased in 1907 in *Indian Opinion*.[50] At the end of chapter 6 Salter wrote, 'All the separate moral rules may be resolved into the supreme one, to seek the general welfare, the universal good.'[51] Gandhi paraphrased this as, 'If we take out the essence of all moral laws, we shall find that the attempt to do good to mankind is the highest morality.'[52] This idea was further explored in chapter 7, entitled by Gandhi with Salter's title 'The

Social Ideal'. Gandhi condensed Salter's chapter to one-tenth of its length, and made the idea of service its dominant theme:

A man is an animal or imperfect [as a human being] to the extent that he falls behind in his service to humanity. We have neither practised nor known ethical religion so long as we do not feel sympathy for every human being . . . Considering our relation to mankind, every man has a claim over us, as it is our duty always to serve them . . . It is a universal experience that God always saves the man who whole-heartedly devotes himself to the service of others.[53]

It is interesting that in these quotations Gandhi, who previously used various expressions, now used the word *seva*, service, which from then on became a standard term in his religious vocabulary.

Looking over the South African period, we see that from 1896 onward Gandhi sought out opportunities to serve in a special way, over and above his familial and professional duties: during the 1896 Bombay plague, and at the deathbed of his brother-in-law in Rajkot. After his return to South Africa, in 1898, he took a leper into his home and then sought regular nursing work in a small local hospital. In 1900 he served for two months in the Indian Ambulance Corps. When the Black Plague erupted in Johannesburg in 1904, Gandhi took charge of looking after the victims. In 1906 he served for six weeks in the Indian Ambulance Corps he organised in the Zulu Rebellion; and its patients were all Zulus.[54]

We have indicated that two authors, Tolstoy and Salter, proclaimed the moral supremacy of the service of human kind, and influenced Gandhi in his ideas about, and in his practice of, service. However real these influences were, they were not the origin of Gandhi's thought and practice. They originated in his childhood, when the example of his mother, for whom service was the totality of her life, forcefully imprinted itself on his young mind. His father's high conception of the duties of 'public service' reinforced that influence. In South Africa, first in his enlarged family, and afterwards in his ashrams, Gandhi imitated and recreated the family atmosphere he grew up in. It was a large family within which his mother was the paragon of service. It also was a family which served the larger community through its men, who served the State with devotion, honesty, and selflessness. In South Africa Gandhi communicated to his friend Joseph Doke his memories of his mother:

If there were sickness in the home, she would sit up night after night discharging the duties of nurse. If anyone nearby was in need,

Brahman or Shudra, she was the one to render help as soon as possible. Every morning the old gateway was besieged by twenty or thirty poverty-stricken people, who came to receive the alms or the cup of whey which was never refused.[55]

Gandhi's portrait of his mother made Doke reflect in 1909: 'just as though the house were a mediaeval convent, and she an Indian Saint Elizabeth'.[56] In 1909 Gandhi wrote some letters from prison to his son Manilal, the theme of which was that 'service' was the best possible education he could get:

What can be better than that you should have the opportunity of nursing mother and cheerfully bearing her ill-temper, or than looking after Chanchi and anticipating her wants . . . or again than being guardian to Ramdas and Devadas? . . . It is true that you have had to give up reading and writing, but one does not always get the opportunity of serving others.[57]

There was another way in which the idea of service came to Gandhi via his family tradition: through the hymns of the Vaishnava saints. These hymns were very much part of the Gandhi household, and especially dear to his mother, who

hailed from a village near Junagadh where Narsimh Mehta lived during the fifteenth century. This saint-poet, specially beloved of Gandhi throughout his life, was a Brahmin, but he used to visit the quarters of untouchable friends and sing bhajans [hymns] in praise of Vishnu.[58]

In South Africa Gandhi rediscovered that Gujarati *bhakti* heritage, mainly through Gujarati books sent to him by Raychand, who himself was a great devotee of the *bhakti* poets of Gujarat. As Devanesan wrote, 'before he finally left South Africa, Gandhi would be familiar with a body of literature extending from the poetry of Narsi Mehta in the fifteenth century to the writings of Narmadashankar [in the nineteenth century].'[59] He used the hymns in his ashrams and also published some of them in *Indian Opinion*.[60] Of all the Gujarati *bhakti* poets, Narsimh Mehta was Gandhi's favourite, as he was the first and best to all Gujaratis. The poem Gandhi loved most was the one about the true Vaishnava:

A true Vaishnava is he
Who is moved by others' sufferings;
Who helps people in distress,
And feels no pride for having done so.

Shamal Bhatt's stanza was another he loved to quote:

For a bowl of water give a goodly meal;
For a kindly greeting bow down with zeal;
For a simple penny pay thou back with gold;
If thy life be rescued, life do not withhold.
Thus the words and actions of the wise regard;
Every little service tenfold they reward.
But the truly noble know all men as one,
And return with gladness good for evil done.[61]

SATYAGRAHA, THE MERGER OF POLITICS
AND RELIGION

The idea of passive resistance to evil came to Gandhi from a variety of sources, as he himself acknowledged at the time of his conversations with Doke, his first biographer. It is not possible to disentangle those various influences. Some came from the Hindu tradition like *dharna* [an old Indian form of a fasting sit-in], the *Bhagavadgita*, and Shamal Bhatt's poem 'For a Bowl of Water'. Others were Christian sources such as the Sermon on the Mount, and the writings of Tolstoy. Some came from contemporary political movements like the Passive Resistance Movement in England, the agitation of the Suffragettes, and the writings of Thoreau. It was at the time of a serious political crisis in 1906 that Gandhi, at a mass meeting, proposed a campaign of mass civil disobedience in order to put a new kind of pressure on the government. From the point of view of this work, the most important aspect of this innovation was the re-interpretation of both the political action and the political aim in religious terms.[62]

In both his autobiography and his *Satyagraha in South Africa*, Gandhi tended to see the satyagraha movement as an intensely religious phenomenon from its very inception. However, that is a view strongly coloured by later developments. The growth of the beginnings of passive resistance into the full doctrine of satyagraha as a religious movement was slow. The way to discover that process is a close inspection of volumes

5 to 9 of the *Collected Works*, where all Gandhi's statements between
the middle of 1905 – when the famous decision to go to jail rather than
to obey the proposed law was passed by a mass meeting – and 1909 are
recorded.

The following two texts clearly illustrate the distance travelled by
Gandhi during that period. Before going on his first visit to London on
10 October 1906, Gandhi wrote about the famous resolution:

> The Resolution passed by Indians is, and at the same time is not,
> unique. We consider it unique, because nowhere else in the world
> have Indians so far resolved, as they have done now, to go to gaol
> rather than submit to a law. On the other hand, we do not consider it
> unique because a number of similar instances are found [in history].
> When we are dissatisfied with anything, we often resort to *hartal*
> [strike] . . . in order to obtain redress of our grievances . . . The
> *hartal* only means that we do not approve of a certain measure taken
> by a ruler. This tradition of resisting a law has been in vogue among
> us from early days.[63]

There is no specific religious dimension given to this procedure, and the
other examples Gandhi gave in the same text of similar actions among
South African Indians, Zulus, and Englishmen, confirm that conclusion.

When one compares the above statement with the following one
delivered by Gandhi shortly before he left South Africa, the view of
satyagraha is considerably different:

> A satyagrahi does not deliberate in advance when embarking on
> satyagraha. When he finds anything done that violates his conscience,
> he should use soul-force against it. Even at the time when I first
> started satyagraha, I considered it to be but a part of dharma. I have
> discovered from experience that it is the only religion and the only
> *chintamani* [the philosopher's stone that yields all desires], and it has,
> therefore, developed in me especially in its aspect as dharma.[64]

For the first two years of agitation against the proposed regulation,
there is no evidence at all that there was a special religious significance
to the movement. It was a movement of 'passive resistance' in a just
cause against an unjust law; the decision was to go to jail rather than
obey the law. This would draw attention to the cause and was a 'method
of obtaining redress.' It was the 'only effective way to oppose the law',
and it would be dishonourable not to stick to the pledge to resist.[65]

In the middle of 1907, there was a shift in Gandhi's explanation of passive resistance. He referred to 'so-called passive resistance, because in my opinion, it is really not resistance but a policy of communal suffering'.[66] He elaborated on that a little later, as the day approached that the Government was expected finally to implement the law and take action against non-compliance.

We have already examined the various reasons why we ought not to submit to the obnoxious law. It should be noted that in defying this murderous law we obey the divine law. To submit to the unjust law will be a sin. Likewise, it will be a sin to violate the divine law . . . What is this divine law? It is that one has to suffer pain before enjoying pleasure and that one's true self-interest consists in the good of all, which means that we should die – suffer for others.[67]

Another new idea now came to the fore that civil disobedience was a duty, because it preferred to obey God's law rather than human law. This idea came primarily from Thoreau, whose essay 'On the Duty of Civil Disobedience' greatly influenced Gandhi, and made him write two articles on it. Passive resistance was not just a tactical political man-oeuvre against undesirable legislation, it now became a duty, a religious duty to give precedence to divine law over human laws. Therefore, obeying the new law was an act 'against religion', and the reason for opposition to the law was in essence a religious reason. As Gandhi said on 4 January 1908 in a speech in Johannesburg, 'All who considered [that] this was not a religious struggle, that this was not a religious cause, did not know what religion meant.'[68]

By the time Gandhi went to jail for the first time in January 1908, he had given a strong religious slant to the movement of passive resistance, and a new name: satyagraha. The struggle was now 'a struggle for religious liberty' and he continued:

By religion he did not mean formal religion, or customary religion, but that religion which underlay all religions, which brought them face to face with their Maker. If they ceased to be men . . . if they broke that vow . . . they undoubtedly forsook their God.[69]

This religious slant became quite dominant in the important article he wrote at the end of May 1909 entitled 'Who can offer Satyagraha?' Here he described at length for the first time what the necessary qualities of a satyagrahi were. He had to be fearless, and have more courage than the one who relied on physical strength. He should be totally dedicated to truth, and never compromise with untruth, completely indifferent to wealth, and free from family attachments, so that the present and the future needs of the family never interfered with his duty. Gandhi summed it all up in conclusion, 'he alone can offer satyagraha who has true faith in religion. The name of Rama on the lips and a dagger under the arm – that is no faith.'[70]

A little later he made this thinking even more religiously explicit. 'After a great deal of experience it seems to me that those who want to become passive resisters for the service of the country have to observe perfect chastity, adopt poverty, follow truth, and cultivate fearlessness.' Here, in *Hind Swaraj*, we hear Gandhi formulate for the very first time the essential programme for the training of the freedom fighter, the satyagrahi. He was not able to implement it in South Africa, but as soon as he arrived back in India, he organised an ashram for the training of such freedom fighters, who would bind themselves by vow to the above observances.[71]

SOUL-FORCE

It was in the context of the transformation of satyagraha into a religious endeavour, that the idea of soul-force emerged in Gandhi's mind. On the occasion of the 1909 New Year, he wrote a reflective piece in *Indian Opinion* as follows:

> Swadeshi means reliance on our own strength . . . the strength of our body, our mind and our soul. From among these, on which should we depend? . . . The soul is supreme, and therefore soul-force is the foundation on which men should build. Passive resistance or satyagraha is a mode of fighting which depends on such force.[72]

In June he came back to this idea in a speech on 'The Ethics of Passive Resistance':

> Passive resistance, (the speaker proceeded), was a misnomer . . . The idea was more completely and better expressed by the term 'soul force'. As such it was as old as the human race. Active resistance was better expressed by the term 'body force'. Jesus Christ, Daniel and Socrates represented the purest form of passive resistance or soul force . . . Tolstoy was the best and brightest exponent of the doctrine

. . . In India, the doctrine was understood and commonly practised long before it came into vogue in Europe.[73]

However, he wrote to Narandas Gandhi: 'the knowledge of soul-force that our forefathers had is lost in darkness'.[74] He reiterated his idea in London in a speech to the Emerson Club – 'soul force is far superior to brute force and it is invincible'.[75] Gandhi acknowledged his indebtedness to Tolstoy with whom he was at that time corresponding:

> He offers uncompromising opposition to oppressive laws in Russia and exhorts others to do the same but he never employs physical force and forbids others to employ it. He relies entirely on spiritual force .
> . . He places his trust in God alone . . . His letter shows us convincingly that soul-force – satyagraha – is our only resort.[76]

He also passed on his opinion to the forthcoming meeting of the Indian National Congress, stating that the Indians in South Africa were fighting for a national cause: the honour of India. Their method was 'to oppose the brute or physical force by soul-force'. He suggested that Congress should carefully study the method and, 'perchance find out that for the many ills we suffer from in India passive resistance is an infallible panacea'.[77]

HIND SVARAJ

At the end of that pivotal year of 1909, Gandhi wrote in a hectic ten days his pamphlet *Hind Svaraj* on board the SS *Kildonan Castle* on his way back from London. This is a very important document in the development of his ideas; our interest is in how it refers to religion. *Hind Svaraj* is primarily a savage indictment of western civilization:

> This civilization takes note neither of morality or religion . . . it is irreligion, and it has taken such a hold on the people in Europe that those who are in it appear to be half mad . . . According to the teaching of Mohamed this would be considered a Satanic Civilization. Hinduism calls it the Black Age [Kali Yuga].[78]

In contrast, true civilization was described as 'that mode of conduct which points out to man the path of duty . . . To observe morality is to attain mastery over our mind and our passions'.[79] This civilization characterised traditional India, and its quality was moral and religious, 'based on a belief in God'. Gandhi's aversion to western civilization had grown by his stay in Johannesburg, the city built on the gold mines, as Devanesan perceptively noticed. It was a 'Monte Carlo superimposed on Sodom and Gomorrah, the central sin spot of civilization . . . with the incessant roar from the mines.'[80]

It is not surprising, therefore, that we hear the first rumblings of Gandhi's thunder against western civilization in South Africa. The first attack happened in May 1908, when in a debate in the YMCA on the question 'Are Asiatics and the Coloured Races a Menace to the Empire?' Gandhi argued that there was a great difference between western and eastern civilizations:

> It appears that western civilization is destructive, eastern civilization is constructive. Western civilization is centrifugal, eastern civilization is centripetal. Western civilization is disruptive whereas eastern civilization combines . . . western civilization is without a goal, eastern civilization has always had the goal before it.[81]

Although it is clear that Gandhi ranked eastern civilization higher than the western one, he did not at that time consider the latter destructive and beyond redemption. He considered that their meeting, as it had happened in the British Empire, was one that could produce a better world.

But it is really during his four months' stay in England from July to November 1909 that his view of the British Empire and of western civilization drastically changed. The occasion of Louis Bleriot's first crossing of the English Channel by plane caused an outburst entitled 'This Crazy Civilization', with its mad rush of trains and planes, its mad rush after luxury. 'Unless its whole machinery is thrown overboard, people will destroy themselves like so many moths.' Later he attacked the spread of processed, adulterated foods under the title 'Civilization or Barbarism'. In a speech at Hampstead, he spoke on 'East and West' and claimed that 'The chief characteristic of modern civilization [was that it] worshipped the body more than the spirit.' He condemned the destructive role of railways and telegraphs, creating a rush leading to calamity. In a long letter to his friend Polak, written on 14 October 1909, he went into great detail and practically enumerated all the questions he developed in his *Hind Svaraj*.[82]

The influences that changed Gandhi's concept of modern civilization so dramatically were many. There were the books he read in London, a

list of which he appended to his *Hind Svaraj*. Among these, Edward
Carpenter's *Civilization, its Cause and Cure*, was most important, as he
wrote to Polak.[83] He was also inspired by the conversations he had with
extremist young Indian revolutionaries, who all favoured a violent
overthrow of the British Raj, and by conversations and discussions with
English friends. James Hunt has provided in his book *Gandhi in London*
an excellent analysis of all these influences that worked on Gandhi
during those decisive four months in London.[84]

After condemning western civilization, Gandhi made it clear that the
freedom he desired for India was a freedom from the curse of modern
civilization, and a return to the ethico-religious culture of traditional
India. That freedom was not to be fought for with the weapons of
violence, but with soul-force. That is why we find in *Hind Svaraj* the
first extensive description of soul-force as a political tool with a purely
religious essence.[85]

THE MAHATMA

The mature Gandhi who in 1914 forever left the shores of South Africa,
'that God-forsaken continent where I found my God', was very different
from the diffident, naive, yet ambitious young man without much idea of
or involvement in religion, who had arrived there two decades earlier.
An astounding, slow and gradual but radical change had taken place in
his practical, active religion. This was the transformation of a typical
British-educated lawyer, top-earning, well-living, ensconced among the
wealthy, and wishing to succeed his father and grandfather in worldly
prominence and success, into a Mahatma, clad like a coolie, without
home and without position, tied by vows of chastity and poverty of
Carthusian rigour, and totally dedicated to the service of the poorest of
society. His practice of religion had made him into a different man. The
vow of chastity had freed him from the restrictive duties of husband and
head of family; the vow of poverty had terminated his promising professional career and his hold on any property. He had become an ashram-
dweller. But he was very different from the traditional Hindu *sannyasi*.
He had not cut the bonds of family and property in order to flee from
'the world' into the seclusion of mystical pursuits. He had cut himself
free in order to be able to devote all his energies to the service of the
people. This service was simultaneously rendered in two theatres: the
micro theatre of the enlarged family, the ashram, and the macro theatre
of the nation. Having resorted to a wide range of political methods in his

fight for the Indians of South Africa, he had slowly come to the conclusion that satyagraha and soul-force were to be his principal weapons. So it was that the creativity of his mind expressed itself fully in the practical side of religion. The combination of service, satyagraha, and soul-force as an all-encompassing ethic that was meant to achieve both *moksha* and *svaraj*, was an astoundingly original achievement. Gandhi had in a way achieved the nearly impossible: the marriage of politics and religion in a way that far from demeaning either, enhanced both. This was his precious personal creation that he was taking along to India, to wage there, as Mahatma Gandhi, his new battle for the liberation of India – the battle for *Hind Svaraj*.

2

Bewildering Doubts and Convincing Answers, 1893–5

The first chapter described the arduous, excitingly original journey of Gandhi to a high level of religious commitment. We now step back in time to the very beginning of the South African period. In the first two years, Gandhi faced what could be called, if not a crisis of faith, then at least an agony of religious confusion. This chapter describes that crisis and how Gandhi worked his way through it towards religious certainties that would sustain him throughout his life.

Albert Baker, the South African attorney who received Gandhi on his arrival, was a preacher and a director of the South Africa General Mission. Right away he asked Gandhi to join him and his colleagues in their daily short prayer after lunch. So, next day Gandhi met Miss Clara Harris, Miss F. Georgina Gabb, and Mr Michael Coates. The two women invited him to the four o'clock tea at their house every Sunday, where the main topic of conversation was religion. These new friends of Gandhi were not only very nice people, they were also Christians burning with evangelical zeal. They soon added to their prayers a special prayer for their new Indian friend, who being a Hindu, was missing out on salvation. 'Lord, show the path to the new brother who has come amongst us. Give him, Lord, the peace that thou has given us. May the Lord Jesus who has saved us, save him too.'[1] These new friends all belonged to the South Africa General Mission, and shared the basic Evangelical non-conformist beliefs: 'a gospel of individual salvation, based on a literal belief in the Bible, and delivered with personal dedication to others who were perceived to be lost in darkness and ignorance.'[2] The cornerstones of their creed were the Bible, as the infallible source of all truth, and Christ the Redeemer, who has saved mankind by his suffering and death. These were the ideas they tried to convince him about in an intensive five months from June to October 1893. Besides their talks, they also gave him books to read. Gandhi recalled three of them specifically in his autobiography; but none made a great impression on him.[3] Some ponderously proved the existence of God, about which there was no doubt in Gandhi's mind. Others concentrated on proving the unique truth of the Bible and of Christianity by the prophecies fulfilled and the miracles accomplished. Prophecies and miracles would evoke in a Hindu's mind the much more spectacular wonders related in the *Puranas*.

Mr Baker was getting desperate about the conversion of Gandhi, and decided to take him along to the three-day Wellington Convention, a revival meeting with an atmosphere of religious exaltation, which, he thought, was bound to bring Gandhi to the brink of conversion. But his hope was not fulfilled, although Gandhi did appreciate and admire the sincerity, conviction, and devotion of the participants; but conversion to Christianity was not something he could contemplate. In his autobiography he tried to state in summary the form of Christianity that was so passionately presented to him:

> It was more than I could believe that Jesus was the only incarnate son of God and that only he who believed in him would have everlasting life . . . My reason was not ready to believe literally that Jesus by his death and by his blood redeemed the sins of the world. . . . Again, according to Christianity only human beings had a soul, and not other living beings . . . while I held a contrary belief. I could accept Jesus as a martyr, an embodiment of sacrifice, and a divine teacher, but not as the most perfect man ever born. His death on the Cross was a great example to the world, but that there was anything like a mysterious or miraculous virtue in it my heart could not accept . . . Philosophically there was nothing extraordinary in Christian principles. From the point of view of sacrifice, it seemed to me that the Hindus greatly surpassed the Christians. It was impossible for me to regard Christianity as a perfect religion or the greatest of all religions . . . neither was I convinced of Hinduism being such. Hindu defects were pressingly visible to me. If untouchability could be a part of Hinduism, it could but be a rotten part . . . I could not understand the *raison d'être* of a multitude of sects and castes. What was the meaning of saying that the Vedas were the inspired Word of God? If they were inspired, why not also the Bible and the Koran?[4]

This is a very revealing text, but it should be read with caution: Gandhi wrote it over thirty years after the event, with the clear knowledge of hindsight. He certainly would not have been able to write those paragraphs at that time. Nevertheless, they do inform us of his general state of mind. The strong dose of Christian propaganda had churned up in his mind doubts and uncertainties, and particularly about the Christian claim of the unique divine provenance of the Bible, and the unique role of Christ in salvation. He had great difficulties with the Christian claims, and equally great doubts about the tenets of his own faith. The difficulties, he decided, were primarily the result of ignorance. The first step on the way out of his difficulties and doubts had to be to inform himself of the fundamental tenets of Hinduism. No wonder that he thought of Raychand, a man 'who captivated my heart in religious matters as no other man till now,' he reminisced in 1930.[5]

LETTER TO RAYCHAND

In June 1894 Gandhi sent Raychand a letter containing 27 questions about religion.[6] This letter is unique in the voluminous writings of Gandhi, which mostly consist of articles, speeches, and letters. There the author was primarily adviser, teacher, guide and enthuser, one who knew his mind and felt sure about the truth and validity of his pronouncements. In his letter to Raychand, on the contrary, he was the one who sought advice and guidance, who was at a loss about important issues and assailed by anxious doubts. This letter is uniquely important because it reveals the issues, the questions, the uncertainties that troubled his mind in that most critical stage of his religious development, about a year after his arrival in Pretoria.

The list of questions divide into four distinct sections. The first section (questions 1–11) deals with the essentials of Hinduism, the second (12–16) with Christianity, the third (17–26) with specific aspects of Hinduism, and the last question raises a moral issue. This simple listing makes some things immediately obvious. Gandhi's prime concern was his ignorance about his own faith, as 20 questions refer to Hinduism. Secondly, he was very disturbed about various claims by his friends about Christianity, and felt ill-equipped to deal with them. Thirdly, moral issues as such were not high on his agenda at that time.

The first block of questions about Hinduism show that Gandhi already had a clear idea what the essential pillars of religion were: he jumped right into the heart of the matter. 'What is the soul? What is God? What is rebirth and deliverance from rebirth? What is revelation?' The first question was not about God, but about the human spirit and its relation to action: 'Does the spirit (*atman*) perform actions?' Gandhi already surmised that all questions about religion had to start from here: the human spirit and human activity. His question about God used the word

Ishvar, the Hindu term that always refers to the personal divinity; he did not use the term *Brahman* of the Vedantic tradition, which refers to the 'impersonal' absolute. To the question 'What is God?' he attached another one: 'Is He the creator of the universe?' His Christian friends frequently referred to the God-creator, so emphatically described at the very beginning of the Bible. Obviously this idea was not as self-evident to Gandhi: in London, he had read in the writings of both Madame Blavatsky and Annie Besant that they rejected the idea of a creator God.[7] The only other question asked about God was question 26, as it were in an afterthought: 'Who is Brahma, Vishnu and Shiva?' He seems to have already accorded mythology a very minor rank.

The next five questions concerned ideas that most profoundly differentiate Hinduism from Christianity: rebirth and deliverance from rebirth, *moksha*. Gandhi knew that they were key concepts of Hinduism, which were accepted by the Theosophists, and rejected by Christians.[8] He asked Raychand if it was really true that one may be reborn, according to one's deeds, as an animal, a tree, or even a stone. Whereas rebirth in animal form was a general Hindu belief, rebirth as a plant or a stone is rather related to Jain doctrine. One is reminded that Gandhi's family had many Jain friends and also Jain monks as spiritual advisers. His questions about *moksha* and reincarnation suggest that he knew little on the subject at that time.

He introduced his questions about revelation thus: 'What is Arya Dharm? Have all religions their origins in the Vedas?' It is interesting that Gandhi did not use the term Hindu Dharm, but the term used by the Arya Samaj, and that his question about the Vedas being the origin of all religions is also a typical Arya Samaj tenet. One wonders if he got these ideas from the Theosophists. He probably remembered that Madame Blavatsky preferred using the term Arya and the fact that she attributed great antiquity to the Vedas.[9] Next Gandhi asked, 'Who composed the Vedas? Are they without beginning? If so, what does that mean?' Obviously, Gandhi was baffled by the idea of a scripture that is supposed to be without a beginning and yet has a human form. He then continued the same question about the *Bhagavadgita*, the sacred text he was most familiar with; 'Who is the author? God is not the author is He? If He is, is there any evidence for that?' These questions about scripture were evidently the results of the claims of his Christian friends about the Bible.

His final question in this section about Hinduism was totally different, asking if any merit at all would be acquired from the sacrifice of animals or other things. Gandhi came from a very strong non-violent tradition of

Vallabhacharyas, but he knew about the practice of animal sacrifice in Hinduism. He must also have heard Christians condemn animal sacrifices, and also refer to the 'sacrifice' of Christ that redeemed the world. He was unsure what, if any place, animal or other sacrifices had in religion.

The section of questions about Christianity strongly reflected, the essential Christian tenets his South African friends reiterated. The first one set the general tone: 'If it is claimed that a particular religion is the best, may proof of that not be asked?' He obviously had Christian claims in mind and he had read Blavatsky's rejection of it. This was followed by a general question: 'Do you know anything about Christianity? If so indicate what you think of it.' Then he moved on to the very heart of the matter: the Christian claims concerning the Bible and Christ.

> [The Christians say] that the Bible is inspired by God, and that Christ was an avatar of God, and that he is, and was the son of God. They say that the prophecies of the Old Testament were fulfilled in Christ. It has been written about miracles performed by Christ.[10]

These were the fundamental beliefs of Gandhi's friends; the infallibility of the Bible, proven by the fulfilment of prophecies and the accomplishment of miracles. Gandhi probably remembered that the Theosophists denied these miracles.[11]

The remaining questions all related to Hinduism, but not in any particular logical order. Some dealt with the knowledge of previous births, and the certainty of salvation.[12] Three questions dealt with cosmic eschatology. Here too, one suspects a Christian context. Christianity proclaimed its own eschatology of 'the end of the world', which was characterised by the resurrection of the dead, the final universal judgement, and the advent of the glorious, everlasting Kingdom of God. This contrasted with Hindu beliefs. Hinduism had its own view of 'the end of the world' in its concept of cosmic cycles, in which a process of progressive deterioration leads to a cataclysmic end of the cycle, which is followed by the birth of a new cycle, starting with a 'Golden Age'. Madame Blavatsky referred to this cyclic emanation and re-absorption of the cosmos as the 'Cycle of Life'.[13] Gandhi asked, 'What will the final condition of this world be? Will out of the current lawlessness righteousness arise? Does the world *pralaya* [dissolution of the world] exist?'

From his Vaishnavite background Gandhi knew the importance of Krishna as avatar, and of *bhakti* for salvation, but he knew also about the preferences for knowledge in Vedanta. He probably had heard his friends speak about being saved 'by faith in Christ'. This was all very confusing, and gave rise to the next questions: 'Is it possible for a person without knowledge to attain *moksha* by *bhakti*? Are Krishna-avatar and Ram-avatar real? Are they God or only part of Him? Can *moksha* be attained by believing in them?' Krishna was at the centre of Vaishnava devotions, but the great gods of Hinduism were not. Gandhi did not understand what they were, and asked 'Who are Brahma, Vishnu and Shiva?' It is interesting that the question was not part of the first section about the essentials of Hinduism, but rather tacked on to the end of the list. It seems to indicate that Gandhi already ranked mythology low among his religious concerns.

The very last question was the only one that tackled a moral issue: 'If a snake approaches to bite me, should I let it bite me or should I kill it, supposing I have no other way of removing it?' It is not surprising that the moral issue has to do with non-violence, *ahimsa* , because of Gandhi's Vaishnavite background. In fact, non-violence would increasingly become a major preoccupation during Gandhi's life. What is most striking about this question is that it is the only one that refers to ethics in a long series. Moral action will become the very centre of Gandhi's religious endeavours. At this particular time his uncertainties and doubts were totally concentrated on what one may call the theological or ideological issues of religion, and not on moral action.

Gandhi's list of questions reveals on the one hand a very clear mind that could formulate pertinent and penetrating questions about the very essence of religion. On the other hand, it also shows that he was aware of his ignorance about Hinduism, although he knew that there was no need to be ashamed of it. He wanted to learn about his own religion so that he could for himself satisfactorily deal with the claims of his Christian friends. In a way it was to these friends, and their concern, that he owed his urge to learn about Hinduism. He desperately needed help to clear up his doubts and decided to ask for the assistance of the one man he knew whose religious ideas and writings, and whose religious way of life had impressed him enormously – Raychand.

RAYCHAND'S REPLY

Raychand answered Gandhi's letter in October 1894.[14] His letter needs to be analysed in great detail because it put forward firm, lucid principles with a very strong logical coherence, which impressed Gandhi so overwhelmingly that they reverberated throughout his life. Raychand's answer to Gandhi's first question about the nature of the spirit (*atman*) was at least three times as long as any other answer, showing the priority it deserved in his eyes. It set out the basis of his religious ideology. Its starting-point was the total opposition of spirit and matter (*atman-jar*). Whereas the spirit is eternal, and its essence is knowledge, matter is impermanent and its main characteristic is the absence of knowledge. The spirit exists in two conditions: the state of knowledge and that of ignorance. In the state of knowledge, the inner being of the spirit is totally illumined and it is in an all-encompassing trance of enlightenment (*samadhi*). The spirit itself is the creator (*karta*) of that state, which is the state of liberation from body and transmigration (*moksha*). In the state of ignorance the spirit is entangled in emotions and passions, imprisoned in a decaying body, and engaged in the production of material things. These activities (*karma*) performed in the state of ignorance are the seeds of necessary consequences such as sickness, old age, death and rebirth. The spirit has the power to dissociate itself from this condition and to achieve the state of total freedom. Liberation (*moksha*), as Raychand defined it in answer to question three, is the total elimination of the bonds that shackle the spirit: the passions, the body, and the material world; this liberation is totally within the power of the spirit.

It is striking that in each of his succeeding letters (one in March 1895, and another in early 1896), Raychand repeated these basic ideas by condensing them in a short list. In his second letter he referred to the 'six principles' which constitute the discriminating knowledge that leads to *moksha* according to Jina, the legendary founder of Jainism. These principles are:

> The spirit exists; it is eternal; it is the performer of deeds; it must suffer the consequences of its deeds (*karma*); it can detach itself from *karma*; the method of achieving that detachment.

In his third letter Raychand explained that Aryan thought included the same foremost principles.

These same ideas were reinforced about the same time in the following manner. In his first letter Raychand, in answer to the first question about the nature of spirit, wrote that this question was most important and required elaborate answers. Such answers could not be adequately given in a letter, and therefore he was sending a book, the *Saddarshana Samucchaya*, for Gandhi to study. He repeated that advice twice in his first letter.[15]

This booklet, 'Compendium of Six Systems', was attributed to Haribhadra, a convert to Jainism who probably lived in about the fifth or sixth century AD. His very short compendium describes six Indian systems, or philosophies: Buddhism, Nyaya – Vaisheshika or Logic – Atomism, Samkhya or Dualism, Mimamsa or Vedic Exegesis, Lokayata or Materialism, and Jainism. The presentation of the first five is an arid enumeration of a number of logical, psychological, and ontological categories, without any attempt at showing their relations or their integration. The section on Jainism stands out by the clarity and logical development of its argument. Haribhadra offers no criticism of the other systems, but at the end of his exposition he describes the Jain system as 'being free from all defects and . . . internal contradictions'. This comment was later on echoed by Gandhi when he called Jainism 'the most logical of all faiths'.

Haribhadra's description of Jainism was as succinct as Raychand's, and even in detail it was identical with the three summaries of the essence of religion presented by Raychand in his letters to Gandhi. This essence is summed up in just a few principles that represent not only Jainism, but the very core of Arya Dharm, Indian religion, as his answer to question eight clearly showed. These principles are:

- spirit and matter are radical opposites;
- in the state of bondage spirit is enslaved by matter;
- total liberation from bondage is possible;
- the means of liberation are knowledge and action.

The two most striking aspects of these principles are that they totally ignored the idea of a creative divine principle, be it a personal God or an impersonal Absolute, and, secondly that they kept the process of liberation totally and squarely within the sphere of human endeavour. In these two respects these principles differed fundamentally from most schools of Hindu theology.

A good number of Gandhi's questions pointedly directed themselves to that very problem of the nature of God. The second question – 'What is God? Is He the creator of the universe?' – goes right to the heart of the matter. Raychand answered as follows:

Divinity (*Ishvaratva*) is nothing else but the natural condition of the spirit (*atman*), when totally free from all *karma,* a state which is not revealed as long as the spirit is bound by *karma* . . . It is my firm belief that *Ishvar* is not a separate being endowed with immense power.[16]

So, God is to Raychand not the creator of the universe or of the individual spirits, nor is He the dispenser of the fruits of man's deeds. This conforms with the classical Jain belief that reality consists of matter on the one hand, and on the other a multitude of spirits. Any spirit who attained *moksha* may be given the title of *Ishvar* [God]. In this respect Jainism is very similar to the Hindu Samkhya system, which in its classical form also subscribes to a dualism of matter and spirits, and denies the existence of a creator God.

Gandhi's penultimate question, 'Who are Brahma, Vishnu and Shiva?', is an appendix to question two, because they are after all the names, singly or collectively given to the personal God in traditional Hinduism. Here is Raychand's answer. The Hindu tradition believes that all material nature is a mixture, in various proportions and combinations, of three constitutional elements (*gunas*). The action, and intermixture of these elements produce the emanation of the cosmos from its dormant state into its creative phase. Raychand says that it would make good sense to consider the three great Gods as personified representations of these three basic elements of the universe. However, that is not how the *Puranas* describe them. There they are involved in a myriad of mythological tales and allegories for the instruction of the faithful. As morality tales, says Raychand, they should be taken to heart. But one should not waste one's time in futile theological speculation about Brahma, Vishnu and Shiva as divine principles or personalities.[17]

Whereas Brahma, Vishnu, and Shiva were but remote figures on Gandhi's religious horizon, Rama and Krishna were very much at the centre of his religious world. Among the Vallabhacharyas, Krishna was not only an incarnation of Vishnu, but was actually adored as the Absolute Godhead himself. Gandhi asked if they were 'incarnations of God, God himself, or part of Him?' Raychand answered that, no doubt, they were 'great spirits' (*mahatma*). By the very fact of being a spirit (*atman*), they were potentially God, just like every other spirit. If they indeed had shed all their *karma* and attained *moksha*, they really were 'divine', but that was disputable. In this answer Raychand applied to Krishna and Rama all the principles about the nature of the spirit which he had stated earlier.

The answer to the second part of that same question ('Can we gain salvation through faith in them?'), is also very revealing. Raychand wrote that the answer was simple. *Moksha* meant the total absence of all passions and of ignorance. The only kind of faith that could help towards gaining that deliverance would be such faith that helped us to free ourselves from attachment and ignorance. Since a person's own actions were the only means to achieve *moksha*, faith in a person could be no more than a help in that direction, and in itself could not achieve anything.

Question 24 actually dealt with the same problem. 'Is it possible that an uneducated person can achieve *moksha* by *bhakti* alone [devotional love of a personal God]?' Raychand answered that *bhakti* cannot be a direct cause of *moksha*, but it can increase the power of knowledge and thus help the spirit to achieve liberation. Neither faith nor *bhakti* have in themselves liberating power; all they can do is assist the spirit in its striving for pure knowledge.

The other major problem for Gandhi in dealing with Hinduism and other religions, was the question of revelation. Both Christianity and Hinduism claimed that their scriptures were revealed by God and therefore eminently truthful. Raychand started his answer by making the following distinction: the scripture taken as a book, composed and written by a human being, could not be claimed to be eternal; but the scripture as a set of ideas could be considered to be beginningless, and expounded by various saintly teachers, in various forms, at various periods of human history. This statement puts all scriptures, as 'sets of books', in the same category of being human creations. A scripture could only be described as divine, if it were composed by a spirit totally liberated, and in possession of full knowledge. But Raychand felt that even if we considered Rama and Krishna to have been 'great souls', it would still be doubtful whether they really had achieved full divinity. Therefore, all scriptures were human creations and inherently fallible and imperfect.

Raychand did not believe that the Vedas were the origin of all religions. He admitted that the Vaishnavas and other sects had their origin in the Vedas, but 'The knowledge revealed by the Jain saints is a thousand times deeper than that of the Veda', and could, therefore, not have derived from it. He admitted that everyone tended to consider his own religion, be it Jainism, Buddhism, or Vedanta as *the* Arya Dharm but he added that 'those who really know, describe as Arya Dharma only that path (*marga*) by the help of which the soul can achieve its own true nature'. In answer to question twelve about the claims to superiority of a particular religion, Raychand stressed that the comparative test of religions does not consist of a study of doctrines or scriptures, since these are all human, imperfect and historical. It is a practical test that should be used: 'that religion only is the best and truly effective, which is effective in destroying the bondage of this world and in establishing the spirit in its essential nature.'

Raychand simply applied these general principles in answering Gandhi's questions about Christianity. He felt that Christianity did not in any way reach the standard of Aryan religions because it did not accept the basic truths of 'essential religion': the eternity of the soul, the law of *karma*, and the method of putting an end to *karma*. In fact, it believed in the eternal subjection of the soul. How, then, could it possibly be the best religion? As for the question of the Bible being divinely inspired, the same principles applied as were applied to the Vedas. The claim that Christ was the incarnate son of God constituted a logical impossibility; at most one may accord the expression the status of allegory. Gandhi had also asked about the two 'evidences' of the divine origin of Christianity which his Christian friends proclaimed: the fulfilment of Old Testament prophecies in Christ, and the miracles performed by Christ. Raychand answered that even if prophecies were fulfilled, which cannot be rationally proved but only accepted in faith, that did not prove divine provenance. Astrologers too can predict the birth of a great soul. As for miracles, bringing a dead person back to life is impossible: it would totally negate the law of *karma*. Moreover, Yoga techniques can also create certain 'miracles', and it could not be proved if Jesus had such powers or not. But, most importantly, such yogic powers are of little or no importance when compared to the divine power of the spirit (*atman*).

Questions 21, 22, and 23 dealt with cosmic eschatology, 'the end of the world'. Gandhi's Christian friends must have spoken to him about the Christian doctrine of 'the end of the world', and the paradisal 'Kingdom of God' that would be established for eternity. He also knew something about the Hindu concept of the periodic emanation and dissolution of the universe, which was endorsed by Madame Blavatsky.[18] Raychand could not accept either of those scenarios for the future of the world. He considered it rationally impossible that 'all souls will attain *moksha* and that the world will totally perish'. Continuous change was of the essence of the universe, and it would be so without end. Morality and immorality would always coexist. The idea that a perfect reign of law would sometime arise was just an encouragement for people to persist with their immorality.

At the end of his first letter Raychand dealt with the one question about what to do in case of a snake attack, when faced with the alternative: either be bitten or kill the snake. He wrote, 'One hesitates to advise you that you should let the snake bite you.' He went on to explain. The principle was simple enough: to kill is not acceptable. But only those who were filled with the desire for spiritual well-being could be advised to let the snake kill. One could only give the advice to kill the snake to someone who 'is un-Aryan of disposition, in other words who does not believe or live by the Aryan ideal of non-violence'. Raychand stuck firmly to the Jain doctrine of non-violence which did not allow for exceptions or subterfuges.

Raychand's third letter, written about two years after the first, was very different in that it primarily dealt with matters of conduct.[19] It answered queries of Gandhi about proper behaviour in relation to caste duties in the circumstance of living outside India. Raychand praised Gandhi for the way he had developed his gifts in that foreign place Natal, which had one advantage in that it did not offer him the many occasions of intrigue that Rajkot presented by family and social pressures. Yet he felt that Gandhi's virtues would have flourished more in the land of the Aryas, because of the support of the *satsang*, the company of good and saintly people, which was absent in Natal. Moreover, Natal offered many situations where proper conduct was difficult to uphold.

Raychand then proceeded to give some advice about proper conduct, *Arya Achar*, which consisted primarily of 'the practice of the virtues of mercy, truthfulness, forgiveness, etc.' The foundation of proper Aryan conduct consisted in the observance of *varnashrama dharma*, the rules of caste and stage of life, which had to be followed until one entered the final stage of *sannyasa*. Next, Raychand gave examples of proper caste behaviour in food consumption: one should not eat forbidden foods, one should not eat with different castes, and one should certainly not eat with Muslims. Even if Gandhi did this out of kindness, and felt it did him no harm, he should abstain because it would set a bad example to others, who may not have the spiritual strength to cope with the temptation. This was a counsel Gandhi would find impossible to follow.

ANSWERS FROM ADVAITA

Raychand sent Gandhi in 1894 three ancient Hindu texts that belonged to the Hindu system of Advaita Vedanta. This system was codified in a masterly fashion by the great philosopher Shankara in the ninth century AD, but its main tenets originated in the ancient *Upanishads* of the pre-Christian era. Its basic doctrines are as follows. The only eternal, perfect reality is *Brahman*, pure spirit, impersonal absolute, which underlies all else. The individual spirit, *atman*, is fundamentally identical with *Brahman*. However, caught in the wheel of illusion by ignorance of its true nature, it is imprisoned in the body and the web of transmigration.

It believes that its mundane existence is its real being. When it fully realises its real nature, its identity with *Brahman*, then the illusion of its earthly existence will disappear and it will merge into *Brahman*. Thus it will achieve *moksha*, liberation from the cycle of transmigration.

The longest of these works was the *Yoga-Vasishtha-Maharamayana*, attributed to Valmiki, the mythical author of the original *Ramayana*.[20] In his autobiography Gandhi wrote that he read the *Mumuksha Prakarana* (chapter on the Aspirant to Liberation), whereas in his introduction to Raychand's works he mentioned the *Vairagya Prakarana* (chapter on Renunciation).[21] These were, in inverse order, the first and second chapter of the work, and Gandhi read both. The work is a massive philosophical poem of great beauty composed between the tenth and fourteenth century AD. It explains Advaita Vedanta and its relationship with Yoga, in the form of a dialogue between Rama and the great Vedic sage Vasishtha. It treats with great subtlety the fundamental philosophical tenets of the system. However, these are not the topics discussed in the first two chapters of about 100 pages each which Gandhi read. These concern themselves with practical as distinguished from philosophical concerns: how one can achieve the realisation of *moksha* in this life. In fact, their concern is with the initial necessary intellectual and moral training that is a prerequisite for the climbing of the seven stages of yogic exercises leading to the supreme goal. A short description follows of the basic ideas that are presented in these chapters with great poetic force.

The chapter on Renunciation is concerned with indifference to desire, self-denial, freedom from all attachments, asceticism. The story is recounted, 'how the high-minded Rama attained the status of liberation in life'. After a long pilgrimage, the young Rama returned home and soon fell into a state of total dejection and apathy, to the great anxiety of his royal father Dasharatha. The sage Vishvamitra was called in to diagnose and cure Rama's condition. The bulk of the chapter is taken up by Rama's own description of his own state of mind: 'no wealth, offspring, consorts, or palace give me any pleasure, but they are rather the causes of my misery.' He goes on to detail the vanity, decay, fleetingness and suffering life offers; the horrors of childhood, youth and old age; the curse of women, amalgams of 'blood, flesh and bones, caskets of all gems of vice'; the ravages of fleeting time, the total instability of all. Rama's speech strongly reminds one of the ascetic chapters of *The Imitation of Christ* of Thomas à Kempis. He is so totally disgusted by his insight into the real nature of the world that he has decided to abstain from all involvement in it. He would withdraw himself totally, refrain from eating, drinking and even breathing, unless he was told how to escape that life of total misery.

The chapter of the Aspirant to Liberation provides the first answer to Rama's despondency. It is spoken by the great sage Vasishtha, who gave his name to the work. This section totally concentrates on the answer of Agasti to Sutikshna's question, related at the very beginning of the work.

SUTIKSHNA: Tell me, is action the cause of emancipation or is it knowledge, or is it both together? AGASTI: Like the flight of birds in the sky depends on both their wings, even so emancipation is gained by both action and knowledge.[22]

This is the basic thrust of the chapter. It is a song of praise to action and to reason, the two wings by which the bird of the soul performs its journey to *moksha*.

Page after page insists that liberation can only be approached by personal exertion; those who think that they are being impelled by God are like dumb animals dependent on someone else. The words 'fate' and 'destiny' are empty expressions without any foundation. Vasishtha recalls the example of Vishvamitra who cast away his destiny as Kshatriya, and who by his own exertion attained the status of Brahmin.[23] Gandhi must have been enormously impressed by this vigorous affirmation of the primacy of personal endeavour in the pursuit of religious fulfilment. This was very different from the approach of his own Vaishnavite tradition where the causes of liberation were primarily the initiative of the loving God and his avatar Krishna, and man's submission to the sacerdotal injunctions. In that process the accent was firmly placed on the devotee's dependence and passivity.

The chapter's insistence on 'reason', personal thinking, and assessment of truth was equally far removed from the approach of the Vallabhacharya sect to truth. For them truth was revealed and fixed in the sacred writing, and it was interpreted by the living incarnation of Krishna, the Maharaja. It was a system in which personal reasoning was given no place at all.

The chapter devotes no less than six long sections on the discussion of knowledge and reason. Vasishtha declared that Brahma decided that 'the means for man to cross the ocean of *samsara* was knowledge, not asceticism, gifts or pilgrimages'.[24] This knowledge is not a sudden illumination, but it is acquired by constant application of reason to discern the truth without which there is no way to avoid evil and embrace good; all good comes from the tree of reason, a truly divine power that causes supreme bliss. Truth takes its origin from reason, and truth gives peace of mind and dispels all misery.[25] A judgement is not to be accepted because of the status of the speaker, even if it be the god Brahma, but because it is in conformity with reason, even if it was uttered by a child. 'One's own direct experience is the source of knowledge and the source of all other proofs, like the ocean is the origin of all waters.' Vasishtha's final advice to Rama is: continue to ponder the doctrines of the great teachers until you yourself in your own mind can arrive at the knowledge of the supreme.[26]

The other two works recommended and sent by Raychand to Gandhi were very small compositions. They are very different presentations of essential aspects of Advaita Vedanta, and both were attributed to Shankara by the tradition. The *Panchikarana* consists of only seven verses, and attempts to present in a concise way some of the main dogmas of that system. The *atman* is totally distinct from the three 'bodies' that envelop it, the gross body, the subtle body, and the causal body. These three bodies have also cosmic equivalents that are symbolised by the letters A, U, and M, which combine to form the most sacred and symbolic syllable OM. By meditation on this sacred symbol, man can penetrate through his three bodies to the very centre of his *atman*; when he realises that this is totally different from all that exists, he will experience that his *atman*'s identity with *Brahman*; this is the supreme truth of Advaita Vedanta.[27]

Although the text brought home the most central dogma of the system, it is difficult to imagine that Gandhi would have been very impressed by that aphoristic and symbolic presentation of abstruse dogmas. The *Maniratnamala* must have been more to his taste.[28] It presents 30 aphoristic verses, which each contain two to four questions and answers. Although the work gives clear indication of being written by a follower of Advaita Vedanta, the content is not concerned with Vedantic metaphysics. In fact, there are two themes that dominate the work; *vairagya*, non-attachment, and *vichar*, reflection, the same two themes that dominate the two chapters of the *Yoga-Vasishtha* Gandhi read.

The first two verses set the agenda for the whole work by stating the general principles which are elaborated throughout. Verse one puts non-attachment forward as the prime quality by which one recognises the person who has been liberated, whereas attachment characterises the person bound to the world. The main causes for attachment are identified: the objects of the senses, and specifically woman, who is the door to hell. The second verse adds the most important principle when it answers the double question: What destroys *samsara* and what is the cause of *moksha?*, with the simple answer *atmabodha*, knowledge of the self. The body of the work keeps reinforcing the message of the first two verses by praising the cultivation of non-attachment and the pursuit of knowledge as the two most basic means for the attainment of liberation, which are in the hands of the individual, and belong to a moral and intellectual order, and not to a divine or magical sphere.[29]

These three texts totally concentrated on describing the means to attain emancipation. Their message was emphatically clear: to attain liberation one had to perform the task oneself; there was no other way. This action had to proceed along two fronts: renunciation and the search for knowledge. It is interesting to note that these Advaita Vedanta texts were sent to Gandhi by Raychand who was a Jain. It shows that Raychand was not a narrow-minded theologian, but a spiritual sage of broad intellect, who was able to appreciate the positive value of Advaita Vedanta, and to recommend its writings as primary reading to Gandhi in his hour of confusion.

ANSWERS FROM CHRISTIANITY: MAITLAND

Towards the end of 1894 Gandhi acquired books of the Esoteric Christian Union, an offshoot of the Theosophical Society. He became an Agent for that Union, sold their books, and praised them highly in letters to the press.[30] Their new interpretation of Christianity was radically different from the Christianity of his friends and that presented in his readings so far. He praised it because it was universal, not based on historical facts but on eternal truths; it affirmed that all religions presented the same eternal truths, and avoided reviling other religions. Moreover, it was primarily concerned with the needs of the spirit, and fought modern materialism with conviction. Gandhi corresponded with the author Maitland until his death in 1897, and in his autobiography he acknowledged his influence.[31]

In various ways the fundamental ideas of Maitland, co-author of the book *The Perfect Way*,[32] strongly reinforced those presented by Raychand to Gandhi in his letters. Some aspects of Maitland's ideas would not have appealed to Gandhi, but they were rather peripheral. We will successively look at the basic ontology of Maitland, his concept of salvation, and his approach to the interpretation of scripture.

First of all, Maitland's ontology was firmly built on the idea of the opposition of Spirit and Matter, 'Matter is the antithetical ultimate of Spirit . . . Spirit alone is good, is God. Matter is that whereby Spirit is limited, and is, therein, the cause of evil; for evil is the limitation of good.'[33] This is very similar to Raychand's concept of spirit and matter. However, there is an important difference. Whereas Raychand denied the existence of a God-creator, Maitland acknowledged the existence of God, but not of a personalised God-creator, but rather of God as 'universal soul', as 'the substance of existence'. In fact, Maitland's idea of God was much closer to the concept of *Brahman* of Advaita Vedanta than to the personal divinity of Christianity.[34]

The parallelism between Maitland and both Raychand and Advaita becomes even more striking when we look at Maitland's concept of salvation. Firstly, what does it mean to be liberated? Maitland used the Christian term 'Redemption' for the process, which is 'brought about by the return from Matter of Spirit, to its original condition of purity . . . The great object to be attained is emancipation from the body – the redemption, that is, of Spirit from Matter.'[35]

Secondly, how is this liberation to be achieved? Maitland clearly affirmed that no external agent could accomplish this for man:

> But the notion that man . . . can be redeemed only by a personal Saviour in the flesh . . . is an idolatrous travesty of the truth. For that whereby a man is 'saved' is his own rebirth . . . and this process is altogether interior to the man, and incapable of being performed from without or by another.[36]

This process of self-purification of necessity involves asceticism. 'The body is but an instrument, existing for the use and sake of the soul, and not for itself . . . Whatever is given to the body is taken from the Spirit.'[37] It must have pleased Gandhi that Maitland accepted that the soul on its pilgrimage to redemption had to be reborn again and again: 'The doctrine of the Progression and Migration of Souls constituted the foundation of all those ancient religions out of which Christianity had its birth.'[38] Maitland's conception of man's pilgrimage to liberation was very similar to Raychand's: it was a process of freeing spirit from matter, a process totally within man's power, and a process spread over a series of reincarnations.

Finally, what was Maitland's concept of revelation and of the interpretation of scripture? Like Raychand, he accepted that there were a set of eternal truths, 'an original system which was the basis of all religions', and that, therefore, 'the doctrine of religion as present reality, needs no historical basis'. The scriptural accounts of Creation and the Fall were not histories, but allegories.[39] The same was true of the Gospel accounts:

They deal, primarily, not with material things or persons, but with spiritual significations . . . the narratives concerning Jesus are rather parables . . . And it is with this spiritual import, and not with the physical facts, that the Gospels are concerned . . . And miracles may indeed be proofs of occult power and skill, but are no evidences of the truth of any doctrine.[40]

Thus Maitland presented an interpretation of Christianity diametrically opposed to that of the Evangelicals. The central pillar of their faith was the historical Christ, the only son of God who had become man, and had redeemed all mankind through his actual death on the cross. Maitland wrote:

Christ, then, is primarily not a person, but a principle, a process, a system of life and thought, by the observance of which man becomes purified from Matter and transmuted into Spirit. And he is *a* Christ who, in virtue of his observance of this process to its utmost extent while yet in the body, constitutes a full manifestation of the qualities of spirit. Jesus is thus the name, not of one but of many, not of a person, but of an Order, the Order of regenerated Selfhoods . . . Between the man who becomes a Christ, and other men, there is no difference whatever of kind. The difference is alone of unfoldment of the spiritual nature possessed by all in virtue of their common derivation.[41]

This idea that Christ is not ontologically different from other men, and that each person is a potential Christ in that everyone has the power to completely purify his spirit from the contamination of matter, is surprisingly similar to what Raychand wrote about Rama and Krishna. They were not incarnations of God, but being spirits, they had, like every other spirit, the potential of totally purifying themselves; that total purification brought them back to their natural state, totally free from matter and *karma*, a state which Raychand called 'a god-like state'.

ANSWERS FROM CHRISTIANITY: TOLSTOY

Towards the end of his stay in Pretoria, Gandhi read the recently translated work of Leo Tolstoy, *The Kingdom of God is Within You*.[42] Later on he read more of his works, but for now, it is proper to concentrate on that work, because it reinforced in many ways the ideas he had been gathering from his other readings. Gandhi acknowledged the great influence Tolstoy had on him, and he corresponded with him.

Tolstoy was not one to indulge in metaphysics as Raychand and Maitland did. However, there are clear indications that his conception of life as the basis of religious endeavour did lean towards the dualism and antithesis of spirit and matter found in the others: 'Christ recognises the existence of both sides of the parallelogram, of both the eternal, indestructible forces of which man is composed, – the force of the animal nature and the force of the consciousness of a filial relation to God.' Christ was calling man 'to free it (the divine force) as much as possible from what is retarding it.' And life, according to Christ's teaching, consists in, 'only this liberation of the son of God, who lives in every man, from the animal, and his approximation to the Father'. Tolstoy did not theorise about the nature of God because to him religion was about man's striving, not about divine mysteries.[43]

But what, then, is the religious aim of man, what is that salvation he strives for? The term salvation was carefully avoided by Tolstoy because of its doctrinal implications in the Christian church. 'Life according to the Christian teaching, is a motion towards divine perfection . . . which reflects the direction of man's life from the animal condition towards the divine.' Tolstoy wrote that he 'advanced the model of an inner perfection of truth and love in the person of Christ'. This perfection consisted of the total renunciation of all violence, because 'the sacredness of every man's life is the first and only foundation of all morality'. This ideal, 'the divine law of love', was propounded by Christ in his Sermon on the Mount, but it was not a new revelation but an ideal 'borne in the soul of every man'. In other words, Christ's message was intended to make men aware of that inherent love that existed in them.[44]

In answer to the question how man achieved that ideal, Tolstoy vehemently rejected the methods proposed by the churches:

> If a man can save himself through redemption, sacraments, prayer, he no longer needs any good deeds . . . Men who believe in a bad and senseless God who has cursed the human race and who has doomed his son to be a victim, and has doomed a part of humanity to everlasting torment, cannot believe in a God of love. A man who believes in a God-Christ who will come again in glory to judge and punish the living and the dead, cannot believe in Christ, who commands a man to offer his cheek to the offender, not to judge, but to forgive, and to love our enemies.[45]

He put the work of salvation totally in the hands of man, and he insisted that this personal effort entailed suffering. 'The Kingdom of God is taken by force and only those who make an effort can get hold of it.' This effort could not be undertaken 'without self-renunciation, privation, suffering, and in extreme cases, the loss of life itself.'[46]

Finally, what was Tolstoy's conception of revelation and scripture? As we have seen, the supreme law of love has been inherent from all times in the very nature of man. Tolstoy accepted the importance of scripture: Christ, as the Gospels tell, tried to make men aware of that law of love, and he did this primarily in his Sermon on the Mount. But this direct teaching of Christ is but a small part of the Christian Bible, and even of the New Testament, which includes the Acts of the Apostles and the letters of the Apostles. One characteristic of these writings was their emphasis on the miraculous and the supernatural. Tolstoy rejected these episodes as adventitious, as inventions of the early church. So, 'stories of miracles heaped upon one another', and as the need for authority and certainty increased, dogmatism set in. Blind faith was demanded, and man 'no longer believes in God, nor in Christ, as they have been revealed to him, but in what the church commands him to believe.'[47]

In the same passionate way he rejected dogmatism, Tolstoy rejected the external rituals of the church, 'its ablutions, purification, fasts, Sabbaths', because the Gospel said that 'not the things which enter man's mouth, but those which come out of his heart, defile him.' But he went even further and repudiated the very concept of a church. Christ could certainly not have founded a church, because there was neither in Christ's words nor in the conceptions of his times 'anything resembling a concept of a church as we know it now, with its sacraments, its hierarchy, and above all, its assertion of infallibility'.[48]

CONVERGENCE OF ALL THE ANSWERS

The readings considered in this chapter were all studied by Gandhi in a short period of time, and thus they were bound to have a cumulative influence. They consisted basically of three different approaches with different sources. First there were Raychand's letters and the *Saddarshana Samucchaya*, which presented a strong Jain point of view. Secondly, there were three classical Advaita Vedanta texts pursuing a common approach. And thirdly, there were two works written by contemporary Christian thinkers, whose importance in the development of his own thought was clearly acknowledged by Gandhi; he actually had a prolonged correspondence with both authors. The influence of the totality of these writings on Gandhi cannot be overestimated. It seems important, therefore, in order to assess that influence, to systematically draw together the convergences of these texts.

In the matter of revelation, Raychand, Maitland, and Tolstoy agreed that there existed from the beginning of the world a set of fundamental truths, and that the scriptures of various religions were but man-made, and therefore fallible, attempts to formulate these truths. They also agreed that miracles either do not exist, or if they exist, are in no way proofs of the truth of anything. Raychand and Maitland also agreed that the avatarhood or divine incarnation of Krishna or Christ did not mean that they were God born on earth, or son of God, but that they were individual spirits who had reached the full perfection of liberation, an ideal achievable by every single spirit.

All the writers affirmed that at the basis of their conception of reality lay the radical opposition of spirit and matter – of 'animal and spiritual' in Tolstoy's case. Raychand and Maitland both denied the existence of a Creator-God along Christian lines. The three Indian Advaita Vedanta works affirmed the existence of *Brahman*, the Ultimate Absolute Reality. Maitland's idea of the divine was very similar to that. Raychand obviously supported the absolute duality of matter and spirit of Jainism, but did not explicitly deny the concept of *Brahman*, whereas Tolstoy did not philosophise at all about ultimate reality.

Finally, we find a strong convergence in their conception of liberation, the final goal of existence. All writers agreed that liberation consisted in the ultimate perfection of the spirit and its total freedom from the bonds of matter. The Vedantic writers called that state 'identification with *Brahman*'. As for the means of achieving that liberation, all strongly affirmed that only personal effort was the real means. They excluded all other non-personal, 'extraneous means' such as faith or *bhakti*, grace, or rituals, or the action of a Redeemer (Maitland and Tolstoy). They all put forward as the effective means of liberation the personal efforts of asceticism and renunciation, of understanding and wisdom, and of mercy and non-violence.

That is the convergence of ideas that impressed itself on Gandhi's mind during these months of reflection and study, at the end of which his mind had overcome all his anxious doubts and found peace. Firstly, his readings totally cancelled for ever whatever uncertainties the arguments his Christian friends had engendered. The concept of revelation he was now presented with was of a treasure of ancient truths that were proclaimed by different cultures in their sacred books. All these scriptures were man-made and intrinsically fallible. The Evangelists' claim of unique and total truth for the Bible became very unbelievable. His reading also totally discredited the claim that prophecies and miracles proved the divine authenticity of the Bible. The claim of these Christians that Christ was the only son of God and uniquely the redeemer of all mankind seemed rather unreasonable compared to the acceptance that great men in various cultures, such as Christ, Buddha, and Krishna, had progressed so far on the path to spiritual perfection that their cultures revered them as exemplars of what every man could achieve. The claim of the Evangelicals that man's redemption comes through the sacrifice of Christ, and through faith in Christ alone, must have seemed narrow and unfair to most of mankind, compared with the challenging doctrine that liberation had to be and could be achieved by the very action of each individual.

But his reading did not only provide Gandhi with strong and logical answers to all the passionate claims of the Evangelicals, it also provided him with some very important basic ideas about the structure of reality and the function of religion. The most basic fact affecting man was the opposition of matter and spirit. Essentially man is a pure spirit caught in and contaminated by matter. Religion presents the way of freeing the spirit from this bondage and restore it to its pristine glory and purity. That process is totally in the hands of each individual, and it consists primarily of moral action and deep understanding. Avatars and divine incarnations describe individuals who have approached that ideal of liberation of the spirit. An important branch of Hinduism, Advaita Vedanta, held that total liberation of the individual spirit meant its conscious identification with *Brahman*, the absolute spirit that upholds all that exists. We will see how strongly these ideas influenced Gandhi's concept of religion throughout his life.

3

The First Definition
of Hinduism

In March 1905, Gandhi gave four lectures on Hinduism under the auspices of the Johannesburg Lodge of the Theosophical Society. This constituted his first attempt at formulating how he understood Hinduism. By now the basic ideas he had gathered from his readings during 1894 had coalesced into a fairly clear schema of what religion and Hinduism meant to him.[1]

The first two lectures, which were published in English in *The Star*, presented a historical perspective on the development of Hinduism. They obviously depended strongly on the writings of British historians, especially W. W. Hunter's whom he often quoted in his memoranda, and present in themselves no strong personal views of Gandhi.[2] Nevertheless, some convictions and tendencies emerged there that would persist throughout his life. He accepted that India was invaded by 'a branch of the Aryan peoples' who colonised the subcontinent. Their scriptures, the Vedas, were very ancient, and were 'claimed to be God-given'. The rise of Buddhism constituted a reform of Hinduism, and had a lasting effect on it by its condemnation of animal sacrifices, which were part and parcel of early Vedic religion, and by its spirit of tolerance. Whereas Hinduism was never a missionary religion, Buddhism spread to Tibet, China, Japan, Burma and Ceylon. Jainism arose about the same time as Buddhism, independent from it. Gandhi's remarks about Jainism are of the utmost importance, because here he echoed what Raychand wrote, and what was also stated in the *Saddharma Sammucchaya*.

> Unlike others, they did not claim for the faith that it was of Divine origin, recognising that its sacred writings were the results of human workmanship. Jainism was, perhaps, the most logical of all faiths, and its most remarkable characteristic was its scrupulous regard for all things that lived.[3]

The second lecture continued the historical survey with the rise of idolatry. Although the 'Hindu philosophies' recognised God as the purest spirit, the masses sunk to 'the lowest depths', and worshipped God through his various manifestations, 'a mode of worship to which philosophical Hinduism with its tolerant spirit, had no difficulty reconciling itself.'[4] The next period was inaugurated by the advent of Islam in India. Gandhi was very positive about Mohamet and Islam, the key-note of which was 'its levelling spirit' of equality for all. Next an attempt was made by Kabir to bring about a conciliation of Islam and Hinduism. Guru Nanak combined the doctrines of Kabir with militant Hinduism and created the Sikh faith. Besides the creation of Sikhism, the main influence of Islam on Hinduism was that it 'brought out one of the chief characteristics of the religion, namely, toleration, in its true light and fullness'. Gandhi also mentioned Akbar's attempt at integration and toleration.[5]

The third lecture was devoted to the advent of Christianity in India. The missionaries converted Hindus partly by force and partly by persuasion. But later on Christianity became associated with Western civilization and Hindus began to look upon it with disfavour. Christianity had considerable influence by pointing out some of the glaring defects of Hinduism, which gave rise to reform movements such as the Brahmo Samaj and the Arya Samaj.[6]

The fourth lecture, on the tenets (*Tattva*) of Hinduism, was the most important one, because here Gandhi tried to explain 'what the followers of this religion, Hinduism, believe'. Whereas for the previous three historical surveys he relied on English secondary sources, in this lecture he explained his own conception of Hinduism. The third and fourth lectures were not published in *The Star*, but Gandhi published a synopsis of all four lectures in *Indian Opinion* on 15 April 1905. The great advantage of this summary was that it was actually written by Gandhi in Gujurati; this makes it possible to discover the exact Hindu terms he used.[7]

The first tenet of Hinduism according to Gandhi, was that God exists. He used the term *Ishvar*, the Lord, which in Hinduism traditionally denotes the personal divinity, mostly Shiva or Vishnu. We should remember that the lecture was originally given in English to a Western audience. To express that you believe in the divine, in English the expression 'God exists' is used. However, his next sentence makes it quite clear that Gandhi was not referring to the personal creator-God of Christianity. He described this 'God' as without beginning, without qualities (*nirguna*), without form (*nirakar)*, all-pervading, all-powerful, whose essential nature (*mul svarup*) was *Brahman*. So, he was not really referring to the personal divinity *Ishvar*, who cannot be described as *nirguna* and *nirakar*; he was speaking about *Brahman*. This is the term which emerged in Upanishadic times, and was taken over by the great orthodox school of Advaita Vedanta to signify the impersonal absolute reality that underlies all that exists. This is clearly confirmed by the next statement: 'He does not act, neither does he cause action; he does not reign over cosmic reality; he is essential pure bliss, and through him this whole creation is sustained.' In other words, the sustenance of the universe is not the result of any action of a personal God, but rather of the simple fact that *Brahman* is the ground of all that exists.[8]

This Advaitic approach of Gandhi becomes even clearer in his second tenet of Hinduism: 'The soul (*atma*) exists; it is distinct from the body; it is also without beginning, without birth; between its essential nature and *Brahman*, there is no difference.' This again is pure Advaita Vedanta, confirmed even further by the statement that when the *atman* is freed from the cycle of births and deaths it achieves deliverance (*moksha*) which means merging into *Brahman*. There cannot be any doubt that Gandhi here affirmed that the very essence of Hinduism is to be found in the basic tenets of Advaita Vedanta. That was in fact what he said in the introductory segment of his summary:

> The main thing that distinguishes the Hindus is their belief that the Brahman or oversoul is all-pervading. What we all have to attain is *Moksha* or liberation, . . . meaning freeing oneself from the evil of birth and death and merging in the Brahman.[9]

The third tenet treated the means of achieving liberation. Gandhi mentioned three: to perform good deeds, to practice compassion on all that lives, and to cultivate truth. However, he went on to say that even when one achieved this to a very high degree, liberation was not attained, because even the fruits of one's good deeds had to be reaped in the body. Therefore, a further step had to be taken. One has to continue to act morally, but in order to prevent one's good actions from producing their necessary result in a future life, one should act without any desire for, or attachment to the results, and dedicate all one's actions to God. Thus one's actions would not produce any more results, and one could escape from the cycle of transmigration into the state of *moksha*, liberation, and oneness with *Brahman*.[10]

The most striking characteristic of Gandhi's description of the means of achieving liberation, is that the central stage is dominantly occupied by moral action: actions that are good, totally compassionate, and in accordance with truth. No single branch of the great Hindu tradition would accept that man's moral action is the principal springboard to liberation. They all accept that moral action is an essential part of the preparation of the aspirant to liberation, but they all require some special and different kind of activity, distinct from moral action, and of a higher quality, that causes the advent of liberation. This may be on the part of the aspirant yogic or mystical endeavours leading to trance, or forms of ecstatic *bhakti*, love of the Lord; some schools, moreover, attribute the actual transit to *moksha* to an action of the loving divinity, a form of effective grace.

Nevertheless, Gandhi's conception of the means to achieve liberation does have a firm footing in the tradition, namely in the doctrine of the *Bhagavadgita*. This work teaches that action cannot be renounced because it is an essential aspect of the human embodiment. Action itself should not be renounced, but the fruit of action should be renounced and all action should be dedicated to Krishna:

> Whatever you do, whatever you eat, whatever you offer in sacrifice or give away in alms, whatever penance you may perform, do it as an offering to me (*mad-arpanam*).[11]

That is exactly what Gandhi wrote: act without attachment to the result, and offer it all to the Lord (*Ishvar ko arpan karen*).

There remains, however, one important difference between Gandhi and the *Gita*. The latter recommends that all actions be offered up to Krishna, who is the full incarnation of lord Vishnu, the supreme personal God of the Vaishnavites. Gandhi did say 'offer it all to the Lord', but, as we have seen, he uses the term *Ishvar* as a convenient translation of the English term God, but the God he described at the start of this section was not a personal God but an impersonal absolute, *Brahman*. He adopts the attitude of offering all as it is found in the *Gita*, but he does not subscribe to the definition of the Godhead as personal. This naturally raises the question: how can one have a devotional attitude of total surrender to an impersonal absolute? Advaitic absolutism and devotional surrender do not seem to fit together, and they do not really co-exist in the traditional schools of Hinduism which require the Lord God to be the object of devotion. However, this unusual combination of Advaita and *bhakti* represents a strong, late and popular stream in Hinduism appropriately named *nirguna bhakti*, love for the unqualified (absolute). This was a fundamental characteristic of the collection of *bhakti* poets often referred to as the 'Sants'. In fact, during this period Gandhi read a lot of these poets and even reproduced their poems in his journal.[12] And he himself, even if he was not aware of the term *nirguna bhakti*, gave a hint to the spirituality of these poets in a letter he wrote eight years later to Jamnadas Gandhi, trying to explain what true *bhakti* is:

> The true meaning of *bhakti* is search for the *atman*. When the *atman* realises itself, *bhakti* is transformed into *jnana* [knowledge]. Narasimha (Mehta) and others gave themselves to such devoted search of the *atman* [*atmaki bhaktipurn khoj*].[13]

Bhakti is here clearly connected with *atman*, the spirit, which is in reality identical with *Brahman*. This is clearly *nirguna bhakti*.[14]

There is a further striking aspect of Gandhi's first statement about the essential tenets of Hinduism: his omission of a number of very important ingredients of that religion. Some of these may have been omitted simply because the audience Gandhi addressed consisted primarily of Christians. But the omissions do have something to tell us about Gandhi's own attitude to Hinduism. He totally disregarded the Vedas and scripture in his summary of the tenets of Hinduism. The Christians certainly would have been most interested to hear about that topic, considering the tremendous importance the Bible had in their own religious beliefs. Gandhi did refer to the Vedas in his first historical lecture and said that they were very ancient. He added that 'very devout Hindus believe that the Vedas are of divine origin and without beginning'. He gave no clear indication that this was an essential aspect of Hinduism, nor that he himself believed in that claim. The opposite can be inferred from what he had to say about Jainism: it did not believe in the divine origin of its sacred writings, which were the result of human workmanship; therefore, 'Jainism was the most logical of all faiths'. It seems Gandhi believed that logically all scriptures, including the Christian and Hindu ones, were human creations.[15]

Secondly, Gandhi totally avoided any mention of the Hindu pantheon, even of the three great Gods, Brahma, Shiva, and Vishnu, and of the avatars. These in fact stand at the very centre of the religious life of most Hindus. Thirdly, the whole world of ritual was omitted, except in the historical introduction. There he stated that animal sacrifice was the essential 'ceremonial characteristic' of early Hinduism. It was Gautama Buddha who was the main cause in the stopping of that practice. Gandhi also referred to idol-worship in his second historical lecture about the period when Hinduism was 'very largely addicted to idolatry', worshipping 'stocks and stones', which 'brought down the ignorant masses to their lowest depths'. These expressions do indicate in Gandhi an aversion to the practice, although he stated that philosophical Hinduism reconciled itself to it. Significantly, Gandhi totally omitted this episode in his summary of the lectures. All in all, Gandhi showed here that he had no positive feeling for any form of ritual, and totally excluded it from the essence of Hinduism.[16]

Finally, there is yet another striking gap in his account: he did not mention the importance of intellectual and psychic practices that play a major part in most schools of Hinduism including Advaita Vedanta. We refer here to the various practices of meditation, concentration, trance, which were first catalogued by Patanjali in his *Yoga Sutras*, and became a very important basic ingredient in many higher forms of Hinduism, even if it was adapted to the various approaches of schools and sects.

When we look closely at the way in which Gandhi presented the tenets of Hinduism, we find a very clear progression structure: God exists, the soul exists, *moksha* exists, and here are the means to achieve liberation. This structure is very simple, and we can trace this simplicity back to the answers of Raychand to Gandhi's questions of 1894. In his first letter Raychand answered Gandhi's question, 'what is the *atman*?', by explicating the nature of the spirit, the possibility of liberation, and the means of attaining it, thus presenting the essence of his Jain belief. In each of his following two letters, Raychand repeated these essentials aphoristically exactly in the same order. Moreover, Gandhi found that same presentation that same year when he read the *Saddarshana Sammucchaya*, sent to him by Raychand. There can be no doubt that these four near-identical presentations of Jainism are the source of Gandhi's own simple structure. In fact, in one of the rare concise statements about religion as a whole during the rest of his stay in South Africa, the identical pattern recurred: 'God is the supreme *atman*. The *atman* exists. *Moksha* is possible for it.'[17] However, there remains one important difference. Whereas all the schemata presented by Raychand totally omitted any mention of God, Gandhi put 'God exists' at the top of his list.

THE DEFINITION MAINTAINED

Gandhi's definition of Hinduism did not change during the rest of his stay in South Africa. The occasions when he explicitly wrote about religion as such were very rare. In the first two months of 1907 he published in *Indian Opinion* a series of essays in which he presented the 'substance of the teachings' contained in William Mackintire Salter's *Ethical Religion*.[18] A close comparison of Gandhi's text with the original clearly shows that he remained throughout extremely faithful to Salter's text, summarising parts, transcribing others nearly literally. He omitted a great amount that he considered of little interest to his readers, such as lengthy passages about the history of Christianity, or excursions of a more philosophical kind.

No doubt Gandhi found in Salter's work a great deal that conformed with and confirmed his own convictions about religion. Salter firmly held that ethical action was the very heart of the meaning and goal of human life, and the most important aspect of religion, because 'without morality, religion cannot subsist'. Ethical teachings are, according to Salter, of universal application and are not transmitted by God through messengers in holy books, but they are in fact a supreme law that dwells in everybody's heart. Salter's stress on moral action was most forcefully expressed in his saying that 'an ethical idea is useless as long as it is not followed by suitable action'. This idea would later find an echo in Gandhi's saw that 'there is nothing apart from conduct which can be defined as religion.'[19]

However, Gandhi did not agree with all of Salter's ideas. First of all, Salter's work reflected a strong prejudice against all forms of established religion. The following quotations make that abundantly clear:

> What does religion, then, add to ethics . . . ? Nothing I can see; and what it attempts to add, is, generally at least . . . superstition. Religion conceives the good in the form of a person, and asserts that he is ruling the world. But this is an illusion, and really a harmful one. A true, sound and wholly rational religion . . . would be simply a perfected ethics.[20]

Gandhi wrote, 'the author adds that there is nothing wrong in calling morality a religion', but what Salter in fact stated was that 'morality alone was fit to be a religion'. Gandhi showed his disagreement with Salter's strong prejudice against established religion, by simply omitting those passages from his summary. After all, his own audience were practically all practising Hindus or Muslims.[21]

Salter also argued very strongly against the concept of God as a person as presented by religions. His rational belief in the divine was expressed as follows:

God is the infinite element in all duty, its eternal basis without which duty and man and the world alike would disappear . . . The deepest, the bottom thing in the universe must be that which is capable of giving a commandment; not matter then, nor force, nor will, but reason, that ineffable reality of which human reason is a poor and shadowy suggestion.[22]

Again Gandhi carefully omitted such statements, and he even went a step further. He actually inserted in several places some sentences that certainly did not come from Salter, and did not conform to the moralist's convictions.

God (*Khuda ya Ishvar*) is omnipotent, He is perfect. There are no limits to His mercy, to His goodness and His justice . . . The result of our action is not within our control. God (*parameshvar*) alone is the giver of fruit . . . One may conclude that the moral law is supreme and divine (*Ishvariya*).[23]

We have seen that Gandhi did not believe in a personal God, but in the absolute *Brahman*; he will reiterate this quite clearly in his later letters to Jamnadas Gandhi. He is writing here for simple believing Hindus, and he is putting the conviction of Salter that the divine is the eternal element of all duty and goodness, into a terminology that is understandable to them.

In his treatise *Hind Svaraj* written at the end of 1909, Gandhi did not directly treat religion as such. Gandhi's references to the essence of religion during this period were sporadic, but they always confirmed the pivotal statements of his 'Lectures on Hinduism'. He reiterated that religion should not be equated with the established religions: 'by religion he did not mean formal religion or customary religion, but that religion which underlay all religions, which brought them face to face with their maker'. He stressed that the essence of religion was action, moral action: 'Knowing the fundamentals means putting them into practice'. Religious rites were 'all right as far as they go . . . but by themselves they are no indication of one's being devoted to God in worship. He alone truly adores God who finds his happiness in the happiness of others,' and performs moral deeds.[24]

In the middle of 1913 Gandhi wrote four letters to Jamnadas Gandhi in which he stated some of his main convictions about religion.[25] They provide us with a clear picture of his ideas towards the end of his stay in South Africa. It is interesting to note that these letters were written in answer to Jamnadas' letters to Gandhi wherein he asked for clarification of his doubts and difficulties. They must have reminded Gandhi of his own correspondence with Raychand nearly twenty years earlier. These letters confirm Gandhi's basic ideas as expressed in his lectures on Hinduism of 1905. It is important to draw attention to the context of these statements. They are contained in personal letters to one of Gandhi's closest followers and collaborators. They are bound to closely reflect Gandhi's deepest conviction. In other texts, for instance, in his periodical *Indian Opinion*, Gandhi's language and expression was often dictated by his audience of devout Hindus who were ignorant of the philosophy of Hinduism. We saw how in that context, Gandhi was not averse to refer to the divinity as *Ishvar*, the Lord, because that was the only term which conveyed to them the idea of the divine. With his pupil Jamnadas he was able to express himself more directly and accurately.

Gandhi clearly reaffirmed his conviction that the ultimate ground of all is not a personal divinity, but the absolute *Brahman*, 'pure consciousness, as described by the adherents of Advaita'. There is no personal God who dispenses rewards and punishments. If anyone can be called God, it is the individual *atman* that has actually reached deliverance from birth and death, and has thus become omniscient. Gandhi strongly reaffirmed his belief in Advaita by explicitly using the following Advaitic maxim, and calling it a first principle: *Brahma satyam, jagan mithya*, Brahman is real, the cosmos is unreal.[26]

Gandhi was forced by Jamnadas' questions into specifying what he understood by avatar, or incarnation of God, a subject he had carefully avoided in his lectures on Hinduism in 1905. Jamnadas did not know how to deal with the stories about Krishna in the *Mahabharata*, and even less with those told about the erotic adventures of Krishna in the *Bhagavata Purana*. Gandhi tried to give him some basic principles that would help him clarify his thoughts. Avatarhood, he wrote, meant the achievement of *moksha*, and as such was available to every single *atman*. Krishna and Rama are called avatars because people believe they achieved *moksha*. In periods of moral degradation and despair, people believe an avatar was sent down from above; and they looked for support from exceptionally great saints they considered avatars.[27]

The stories about Krishna had, according to Gandhi, a double level of possible interpretation. If the story was taken to actually refer to the historic Krishna, an embodied soul, then references to imperfections or even sins, should not disturb one, because the embodied Krishna was not perfect. If, on the other hand, the text was taken to refer to Krishna as the Supreme Being, then a symbolical interpretation was appropriate, because in that form Krishna is imagined to be perfect.[28] It is to be noted how similar Gandhi's conception was to that contained in Raychand's letters of 1894. This connection is confirmed by another related idea presented by Gandhi to Jamnadas. 'The true meaning of *bhakti* is search for the *atman*. When the *atman* realises itself the *bhakti* is transformed into knowledge, *jnana*. [The Gujarati literally reads *bhakti* is dissolved and in its place *jnana* appears].'[29] This is exactly what Raychand wrote to Gandhi about the role of *bhakti* in the process of attaining *moksha*.[30]

On the question of revelation, Gandhi reiterated his idea that the scriptures were not infallible, and that they had to be judged with the yardstick of morality. Anything in them that offended the inviolable principles of morality had to be rejected. The task of identifying later textual interpolations in the scriptures should be left to the pandits, Gandhi wrote, because an aspirant to *moksha* should not waste time on such fruitless exercise. As for a formal comparison of the various religions, Gandhi felt that it was uncalled for. However, he pointed to a clear criterion for the purpose of general comparison; that was *daya-dharma*, the rule of compassion. In other words, that religion is the greater one which gives greater prominence to the observance of *ahimsa*, non-violence. Gandhi knew that when this principle was applied, Jainism would stand foremost among the religions because its concept of non-violence was the most universal and far-reaching.[31]

The letters to Jamnadas in 1913 clearly demonstrate that there was no change in Gandhi's concept of religion since his Lectures on Hinduism of 1905. We have shown how much these ideas were taken from Raychand's letters, and what a great convergence of basic ideas consisted between those letters, the Hindu texts Gandhi read, and his reading of Christian radicals like Maitland and Tolstoy. There is a difference in tone from the Lectures on Hinduism, however. In his letters to Jamnadas, Gandhi sounds very confident of his principles, and he was even ready to apply them to a range of new questions.

CONCLUSION

The mature Gandhi who left South Africa aged 45 was a very different man from the callow youth who arrived there twenty years earlier. His religious baggage was very light then. He knew very little of his own religion, and was not really interested in it. The concerted attempts of his Christian friends left him apprehensive and tongue-tied. His prime ambition was to make good as a lawyer, after dismal failure in India, and to work up to a career that would have made his father proud of him, and bring wealth and prestige to his family. The guidance of Raychand, supplemented by some serious reading, soon gave him a sure knowledge of the essentials of his faith, and a firm theoretical framework to deal with the claims of the evangelical Christians. This insight gave him great confidence in his own ideas and their validity. Once this assurance was firmly established, he started that slow ascent in his practice of his religion that would, by the end of his stay in South Africa, give him a reputation of saintliness. He was no longer the ambitious youngster, proud of his English legal qualification, who imitated the lifestyle of England-educated barristers, serving the wealthy with an eye to his future ambitions. He had become an ashram-dweller who no longer had a home of his own; a political activist whose total energy was dedicated to the cause of the lowliest Indians. In Satyagraha he had created a startlingly original form of political agitation firmly grounded in religion. The mature Gandhi who took the steamer back to India was certainly on the way to an extraordinary, high-profile, and powerful career in his country – but one that had absolutely no relation to the ambition that drove him to South Africa twenty years earlier.

Part II

India: Convictions
and Attitudes

4

A New Definition of Hinduism: 1921

It has been shown how, early in his stay in South Africa, Gandhi explained his understanding of Hinduism in his 1905 'Lectures on Hinduism'. The essential tenets of Hinduism he presented there were basically those of Advaita Vedanta: *Brahman* exists, the *atma* exists, and for the *atma* it is possible to achieve *moksha*, the deliverance from the cycle of transmigration leading to the absorption into that absolute *Brahman*. He also told his audience that Hindus believed that the Vedas were divine, but he later made clear that he himself did not believe in their divinity, but that he ranked them with the Bible and the Koran, as human and imperfect explanations of religion. In that exposé he completely omitted any reference to many theological, mythological, ritual, and social aspects of Hinduism, because he was explaining Hinduism not to Hindus but to Christians. There was another reason for that omission. Gandhi himself knew little about many facets of the Hindu tradition, and among the Hindus of South Africa there was practically no one with a deep and scholarly knowledge who could further or challenge Gandhi's ideas or even discuss them with him. Gandhi had read but little of the Hindu scriptures, and the only stimulus to think about religion was private, coming primarily from his closest associates and family. A clear echo of this is found in his letters to Jamnadas Gandhi written in 1913, which were the most important documents for establishing his personal ideas on religion towards the end of his stay in South Africa.[1]

When Gandhi settled down in India in 1914, the scene changed completely. He was now back in the ancient homeland of Hinduism, a land overflowing with people who claimed to be experts in Hinduism, to know its holy books and its sacred language, and to have a right to give authoritative statements on matters of ethics, doctrine, and scriptural interpretation. Moreover, they had access to a range of newspapers and journals wherein to voice their questions and their disagreements, and to challenge Gandhi's pronouncements on Hinduism. Gandhi quickly became aware of that situation. When in early 1919, in his first call to the nation as a whole, he urged Hindus to read the *Gita* on the Sunday of the declared national strike, the reaction was immediate. Hindu authorities accused him of misunderstanding the message of the *Gita* which, they held, encouraged and approved of violence, and was, therefore, out of place in a setting of non-violent satyagraha. Throughout the next thirty years every pronouncement of Gandhi on Hinduism was thus challenged, providing to Gandhi a constant stimulus to clarify, elaborate, and justify his ideas.

From the start many Hindu authorities rejected as unorthodox his understanding of various facets of Hinduism in crucial issues such as non-violence, caste and untouchability. Gandhi's claim that he was a '*sanatani* Hindu', meaning a Hindu who was grounded in the ancient and traditional beliefs and values of Hinduism, particularly annoyed those who considered themselves custodians of the orthodox establishment. From the beginning Gandhi defended his statements and his approach, but it took him a few years before he felt confident to publicly present a comprehensive exposé of his conception of Hinduism. The two most wide-ranging and balanced accounts were published in 1921: the first was published in Gujarati in *Navajivan* under the title 'Who is a Sanatani Hindu?', the second in October, in English in *Young India* under the title 'Hinduism'.[2]

During his first year back in India Gandhi, following the advice of Gokhale, had travelled around India and avoided making any statements on public matters. He had also organised his new Ashram in Ahmedabad. From 1916 he started to participate in political activities, but he still remained on the sidelines. In early 1917 he organised his first local satyagraha campaign for the indigo-workers of Champaran in Bihar. Later on he staged a no-tax campaign in the Kheda district, and from February to July 1918 he organised and led the Ahmedabad mill-workers strike. These three successful local campaigns made him and his satyagraha method well-known around the country, and he became involved in the agitation for Hindi as a national language, and in recruiting for the British Army. It was in the fateful year of 1919 that he became an all-India political figure of prominence by his organisation of the country-wide public strike against the introduction of the repressive Rowlatt Bills. In 1920 he successfully steered his programme of non-cooperation through the National Congress, and rewrote its constitution. These had been a frantically busy five years, that gave him little time for sustained religious reflection.

In 1919 he took over the running of the English journal *Young India*, and of the Gujarati journal *Navajivan*. Therefore, by 1920 he had achieved a strong national leadership position; revered as Mahatma by the people, accepted by the politicians, respected by the British. He had also acquired press organs through which he could explain and propagate his ideals. No wonder that in 1921 he felt ready to boldly state his concept of Hinduism with authority. The two articles mentioned containing that statement, were meant to prove his own claim, so often negated by the orthodox, that he was a *sanatani* Hindu. They are very important public statements which are used here as a benchmark in the study of the development of Gandhi's concept of Hinduism. On the one hand it will show how his new definition of Hinduism compares with the one he developed in South Africa. Secondly, it will offer a clear starting-point for the next four chapters, which will explore how the various components of his conception of Hinduism evolved during the rest of his life.

Right at the beginning of his exposé Gandhi reaffirmed what he considered to be the fundamental tenets of Hinduism:

A Hindu is one who believes in the existence of the *atman* and the *paramatman*, and believes further that the *atman* is never born and never dies but, through incarnation in the body, passes from existence to existence and is capable of attaining *moksha*, . . . the supreme end of human striving.[3]

This is exactly the concise formula he had already used in 1905 in South Africa. Although the term *paramatman* is one generally used to refer to *Brahman*, this should not be taken as here deliberately signifying an Advaitic framework. In this document Gandhi was not explaining the details of his personal beliefs, but the general tenets of Hinduism, within which various conceptions of the deity were acceptable. In the article 'Hinduism', written in English, he uses the wider term 'God': 'Every Hindu believes in God and his oneness, in rebirth and salvation.'[4]

Secondly, he treated the question of revelation: 'a Hindu accepts the Vedas, the Upanishads, and the *Puranas* as holy books'.[5] Two very important riders were attached to this belief in scripture. First of all:

The reader will note that I have purposely refrained from using the word divine origin in reference to the Vedas or any other scriptures. For I do not believe in the exclusive divinity of the Vedas. I believe the Bible, the Koran, and the Zend-Avesta to be as much divinely inspired as the Vedas.[6]

Secondly, Gandhi warned that he did not have to accept 'every word and every verse as divinely inspired'. Every scripture text has to pass the test of reason and morality which will eliminate whatever is 'inauthentic'. Here, naturally, the question arose of who could apply those tests and give an authoritative ruling. Gandhi's answer was quite categorical:

> I do most emphatically repudiate the claim (if they advance any such) of the present Shankaracharyas and shastris to give a correct interpretation of the Hindu scriptures. On the contrary I believe, that our present knowledge of these books is in a most chaotic state.[7]

Perhaps in the future such 'cultured' persons may emerge but in the meantime, 'we, the common people, may cling to the essentials (*mul tattva*) with a simple faith and live our lives in *bhakti* to God'. Gandhi's general concept of scripture was practically the same as he already had in South Africa. One thing had definitely changed: his five years in India had totally disillusioned him about the value of the traditional interpreters of scripture who claimed authentic interpretations. Their claim may have reminded him of the claim of Christians to infallibility so vehemently attacked by Tolstoy in his works.[8]

Gandhi also succinctly indicated what he considered to be the moral centre of Hinduism, or the 'essence of Hinduism' from the point of view of human aspirations and actions: 'I believe that the essence of Hinduism is truth and non-violence . . . The active manifestation of non-violence is love – absence of ill-will.'[9]

Practically all that has been said so far was for Gandhi not only true of Hinduism, but of every religion, 'because the fundamentals of Hinduism as of every great religion are unchangeable, and easily understood . . . But that which distinguishes Hinduism from every other religion is cow-protection [and] its *varnashrama*.'[10] Both of these were extensively treated in the two articles; in fact their treatment occupies about eighty per cent of each essay. This is not surprising, because it was primarily over his ideas on non-violence and cow-protection, and on caste and untouchability, that Gandhi clashed with the orthodox. In South Africa he had practically never mentioned these topics. But in India he encountered them at every turn, and he had to take a stand. In these essays he wanted to show that his own conceptions in those matters should not be branded as unorthodox, but should make him acceptable as a *sanatani* Hindu, as an orthodox believer, because they were essential ingredients of authentic Hinduism.

Gandhi's praise of cow-protection was nothing short of rapturous:

The central fact of Hinduism however is cow-protection. Cow-protection to me is one of the most wonderful phenomena in human evolution. It takes the human being beyond his species. A cow to me means the entire sub-human world. Man through the cow is enjoined to realise his identity with all that lives . . . Protection of the cow means protection of the whole dumb creation of God . . . Cow-protection is the gift of Hinduism to the world.[11]

In South Africa Gandhi treated the question of cow-protection only once in a chapter of his *Hind Svaraj* entitled 'The Condition of India: The Hindus and the Mahommedans'.[12] He did state that he looked upon the cow with 'affectionate reverence' because of her great usefulness to an agricultural country like India. But that is as far as he went, there was nothing like the paragraph just quoted. In the present text Gandhi elevated cow-protection to be the supreme symbol of the highest ideal of non-violence. About the actual treatment of the cow by contemporary Hinduism, he had three comments to offer. First, they generally treated the cow with great cruelty. Secondly, cow-protection had 'degenerated into a perpetual feud with the Mussulmans, whereas cow-protection means conquering Mussulmans, by our love.' Thirdly, Hindus did not attack the British about the killing of cows but 'tolerate it . . . and . . . salute the British flag.'[13]

Varnashrama, the Hindu system of classes, *varna*, and stages of life, *ashrama*, is the other aspect that, according to Gandhi, set Hinduism apart from all other religions. Again, this was not something that exercised Gandhi's mind much in South Africa. But after his five years in India, he clearly put forward in these two essays the basic principles of Hindu social organisation, which would remain largely unchanged throughout his life. The system of the four classes of Brahmins, Kshatriyas, Vaishyas, and Shudras, was according to him a law of nature which 'Hinduism had reduced to a science'. It was a division of society in four categories according to their innate abilities and consequent tasks, which were basically inherited, and which designated each person at birth to a particular class. They were fundamentally different from the system of hundreds of castes, *jati*, which was rampant in India. Class had no reference to rights, only to duties, and had no implication of superiority or inferiority. Thus classes were totally different from castes which concentrated on rights, and were dominated by the ranking from high to low. According to Gandhi, the myriad regulations about food, drink, social contact, and marriage that utterly dominated the caste system were not essential aspects of society. They were, however, 'a

protective fence for Hindu culture', and were means for the cultivation
of self-control. Untouchability, another dominant characteristic of the
contemporary caste system, was contrary to morality and religion, in fact
it was demonic and a shame on Hinduism. He wrote, that this taint had
become to him 'an intolerable burden'.[14]

That was, then, the way Gandhi understood religion and Hinduism in
1921, at the beginning of his long public, national career. The basic
tenets of Hinduism were still very much as he presented them in 1905:
the centrality of *moksha*, the rationalistic view of scripture, and the
moral core of truth and non-violence. The new slant of his exposé was in
the description of the two elements that made Hinduism different from
every other religion: cow-protection and *varnashrama*. The following
four chapters will explore how these fundamental conceptions evolved
during the next quarter of a century in close and intense encounters with
real Hinduism around him, and in the triumphs and disasters of the
national struggle for independence.

5

Facing the Gritty
Reality of Hinduism

Back in India, Gandhi was surrounded by and immersed in the all-encompassing reality of practical Hinduism in its ritual, social, and sectarian manifestations. His attitudes to these realities are investigated in this chapter.

RITUAL HINDUISM

Gandhi reserved his outright condemnation for only two current Hindu ritual practices, animal sacrifice and the dedication of *devadasis*. In the matter of 'the cruel slaughter of goats before the Mother in the sacred eighth day of *Navaratri*, the day of sacrifice, and on the auspicious Dashera day', he wrote:

> We believe it to be the duty of every Hindu to stop, as early as possible, this violence which some Hindus, believers in the duty of compassion, commit on the pretext of offering a sacrifice to the Goddess. If we appeal to our Muslim brethren to stop cow-slaughter, we on our part must stop this violence.[1]

Apropos of the Kali temple in Calcutta, his plea was passionate:

> The mere thought of the Kali temple fills me with horror. How can the place be called a temple at all? In literal truth rivers of blood flow there every day. Who knows what the thousands of goats slaughtered there in the name of religion say in the court of God? How infinite is Mother Kali's patience? Does she really demand cruel sacrifices? People who offer them tarnish her sacred name.[2]

In 1942, when the President of the trustees of the Sirsi temple in Canara abolished the custom of animal sacrifice, Gandhi rejoiced: 'This is indeed good news. Shri Keshwain deserves congratulations for his humanitarian spirit. Those who wish to may eat what meats they like, but it is defaming God to offer sacrifices in temples.'[3]

In each case, Gandhi put forward that the act of animal sacrifice was one that could not be a religious act because it violated the fundamental moral order of non-violence. When confronted with the fact that sacrifice, and even animal sacrifice, was practised in Vedic times, he explained as follows:

> If the *rishis* and *munis* of the past had sacrificed animals, it is my firm belief that at that time the need for such sacrifice was felt; however, today there is no need for doing so; it is a savage and cruel practice. I regard such acts of offering animals as sacrifices as not only not religious in this age, but as irreligious acts.

He went on to suggest that the *Gita* proposed a new interpretation of sacrifice in tune with our world: 'the meaning of *yajna* approved by the *Gita* is: It is an act which is performed solely for the sake of service or from a purely altruistic standpoint'.[4]

In a speech at a public meeting in Karaikudi Gandhi referred to the persisting custom there of 'consecrating' young girls to God, calling them *devadasis* (servants of God), and actually making them into temple prostitutes.

> A lady doctor . . . tells me that the rich people of Chettinad had a due share in perpetuating a hideous immoral custom of assigning girls of tender age to a life of shame under the name of religion. She tells me that there are many *Devadasis* in your midst . . . Let not possession of wealth be synonymous with degradation, vice, and profligacy . . . There are, I am sorry to say, many temples in this country which are no better than brothels.[5]

When an Andhra graduate who had married a *devadasi* wrote to Gandhi about the ostracism, the stigma of prostitution that clung to them even when they had totally severed their connection with the custom, Gandhi wrote back to him suggesting 'ways of working at the problem'. First the employers of the *devadasis* and the *devadasi* community should be targeted in order to stop the vice. But that was not enough. As 'Hunger knows no sin', an innocent source of livelihood should be found for the *devadasis*, who for the moment had no other way of supporting themselves.[6]

Gandhi's attitude to most other Hindu rituals was a combination of positive and negative. It was in the context of the question of idol-worship that he developed the basic principles which guided his judgement of many ritual practices. In his declaration about Hinduism of 1921 he stated that he was not against idol-worship but he did not clarify why.[7] It was on his visit to the southern tip of India, Kanyakumari, that he tried for the first time to articulate his ideas on idol-worship, because 'While circumambulating the temple, all this became clear to me.' In his article 'The Darshan of Kanyakumari', he described how profoundly the location and the temple impressed him, 'I drank in here the nectar of the mystery of religion . . . my religious yearning grew stronger . . . I sat in silence, my heart filled with the image of the teacher of the *Gita*.' This was one of the very rare occasions that Gandhi waxed lyrical about the influence of a particular place on his mind. It was in this atmosphere that he formulated for the first time his understanding of idol-worship.[8]

'I did not pity the ignorance of the idolatrous Hindu,' he wrote, 'but, on the contrary, realised his wisdom.' By 'discovering' image-worship, the Hindu did not make one God into many, but realised that man can worship God in a myriad ways, because God has so many different forms. This allows everyone to worship God in the form he likes best. This form may be an idol of stone or gold, but it is worshipped as a form of the divine, and this divinity is specifically attributed to it. Thus it becomes an aid to genuine divine worship and a method of reaching *moksha*. Gandhi widened his concept of idol-worship beyond that of iconographic representations. A temple, a mosque, or a church also involved a form of idol-worship, because the faithful imagined that their presence in them increased their own holiness. 'Even the faith that God is revealed only in the Koran or the Bible is idol worship and an innocent one.' These 'enlargements' of the concept of legitimate idol-worship are interesting in that they provide a clever answer to those who considered idol-worship as a particular weakness of Hinduism. Gandhi stated that all religions practised it in some way, but that Hinduism, 'made it its specialty, a result of its wisdom'.[9]

In his next essay about idol-worship Gandhi explained how legitimate idol-worship becomes idolatry. When the object of worship is taken purely as a physical object and its function as representation of the divine presence is forgotten, then it is no more worship, but becomes superstition. In respect of that form of idol-worship Gandhi was an iconoclast, an idol-breaker. He extended the same principle to the wider context of belief in scripture. This belief is acceptable and elevating when it is guided by reason and morality. However, when holy writ is considered to be infallibly true in all its utterances, and is used to prove 'that untruth is truth, cruelty is kindness and hatred is love, then it becomes a form of idolatry, and is to be condemned'.[10]

Gandhi regularly reiterated this conception and never changed it substantially. Idolatry, worship through images, was 'as old as Adam, and, as natural to him as eating and drinking, if not more natural'. Idol-worship was 'investing one's ideal with a concrete shape', and as such 'inherent in human nature'. Elsewhere he indicated the essential role of imagination in the process. 'The devotee . . . conceives of his deity in his own image, which means that it is a matter of imagination, but so long as imagination holds sway it represents the real.'[11] In this context, Gandhi connected the role of the imagination in idol-worship with the worship of avatars:

> For the object of one's worship one can choose either an idea, that is an imaginary figure, or a historical person. I prefer the former. Krishna conceived as *Sampurnavatara*, i.e. a plenary incarnation of God, is an ideal, that is, an imaginary incarnation. A historical Krishna may have defects.[12]

Although Gandhi accepted the religious validity of proper idol-worship, he admitted in a letter to Narayan Khare that idol-worship was not for him personally:

> I have said regarding myself that I am both an image-worshipper and an image-breaker. The God conceived by a human being is bound to be a form, though the image may be only in the mind. In that sense I am an image-worshipper. But I have never been willing to worship any form or image as God. Towards a form or image, I always feel *neti, neti*. Hence I regard myself as an image-breaker.[13]

Here Gandhi revealed himself as a follower of Advaita Vedanta, by using the Upanishadic expression *neti neti* (not this, not this) which is the most famous negative definition of the absolute *Brahman*, which is by nature undescribable.

In the sad last weeks of Gandhi's life, when Hindu–Muslim riots erupted everywhere, some Hindus installed an idol of Hanuman in a mosque in Delhi. In view of the clashes in the early 1990s in Ayodhya over the demolition of an old mosque and the installation of a shrine to Rama, it is of interest how Gandhi reacted at that time.

Some Hindus have installed an idol in some mosque . . . but it is said, and I also believe, that so long as it has not been sanctified and not worshipped by pure hands, in my view it is not an idol but a mere piece of stone or gold. Such idols have been installed in the mosque at the corner of Connaught Place . . . It can only be worshipped if it is legitimately installed and sanctified. But all this was not done. Hence it is the duty of those who have installed the idols to remove them . . . By thus installing idols in the mosque they are desecrating the mosques and also insulting the idols. As followers of Hinduism we are idol-worshippers, but worshipping any idol in this manner is not religion but the opposite of it.[14]

Idols are often connected with temples. Gandhi never was a regular temple-goer, and in that he was not different from many Hindus; temple-going is not an obligatory devotional act in Hinduism, only an occasional spontaneous one, except for the adherents of certain sects. Actually, Gandhi's negative attitude towards temples dated from his youth. He recalled in his autobiography his visits to the Haveli, the Krishna temple of the sect of the Vallabhacharyas to which his father belonged. He did not like its 'glitter and pomp', and had heard 'rumours of immorality'. Hence, he wrote, 'I could gain nothing from the Haveli'.[15]

It was in particular during his visits to South India in connection with his fight for the untouchables, and for their right to enter the Hindu temples, that the question of the religious meaning of temples arose. As with the idols, Gandhi stressed the positive side of temples and temple-worship. 'Some form of common worship, and a common place of worship appear to be a human necessity.'[16] This appears clearly from the 'fundamental fact that no faith has done without habitation'. Gandhi then tried to show that this fact was a consequence of 'the very nature of things'. Man is constituted of spirit and body, and this body has been 'rightly called the temple of the Holy Ghost', because it is inhabited by the divine spirit. The temples are nothing but 'a natural extension of these human temples' and, therefore, temple construction belongs to the very nature of things, is a natural consequence of the human condition and is part of all the religions of the world.[17] Gandhi was not afraid to put it strongly in answer to an American correspondent who expressed great astonishment and disappointment over the fact that Gandhi was promoting temple-entry for untouchables, and had thus become, the reporter stated, 'a defender of the faith of temple Hinduism'. Gandhi wrote: 'To reject the necessity of temples is to reject the necessity of God, religion and earthly existence.' He reiterated it later in equally strong terms: 'Demolish the temples and you destroy religion.'[18] Gandhi recognised, as he did for the consecration of idols, that in the case of temples too, a formal consecration by Hindu ceremonies was needed to make any structure, small or large, into a temple:

> Do you know that in our religion it is not possible to call any single place a temple unless [an] elaborate ceremonial of purification has been made inside that building and unless the spirit of God has been invoked by men full of piety, so that God may reside in that?[19]

Gandhi fought strongly for the right of Harijans to enter the temples, many of which were closed to them in South India. He strongly voiced his disappointment with the people of Madras, who

> have allowed blind religious orthodoxy to take such complete possession of them that mere outward forms of religion remain and the inner spirit has vanished. The *Antyajas* [untouchables] in the region suffer more indignities than they do in almost any other part of the county . . . No other part of the country has so many temples and is so generous in providing for their maintenance.[20]

In a document entitled 'Temple-Entry Satyagraha' he set out the principles and methods of this campaign. The campaign was based on his view of untouchability: it was an un-Hindu, immoral exclusion, unsupported by the Hindu Scriptures, which had unjustly marginalised, stigmatised, exploited, and pauperised a large mass of Hindus. The practice of untouchability should be abolished, and the untouchables should be considered equal to caste Hindus and allowed access to the many temples from which they were excluded. No restrictions that were not applicable to other non-Brahmin Hindus should be applied to them. Therefore, setting aside a corner in a temple for untouchables was not to be tolerated. The Temple-Entry Satyagraha was to be 'a penance on the part of touchable Hindus' for the injustices perpetrated on the untouchables. The movement should, consequently, be shared by untouchables and caste Hindus to become effective at that time.[21]

Although the removal of untouchability was 'essentially and predominantly a religious question to be solved by the Hindus',[22] Gandhi realised very well that temple-entry did not only have a religious aspect, but that it had wider social implications. In his essay entitled 'What does a Hindu Temple Mean?' he explained that wider context, showing that the exclusion of untouchables from temples had deprived them also of much of the cultural and social values of the Hindu community:

> Temples are veritable museums of the cultures of different religions.
> In old times, God dwelt in the temple and godliness too; it housed a
> school, a dharmashala, and it was a place where the leading people of
> the locality met together. Harijans have set their hearts on temples to
> such an extent that they build their own temples of sorts. We discover
> their helplessness in these temples. As long as Harijans cannot enter
> the temples of caste Hindus, their helplessness will never end, their
> Hinduism will remain incomplete . . . By remaining outside the
> temples, they have remained outside everything.[23]

Although Gandhi approved of the religious significance of temples in
all great religions,[24] he did not hesitate to harshly condemn the situation
of some temples. Their connection with the custom of *devadasis* made
him declare, 'Not every structure made of brick and mortar labelled
temple is necessarily a temple. There are, I am sorry to say, many
temples in our midst in this country which are no better that brothels.'[25]
Although 'the putrefaction that has set in is not to be found in all temples',[26] there was, in his opinion, a dire need for temple reform besides
the question of the entry of untouchables. In an article entitled 'A Model
Temple' Gandhi attempted to lay down some guidelines for the larger
reform of Hindu temples. It was not a question of replacing all old
temples with new ones, but 'what the reformer should be concerned with
is a radical change more in the inward spirit than in the outward form.
The first requisite was to have a proper priest who should be 'a man of
God . . . and a true servant of the people'. He should be versed in the
Shastras, and totally concerned with the welfare of his people. As for the
temple itself, no architectural plan was needed. It should be situated in
a large space, easily accessible to the poor, and in healthy surroundings,
if possible slightly elevated over its surroundings. In the middle there
would be a space for daily worship. Around this would come 'a school,
a dispensary, a library, . . . and a dharmsala or guest house'. They
would be much like the village temples of ancient times. He concluded,
'But we must also deal with the existing temples. They can become real
Houses of God today, if the worshippers will insist on the priests
conforming to the ideal presented by me.'[27]

But how about Gandhi himself as a temple-goer? Temple-going was
not part of his regular religious practice: 'I do not consider it a mark of
greatness that I do not visit temples. I feel no need to go to temples;
hence I do not visit them.' Nevertheless, he had often visited temples for

various reasons, sometimes simply out of politeness.[28] And it is from these visits that he learned how important and elevating temple visits could be for many Hindus:

> I have been to the temples at both Kashi and Vishvanath and Puri. I must admit that I was not inspired by faith to visit them, but I had seen innumerable innocent souls going there with devotion. I did not pity them but I fell in love with them and I could understand their devotion. These numerous devotees had no idea whatever of the malpractices prevalent in temples . . . Just as human beings cannot think of the *atman* without the body, similarly they cannot think of religion without temples. The Hindu religion cannot survive without temples.[29]

There was one particular occasion when Gandhi personally experienced the intensely religious atmosphere of the great Hindu temples. It was in January 1937 during his 'pilgrimage to Travancore', after the Maharaja's Ezhava Temple Entry Proclamation which threw the temples open to the untouchables. For eight days Gandhi toured the state, visiting temple after temple accompanied by untouchables: 'I am going to these temples as an untouchable suddenly made touchable.'[30] It was one of the greatest, positive, joyous experiences of his life, and at the end of the pilgrimage he declared:

> I am taking away with me the spiritual treasures of which I had not dreamt before . . . But having the doors of the temples flung open by the very generous act of His Highness, I entered them with the same joy that must have been felt by thousands of Ezhavas, Pulayas and pariahs . . . After having entered the responsible life, I cannot say that I ever was a habitual temple-goer. But the possibility of the spiritual growth by entering these temples in a spiritual and devotional mood has dawned upon me after all these visits to these temples in a devotional and prayerful mood, as it had never before been opened to me.[31]

Gandhi's religious practice as an ashram-dweller was very closely connected with the devotions of the ashram. In a letter to Narayan M. Khare he explained the official policy on idol- and temple-worship in the ashram as follows:

> No inmate of the Ashram who wishes to worship Ganesh or any other deity should be stopped from doing so. However, as an institution we

should, in my opinion, remain equal towards all religions and, therefore, should not permit a public temple with an idol in the Ashram. Our public temple is the open prayer ground with the horizons in the different directions as its walls, the sky as its roof and formless God as the idol in the temple. If we followed any other course, we would be required to provide for a mosque, a fire temple, a church, a synagogue and so on . . . An attitude of equality towards all religions requires us to keep in view from now the necessity for all such places of worship. If we do that, however, we might not be able to keep up our attitude of equality, and therefore, the golden rule for us to follow in this as in other matters is to exercise self-control.[32]

Gandhi's reaction to the practice of pilgrimage and to the great pilgrimage sites of Hinduism was thoroughly negative. In fact, he referred to them only a very few times, and each time he stressed the vices associated with pilgrimages, the venality and low quality of the 'clergy', and the incredible filth associated with them. The superstitious beliefs encouraged were nothing but travesties of religion.[33] Gandhi also largely ignored the Hindu festivals, except on the rare occasions when somebody asked him a specific question.[34]

A couple of times Gandhi was asked his opinion about the *Shraddha* ceremonies. These form part of the death rituals and the commemorative death rituals. In some areas of India they are very extensive and they also, like marriage ceremonies, often include the offering of feasts to relations and Brahmins. Although accepting that some believers may consider the *Shraddha* ceremony essential, and believe it has spiritual utility, Gandhi could not understand how 'a departed person is benefited through it'. He was much more definite in the matter of community-feasts connected with it. These he condemned outright as 'devoid of any religious sentiment, serving neither religion nor reason'.[35]

To many Hindus the sacred thread was a symbol of their high caste status: its wearing was reserved to those who were twice born, *dvija*, who had received the sacrament of initiation, *Upanayana*, which was strictly reserved to those belonging to the three top *varnas*, Brahmins, Kshatriyas and Vaishyas. Gandhi himself had given up wearing the sacred thread. He explained in a letter what the sacred thread meant and why he stopped wearing it.

Those people who described themselves as Aryans adopted the use of the sacred thread in order to distinguish between Aryans and non-Aryans . . . Today there is no distinction – and there ought not to be any – between Aryans and non-Aryans. An admixture of blood between the two races took place thousands of years ago and the present inhabitants of India are the progeny of such an admixture. If the sacred thread is to be worn at all, all [the castes] should have the right to wear it . . . Inasmuch as the practice of wearing the sacred thread is likely to have created the distinction between higher and lower castes, it should be discarded . . . It is the sign of a *brahmachari*. If a person observes *brahmacharya* that itself is the best sacred thread. Why is a cotton thread needed?[36]

SOCIAL HINDUISM

During his stay in South Africa, caste and untouchability were nearly completely outside Gandhi's concerns. There were only two occasions when they were mentioned in his writings of that time or in his autobiography. The latter mentions that he had a serious disagreement with Kasturbai when he expected her to empty and clean the chamberpot of a clerk staying with them, who was a Christian born of untouchable parents. The other occasion is in his description of his life in gaol. Gandhi complained that some Indians objected to sleeping near other prisoners of the scavenger caste, or eating food prepared by them.[37]

Once Gandhi settled back in India, he was completely surrounded, and often overwhelmed by the oppressive and offensive presence of caste and untouchability. Within four months of his arrival he stated as follows in a speech at a Reception in Mayavaram, commenting on his observation of the pitiful state of the untouchables:

Do we propose to perpetuate this state of things? Is it a part of Hinduism? I do not know. I have now to learn what Hinduism really is. In so far as I have been able to study Hinduism outside India, I have felt it is no part of real Hinduism to have in its hold a mass of people whom I would call 'untouchables'. If it was proved to me that this is an essential part of Hinduism, I for one would declare myself an open rebel against Hinduism itself.[38]

He was clear in his mind about untouchability, and we will see that his denunciation of it remained radical and outspoken.

As for the organisation of Hindu society into castes, his ideas were far from clear. He was, after his return to India, hectically travelling all over India and organising the establishment of his ashram in Ahmedabad.

There was not much time for deep reflection. By the middle of 1916, eighteen months after his return to India, he started to formulate some of his ideas about caste. He first presented them in Ahmedabad in a 'Speech on the Caste System', at a conference of caste organisations. He admitted he had 'not come prepared to speak on the subject', although he had thought a lot about it. He said very little; that caste organisation was a necessary structure of society that was found all over the world. The hierarchical structure depended not on scripture, but on occupation. Restriction in interdining and intermarriage were for the purpose of self-control, but were not the essence of caste. There were a number of social evils which had caused serious problems with unmarried girls and widows, but the worst feature was the untouchable problem. One of the ways in which Gandhi's uncertainty and confusion expressed themselves in this speech was the way in which he used two different expressions to refer to the same social system: he mostly used the term *jati-vyavastha*, caste system, where *jati* is the exact Hindi term referring to the multifarious castes; but he also used a couple of times the term *varna-vyavastha* for exactly the same system. We will see how later on he will make a clear distinction between *jati* and *varna*.[39]

Shortly after this he expressed himself in a more organised and thoughtful manner when he wrote in *Bharat Sevak*, a Marathi monthly, an article entitled 'The Hindu Caste System'. Here he always used the technical term *jati*, and not once did he use the word *varna*; he was writing about the caste system as it existed, the system of many social subgroups arranged in a hierarchical order. He called it 'a perfectly natural institution', which was part of society everywhere in the world, but which in India had been 'invested with a religious meaning'. This religious dimension was the result of making the caste system 'an agency for ensuring self-control. The caste defined the limits within which one may enjoy life.' This was done by putting strict limitations on the association with other people in matters of interdining and intermarriage: the caste provided boundaries for both. Nevertheless, in special circumstances there could be exceptions to that general rule. The caste system had been the protector and preserver of Hindu society. Besides its regulations relating to eating and marrying, it also provided other services to society, such as primary education, panchayats, arbitration and caste tribunals. It had been a living and developing institution of great merit, but Gandhi acknowledged that in contemporary times the system had become 'full of evils like ostentation and hypocrisy, pleasure-seeking and quarrels'.[40]

Whereas at that stage Gandhi's ideas about caste were still rather crude, his judgement of untouchability was very clear, and had been so even in South Africa. Soon after his arrival in India he reaffirmed this by including in the third edition of the 'Draft Constitution for the Ashram', published on 7 November 1915, a Vow Against Untouchability. The Ashram inmates were put 'under a vow to regard the untouchable community as touchable'. The Ashram founders considered untouchability 'a blot on Hindu religion', and Gandhi soon called it 'a great crime', which 'can never be part of Hinduism'.[41]

At the end of 1920, six years after his arrival in India, Gandhi published in quick succession two articles, 'The Caste System' and 'Caste versus Class', in which he clearly stated the basic principle of his now matured conception of caste.[42] The four divisions of society, the *varnas* already mentioned in the Rigveda (the Brahmins, the Kshatriyas, the Vaishyas, and the Shudras) are 'fundamental, natural and essential parts of society'. In his commentary on the *Gita* he confirmed that.[43] They saved Hinduism from disintegration. Over the centuries they had subdivided themselves into a multiplication of castes and subcastes which were not essential and often led to abuses. In fact, that splitting up of society should be remedied by fusion. The four divisions according to Gandhi's theory did not constitute a hierarchy, did not imply inferiority or superiority, but recognised and embodied the diverse outlooks and modes of life that were part of society everywhere.

These divisions into *varnas* were under the control of the eternal law of heredity, and therefore they were conferred at birth on all people. They were in a sense an extension of the family. It was the law of *karma* that readjusted the balance that might have been disturbed by re-assigning a new *varna* at every birth of the individual. If, for instance, a Brahmin did not live up to the duties and ideals of Brahminhood, he should not be divested of his status in this life, but the law of *karma* would see to it that his next rebirth would not be in a Brahmin family.

The limits on interdining and intermarriage which at that time were extremely dominant aspects of the caste system, were in themselves not condemned by Gandhi. He saw these restrictions as beneficial restraints promoting self-control, and he did not agree with some radical social reformers that abolishing them would be beneficial to society.

These articles also included a condemnation of untouchability, but a much earlier long article of Gandhi published in 1917 entitled 'A Stain in India's Forehead', had already clearly laid out the principles by which he judged untouchability. The relegation of a great section of society to the category of 'untouchables', Gandhi considered 'a sin, a great crime, and if Hinduism does not destroy this serpent while there is yet time, it will be devoured by it'. He did not deny that some kinds of work made its performers unclean and, therefore, untouchable, but he declared that the dirt that soiled the scavenger was only physical and could be easily removed. In fact their work was not to be despised because 'removing garbage and filth is a necessary and sacred function' in the service of society, and similar duties were also 'fulfilled by doctors and mothers'. Gandhi argued that if the latter could purify themselves simply by cleaning themselves after fulfilling their polluting task, there was no reason why the scavengers could not do likewise. He considered untouchability to always be a temporary condition removable by physical cleansing. The institutionalisation of untouchability by birth was the height of injustice and cruelty.[44]

This crime was aggravated by justifying it in the name of religion. The orthodoxy which supported it was 'nothing but hypocrisy'. Just like people in Europe used to quote the Bible in defence of slavery, Hindus invoked the scriptures to defend untouchability. 'It is no good . . . quoting verses from Manusmriti and other scriptures in defense of this orthodoxy. A number of verses in these scriptures are apocryphal, a number are quite meaningless.'[45]

This outright condemnation of untouchability demanded nothing less than its total abolition. This abolition necessarily raised the following question: since the organisation of society in four classes is essential, what will happen to the untouchables when they are fully accepted as part of Hindu society? In his 1917 article Gandhi gave the following answer: 'The untouchables must not be considered as falling outside Hinduism. They should be treated as respectable members of Hindu society and should be assigned their *varnas* according to their vocations.' This meant that they should be assigned a Shudra status if their work and abilities were in the area of community service, and to the Vaishya *varna* if they were versed in and occupied with some form of trade. This, however, led to difficulties, because the class system was not practised any more in its proper form: many Brahmins did not pursue a Brahmin vocation, but were in trade or in service, – and the same was true of the other *varnas*. Gandhi realised the difficulty of the assignment of *varnas* to the untouchables, but at this stage he only stated the ideal solution.[46]

Gandhi's ideas on caste and untouchability in 1920 thus set forth, the development of these ideas over the remainder of his life will now be considered. Gandhi knew that he changed his mind over the years. In his introduction to *Varnavyavastha*, a collection of his writings on caste and class, he wrote, 'I have never made a fetish of consistency', and advised the reader to reject his earlier statements for his later ones.[47] In the

matter of class and caste Gandhi regularly reiterated his theory because
it was one of the questions which agitated many Hindus at that time,
both conservatives and reformers. Many of his statements came as
responses to queries or objections of correspondents, or as public
speeches in South India.[48] His most extensive treatment was his 'Introduction to *Varnavyavastha*', a collection of all his writings on the topic.
He wrote a shorter foreword to the second edition of this booklet in
1945.[49]

In his large volume of writings in caste there is nowhere any fundamental change to his principles as he enunciated them in 1920, only
additional applications or clarifications.[50] In 1924 he addressed a gathering of the organisation of Rajputs in Vartej, and suggested that they
should take up spinning.[51] He got a strong letter in reaction:

> But why would you a Hindu, a believer in *varnashrama* principles,
> help in the degradation of a Brahmin or Kshatriya by insisting on their
> accepting Vaishya dharma and rejecting or neglecting their respective
> *jati* dharmas. Can a Kshatriya not serve and protect the poor even in
> these days but in the *Vaishya* way . . . Spiritualize your caste people,
> but do not materialize [*sic*] the men of other castes by turning them
> into spinners and weavers with the spell of your personality.[52]

This letter gave Gandhi a chance to clarify his own position: 'I ask no
one to forsake his own hereditary dharma or occupation, but I ask
everyone to add spinning to his natural occupation.' He added that
varnashrama was not 'a system of watertight compartments', but that a
Brahmin was not only a teacher, neither was a good Vaishya without
divine knowledge. 'The spinning-wheel is designed to wake up everyone
to a sense of his duty.'[53] But he also recommended hand-weaving as 'a
bread-winning occupation to all in need of an honest occupation':

> To the Brahmins, the Kshatriyas and others, who are at the present
> moment not following their hereditary occupation, but are engaged in
> the mad rush for riches, I present the honest and (for them) selfless
> toil of the weaver and invite them, with a view to returning to their
> respective dharmas, to be satisfied with what little the handloom
> yields them. Just as eating, drinking, sleeping etc., are common to all
> castes and all religions, so must spinning be common to all without
> exception whilst the confusion, selfish greed and resulting pauperism
> persist.[54]

Although Gandhi accepted that *varna* was based on birth, he admitted that it was possible for people to find a new vocation, and to actually perform the duties of a different *varna* from their own. Already in 1921 he had congratulated two Brahmin brothers of Tanjore who were dissatisfied with their 'lazy life', and took up agriculture. Their fellow villagers excommunicated them, and the Shankaracharya of Kumbakonam rejected their offerings. Gandhi called this action tyrannical, and a 'parody of *varnashrama*'.[55] However, although Gandhi thus approved of the change of occupation, he warned that 'in order to perform the duty of a *Vaishya* one does not need the label of *Vaishya*.'[56] In other words, there was no need to actually transfer during this life from one class to another. Such a method of transfer would result in a great deal of fraud, and would lead to the destruction of *varna* itself. Therefore, the transfer should be left to the law of *karma* which would accomplish it in the next generation.

In a speech at Tanjore delivered in 1927, Gandhi formally proposed an interesting argument for his important principle that *varna* with its inherited abilities and tendencies did not imply that there was also an inherited superiority or inferiority.

> In my opinion there is no such thing as inherited or acquired superiority. I believe in the rock-bottom doctrine of Advaita and my interpretation of Advaita excludes totally any idea of superiority at any stage whatsoever. I believe implicitly that all men are born equal. All – whether born in India or in England or America or in any circumstances whatsoever – have the same soul as any other.[57]

Gandhi occasionally came back to the same argument of Advaita to argue against untouchability.[58]

In the particular matter of the restrictions on interdining and intermarriage, Gandhi's attitude changed with the years. At the beginning he viewed these restrictions as beneficial restraints for promoting self-control. 'The greater the restraint we exercise with regard to our appetites whether about eating or marriage, the better we become from a religious standpoint.'[59] Ten years later he reached a less positive view of these restrictions:

> When Hindus were seized with inertia, abuse of varna resulted in innumerable castes with unnecessary and harmful restrictions as to intermarriage and interdining. The law of varna has nothing to do with these restriction. People of different varnas may intermarry and

interdine. These restrictions may be necessary in the interest of chastity and hygiene. But a Brahmin who marries a Shudra girl or *vice versa* commits no offence against the law of varna.[60]

Shortly afterwards Gandhi wrote: 'If we rob interdining and intermarriage of religious significance in the manner it is understood, it becomes purely a matter of option, where we dine and where our children marry.'[61] By 1933 the whole question seems to have lost any serious positive aspect in Gandhi's mind and had now become a matter of pure personal preference.

I have repeatedly said that marriage is not a matter necessarily connected with varna divisions. It is a personal matter. As a rule, however, people like to enter into matrimonial alliances with their neighbours or with people who are like them . . . Eating and drinking are personal matters. One will eat and drink where it pleases one to.[62]

This gradual devaluation of the importance and meaning of interdining and intermarriage restrictions ran parallel and interacted with another change in conception and attitude that was taking place. From very early Gandhi described the *varna* system as an ideal, and he knew that the social reality of India did not correspond to it. In 1917 he already admitted that 'Varna was not practised as the ideal described'; and in 1925 he said, 'But there is today a travesty of varna.' Towards the end of 1927 during his tour of South India he repeatedly described and sang the praises of the *varnashrama* ideal, and then he wrote a long article in *Young India* entitled 'Varnashrama and its Distortion'. Again he described 'the law of varna' with its hereditary occupations, its denial of superiority and inferiority, its relation to interdining and intermarriage, its denial of untouchability – but he had to admit that *varna* as he described it 'had nothing in common with caste as we know it today'.[63]

Gandhi kept adhering to his ideal of *varna dharma*, but from 1931 on he was ready to admit that 'according to my definition of varna, there is no varna in operation at present in Hinduism'. *Varnashrama* had become 'a lost treasure', it had been 'totally destroyed', 'it did not exist any more', it had 'become extinct'.[64] Right through he added to that statement the observation that in fact, only one single *varna* really survived: the Shudra *varna*, to which everyone now belonged. With only one class remaining, what sense was there in restrictions to interdining and intermarriage? But, though the *varna dharma* was extinct, it could be resurrected. The first step in that direction was the acceptance by all that they now shared the class of service, the Shudra *varna*. From that foundation, he believed a new regime of full *varna dharma* could re-emerge.

So far we have considered the general statements of Gandhi about caste applicable to all Hindus. His own actions, however, were mostly much more radical. This is because Gandhi did not consider himself to be a 'normal' Hindu, but in some way removed from a society and societal dharma in the way the *sannyasi* is removed from and, according to Hindu tradition, free from all social and ritual duties. That aspect will be considered in Chapter 9, 'The Ashram-dweller'.[65]

Gandhi's writings specifically on untouchability were voluminous, at least twice as much as those on caste. Whereas in his writings on caste the responses to queries outnumbered the speeches specifically dealing with the caste system, in the case of untouchability, the speeches very strongly outnumbered the queries, and there were also a very large number of articles on the subject.[66] This clearly indicates that whereas in his writings on caste in general Gandhi was mostly engaged in explanation, in his writings on untouchability he was on the attack, vigorously trying to convince his Hindu brethren. This difference is also clearly demonstrated by the very passion and vehemence of his statements, and the strong language he used. His condemnation of untouchability was total, uncompromising, verging sometimes on the fanatical and the hysterical. Untouchability was 'a great satanism', a 'Dyerism', a 'hydra-headed monster', a 'canker eating at the vitals of Hinduism', 'a thousand-headed monster', and an 'unmitigated curse'.[67]

In various ways Gandhi repeated his passionate desire that untouchability be abolished, and his absolute certainty that he was right in that conviction. His attachment to Hinduism was very deep, but he declared that 'the moment I am convinced that untouchability is an essential element of Hindu religion, I would immediately renounce my religion'.[68] This drastic resolve was repeated by him several times.[69] Gandhi always defended his claim that he was a *sanatani* Hindu, a claim that surely implied that his ideas and attitudes had a close relation to the traditional principles of Hinduism. But in the matter of untouchability such consonance was of no consequence: 'Even if the whole country said that I was not a true Hindu, I would claim that I was the only true Hindu, and assert that others who held the practice of untouchability to be part of dharma were false Hindus.'[70]

In his controversy about untouchability the question of the scriptural basis of the practice was constantly raised. In his Madras speech in 1920 he asked his audience 'to accept the authority of my experiences that there is no warrant in our scriptures for considering a single human being as untouchable'.[71] This conviction that scripture did not approve untouchability was repeated very often because the orthodox defence of the tradition kept referring to scriptural proofs, particularly in South India.[72] But in this matter too Gandhi was prepared to stand by his own interpretation against all. 'I should stand by my interpretation of the Shastras even though I were the solitary one amongst the millions of Hindus.'[73]

And even if it happened that these others convinced him that the scriptures did actually authorise untouchability, Gandhi's answer was equally radical:

> If I discovered that those scriptures which are known as Vedas, Upanishads, Bhagavadgita, Smritis, etc., clearly showed that they claimed divine authority for untouchability . . . then nothing on this earth would hold me to Hinduism. I should throw it overboard as I should throw overboard a rotten apple.[74]

One could not more strongly express an unshakeable conviction. There is yet another way in which Gandhi proclaimed the dedication of his life to the removal of untouchability:

> I do want to attain *moksha*. I do not want to be reborn. But if I have to be reborn I should be born an untouchable, so that I may share their sorrows, sufferings, and the affronts levelled at them, in order that I may endeavour to free myself and them from that miserable condition.[75]

The next statement he made in this connection was different. He did not preface it with the conditional clause, 'If I have to be reborn', but said straightforwardly: 'There can be no *moksha* for me, for I am passionately attached to this cause.'[76] *Moksha* required the total renunciation of all desire. He knew that his desire to deliver the untouchables was one he would not be able, or even willing, to eradicate. And as long as such a desire dominated his spirit, *moksha* would remain beyond his reach because the desire made him cling to his life. One cannot but be reminded here of the Bodhisattva ideal of Mahayana Buddhism: the Enlightened One on the very point of entering *Nirvana*, stepped back to devote himself to the task of continuing his propagation of the doctrine and practice of salvation.

Another argument against untouchability was that it was contrary to reason, a violation of truth.[77] But more convincing even was the argument that untouchability was in conflict with the fundamentals of Hinduism.

> It [untouchability] is in conflict with the fundamental precepts of Hinduism. The first among the three principles I am about to enunciate of Hinduism is *Satyanasti paro dharmah*, i.e. there is no religion other than or higher than truth. The second is *Ahimsa paramo dharmah*, and if ahimsa, meaning love, non-violence, is the law of life, is the greatest religion, is the only religion, then I suggest to you that untouchability is in direct conflict with that truth. The third is that God alone is Truth and everything else is transitory and illusory. If it is so, I suggest to you that it is impossible for us to reconcile untouchability and unapproachability with the grand doctrine.[78]

Among all the certainties in his doctrine about untouchability there was one question in doubt: in which *varna* untouchables should be incorporated at the time of officially rejoining the Hindu commonwealth. Very early, in 1917, Gandhi declared that 'The untouchables must not be considered as falling outside Hinduism. They should be treated as respectable members of Hindu society and should be assigned their *varnas* according to their vocations.' He went on to say that the pure *varna* system did not exist any more, and the members of the classes rarely followed their assigned vocation. 'As a matter of fact,' he added, 'owing to our subjection to foreign rule, we are all slaves and are, in the eyes of the Westerners, untouchables lower even than the Shudras.'[79] He does not seem to have been able to draw all these strands together at this time, and in 1925 he answered the question, 'What would be the religious status of the untouchables when the ban of untouchability is completely removed?', in the following way: 'The religious state would be the same as that of the caste Hindus. They will, therefore, be classed as Sudras instead of *Ati-sudras*.'[80]

It was in 1927 that Gandhi finally formulated clearly his resolution of that problem. The first principle was that history had brought such a degradation to the *varna* system that for all purposes it did not exist any more, and that 'it would be well to recognise ourselves as one *varna*, viz. Shudras'.[81] Once that was accepted, there was no difficulty in saying that untouchables would be absorbed into the Shudra class, because that

would then be the one common class of all Hindus. The third leg of
Gandhi's argument was a vision of the future, a vision of how the ideal
class society would be reconstructed:

<blockquote>They [the untouchables] in common with the rest will be absorbed in
the Shudras. Out of these the other three *varnas* will gradually emerge
purified and equal in status though differing in occupations. The
Brahmins will be very few. Fewer still will be the soldier class who
will not be the hirelings or the unrestrained rulers of today, but real
protectors and trustees of the nation laying down their lives for its
service. The fewest will be the Shudras for in a well-ordered society
a minimum amount of labour will be taken from fellowmen. The most
numerous will be the Vaisyas – a *varna* that would include all profes-
sions – the agriculturists, the traders, the artisans, etc.[82]</blockquote>

Gandhi then reflected, 'this scheme may sound Utopian'. It certainly
was, and it was an essential part of the utopia he was constructing in his
vision of *Ramrajya*.

By the middle thirties Gandhi had fought his great battles for the
untouchables, from 1921 to 1936, and they moved away from the top of
the agenda. But his ideas did not change, and occasionally he repeated
that grand dream, that social Utopia that he had constructed in the late
1920s, which started with the reduction of the four classes into one, that
of the Shudras, and the acceptance of all untouchables into that one
class, in perfect equality.[83]

The classical definition of the structure of Hindu society, *varnashrama dharma*, contains besides the class system also that of *ashramas*,
stages of life. These make for an ideal development of the individual as
a member of society. There are four stages in life, childhood and the
married state, followed by *vanaprastha* and *sannyasa*. The first translates as 'forest abode', and is the retirement of husband and wife to a
hermitage after having brought up their family and seen their grandchildren. *Sannyasa* is the last stage of the wandering ascetic who breaks all
links with family and society, and devotes himself fully to the pursuit of
moksha. This scheme was always an ideal in Hinduism, but only rarely
put into practice as very few ever transferred to the third and fourth
stages of life.

No wonder that Gandhi only very rarely mentioned it in passing. In a
speech at Advait Ashram Alwaye, he said: 'As a result of my limited
reading, reflection and meditation, I feel that human society cannot do
without the four-fold divisions of *varna* and *ashrama*.' In a speech at

Trivandrum he explained the four stages in detail, and praised them, but admitted that '*ashrama* has altogether disappeared'.[84] In his *History of the Satyagraha Ashram* he expatiated on them at length, and wrote that, 'The Ashram is engaged in the great endeavour to resuscitate the four ashramas'; but there is no real evidence of that, and he admitted again that it had practically disappeared in India. He still kept it as 'an ideal', as he wrote in his 'Introduction to Varnavyavastha': 'The law of ashrama is a dead letter today. It can be revived only if the law of varna with which it is intimately interlinked, is revived.'[85]

SECTARIAN HINDUISM

One of the important facts of Hinduism is the penetration of numerous sects into the lives of their adherents. Gujarat had a good number of them, especially Vaishnavite sects. Gandhi's own father belonged to the Vallabhacharyas and his mother to the Pranamis. Both were devout members who took their ritual duties seriously, but Gandhi did not like their sectarian religious activities as a child. During the South African period Gandhi never even mentioned sects. The reason seems obvious. Active sectarian adherence was probably very rare among the Hindus of South Africa, simply for reason of distance. Sectarian devotion requires the availability of sectarian shrines, functionaries, and social groups, all of which tended to be absent from the South African scene. Back in India Gandhi was surrounded by sectarian realities, and somehow he had to respond to them.

First his view of Buddhism and Jainism will be considered. They could not be called Hindu sects but to Gandhi they were integral parts of Hinduism itself. Gandhi admitted that he knew very little about Buddhism, and that he had really only read Sir Edwin Arnold's *The Light of Asia*, a description of the life of the Buddha. Nevertheless he was quite ready to make general statements about Buddhism, which he put forward mostly at meetings of Buddhist organisations such as the Buddha Society of Bombay, the Mahabodhi Society, and at Colombo at a meeting with Buddhist dignitaries and at the Young Men's Buddhist Association.[86] At each of these venues he presented the same basic ideas. First of all, he held that Buddhism arose in India not as a new religion, but as a reform of Hinduism. The Buddha was and remained a Hindu, but he was a great reformer: 'He taught Hinduism not to take, but to give life. True sacrifice was not of others, but of self.' He 'taught the world to treat even the lowest creatures as equal to oneself. He held the life of even the crawling things of the earth as precious as his own.' Hinduism accepted this central message, but it fought Buddhism because it saw in it a new anti-Vedic cult, which it was not. Gandhi did not believe that Buddhism was atheistic, or that *nirvana* equalled total extinction. He also held that the Buddha's message had been best conserved in India, and had lost some of its strength in its migration to other lands. Buddhism was not a vital phenomenon in India at this time, and it only featured in Gandhi's writings when he was invited by Buddhists, who admired him for his stance on non-violence, to speak to them.[87]

Gandhi was much more closely connected with Jainism. The Jain presence was very strong in Gujarat, and, as Gandhi recalled in his autobiography, 'Its influence was felt everywhere and on all occasions.'[88] Socially the Jains shared the same caste system with the Hindus, and they used Hindu rituals for a number of their domestic rites. Gandhi's family had very close Jain connections and he found in the Jain saint Raychand great support and guidance. With his assistance he gained quite extensive knowledge about Jainism, and he readily acknowledged that some of its doctrines had profoundly influenced him. 'I know the Jains. I know them and the principles of their religion as intimately as I do Vaishnavism and Vaishnavas . . . I have learned much from their books. My contact with many Jain friends has helped me much.'[89] He conceived the relationship of Jainism to Hinduism in the same way as that of Buddhism and Hinduism: Jainism did not constitute a separate religion, it was the same as Hinduism, part of the Hindu religious universe.[90]

From the early days of South Africa, Gandhi considered Jainism to be 'the most logical of all faiths', and he held that opinion throughout.[91] The Jain doctrine that influenced him most was the doctrine of *anekantavada*, the many-sidedness of reality which leads to the epistemology of *syadvada*, the doctrine that every statement only presents a partial view of reality, and that therefore all statements should be prefaced by *syad*, 'maybe' or 'from one point of view'. This principle became the basis of Gandhi's conception of religious pluralism.[92] Gandhi considered Sikhism too as a reform movement that remained part and parcel of Hinduism. However, the Sikhs did not agree with that, and Gandhi did not quarrel with them for considering themselves distinct from Hinduism.[93] The Sikhs obviously did not like Gandhi's ideas, but Gandhi did not mind them feeling as they did, and avoided offending them.

Notwithstanding the fact that numerous sects are part of the fabric of Hinduism, one is struck by their practically total absence in the writings of Gandhi. He knew they were there, but he never felt the need to address them, or to confront their shortcomings. Probably this was because he preferred to address the Hindu commonwealth as a whole rather than focus on sects. He knew the limitations, and even the moral degradation sometimes connected with sectarian organisations, but he addressed the faults themselves as sins of Hinduism as a whole. A number of his condemnations about rituals, temples and pilgrimages, were in fact connected with sects, but he preferred to see them as defects the body of Hinduism had to eliminate. The same was true of his condemnation of the infamy of untouchability.

On one occasion Gandhi, who always affirmed he was a Vaishnava, commented on aspects of the sect of the Vallabhacharyas to which his family belonged. Not surprisingly it had to do with untouchables, and Gandhi's reaction and advice are interesting.

> In a small region like Kathiawar, the movement for the abolition of untouchability has created a stir in the *Vaishnava* world. The gates of *havelis* [Vallabhacharya temples] are being closed against those who do not honour the practice of untouchability and regard it as wrong . . . What should they do? There can be only one reply: they should give up the thought of the *haveli* . . . The ultimate *haveli* is one's own heart. The *haveli* walls are what crutches are to the lame. They are merely a support. When they cease to be a support and instead become a burden, we should throw them away.[94]

He went on to give some advice to the priests. If they wanted to remain protectors of religion, they had to wake up:

> If in violation of divine laws, they insist on building walls of superstition and evil, they will not survive long. . . The hereditary seat of honour which they occupy is in danger. I do not want them to cherish untouchability and become untouchables themselves.[95]

There was one religious organisation that he singled out for comment, the Arya Samaj. This was not really a sect in the proper sense, but a modern reform organisation, which tended to make itself clearly distinct from 'Puranic' Hinduism as the protagonist of pure 'Vedic' Aryan religion. In South Africa, where Gandhi never mentioned sects, he did make a comment on the visit of Professor Parmanand, a scholar from the Lahore Anglo-Vedic College, who visited South Africa as a missionary for the teachings of the Arya Samaj. Gandhi then praised the Samaj for its useful and practical work in teaching, disaster relief, and patriotism, but went on to call the mission of the Professor into question:

> The Arya Samaj does not represent any established orthodox religion
> of India. It takes nothing away from its credit when we mention that
> it is still a cult struggling for existence and catering for converts. It
> represents a reformation of Hinduism. We feel that Indians in South
> Africa are not ready to receive any doctrines of reformation. The
> needs of the Indians . . . consists of education and as much of it of the
> right kind as can be had.[96]

In January 1916 he was asked to speak at the Arya Samaj Annual
Celebrations at Surat. After expressing his respect for the Samaj, and
praising its founder Swami Dayananda, he proceeded to suggest that
some changes were needed if the Samaj wanted to do really useful work.
He criticised the tendency of some Arya spokesmen to enter into violent
controversy, and continued:

> The service that the Arya Samaj renders is not different from that of
> the Hindu religion. If one examines different bodies like the Brahmo
> Samaj, the Sikh Samaj, etc., once sees that all of them express the
> truths of the Hindu religion. Only the names differ . . . a time will
> certainly come when all the sects of Hindus will be included under the
> single term 'Hinduism'.[97]

Gandhi presented here a point of view that would not have been acceptable to many Arya Samajists, but one that expressed most clearly why,
as it was noted, he carefully avoided addressing or speaking about
particular sects. Hinduism as one single vital commonwealth of religion
was his conception.

In 1924 Gandhi published a very long article entitled 'Hindu–Muslim
Tension: Its Cause and Cure'. In this article he strongly attacked the
Arya Samaj and got a stormy reaction. This led him to publishing two
articles specifically on the Samaj.[98] What angered the Aryas most was
what Gandhi wrote about their two most revered leaders. Gandhi praised
Dayananda Sarasvati, the founder, as a grand, lofty, and fearless charac-
ter of impeccable chastity. However, he declared that his main work, the
Satyarth Prakash, was very disappointing. It misrepresented Jainism,
Islam, Christianity and even Hinduism to a high degree. Dayananda, the
great iconoclast, also enthroned a new idol: the letter of the Vedas.
Notwithstanding the vociferous protests of the Aryas, Gandhi stood firm
by his criticism. He also admired and loved Shraddhananda, but regret-

ted his irritating, impetuous quarrelsomeness that exacerbated Hindu–Muslim tension. The third main criticism was of the *shuddhi* movement for the re-conversion of Muslims to the Hindu faith; he equally criticised the corresponding *tabligh* movement launched by the Muslims. He condemned the movement as being an imitation of the Christian concept of conversion in a way that was contrary to the Hindu tradition, and he accused the movement of reviling Islam in a scurrilous press.

After the assassination of Swami Shraddhananda in 1926, Gandhi wrote several times about him, praising his bravery and unselfish service. But the main plea in all his writing was a plea to Hindus and Muslims not to let that tragic event exacerbate the bad feelings between the communities. He appealed to both communities 'to purge the atmosphere of mutual hatred and calumny'.[99] Gandhi continued his agitation against *shuddhi* till the movement died out, but he was careful not to direct it against the Arya Samaj as such, but to concentrate on the wrong and un-Indian approach of both *shuddhi* and *tabligh*.[100]

CONCLUSION

Only two Hindu ritual practices were totally condemned by Gandhi: animal sacrifice and the dedication of *devadasis*. In others such as idol-worship and temple-worship, he indicated and condemned their corruption, but accepted that, if properly used, they could help people in their religious endeavours. However, he did not see them as in any way obligatory, and admitted that they were not part of his own private worship. Although he did not outrightly condemn the practice of pilgrimage, and that of participation in Hindu festivals, on the rare occasion he referred to them it was in very negative terms. The one aspect of Hindu ritual he positively looked upon as part of the Ramrajya of the future, was the temple. But this temple was not like the massive buildings dotted all over the land, but it was the village temple, which with its school, dispensary, and guest house, constituted the social and spiritual meeting-place for all the inhabitants of the village.

As for social Hinduism, Gandhi's condemnation of the practice of untouchability was total and uncompromising from his days in South Africa. His attitude to the caste system changed substantially over the years. He learned to distinguish between the caste system (*jati*) and the class system (*varna*). His condemnation of the former grew over the years, while he stuck to the defence of the latter. He ended up by admitting that the class system had in fact totally disappeared, and that for all practical purposes, there remained only one effective class to which all belonged: the Shudra *varna*. But he still remained convinced of the intrinsic value of the system as he understood it, and he anticipated that, as Ramrajya, the ideal commonwealth, developed, the *varna* system, respectful of total social equality of all, would regenerate itself.

Matters of pollution were very important in the caste system, and they had spawned an intricate system of taboos on interdining and intermarriage. At first Gandhi considered them as useful regulations, which promoted self-control. But over the years his support diminished, and by the mid 1930s he had come to the conclusion that it was purely a matter of personal preference with whom one dined, and whom one chose as one's marriage partner.

Gandhi always held that Jainism, Buddhism, and Sikhism were not separate religions, but reformations of and part of the total Hindu commonwealth. As for the hundreds of sects, big and small, that were part of living Hinduism, he had no interest in them at all, and simply ignored them. His criticism of Hindu practices always directed itself at the practices themselves, wherever they occurred, inside or outside sects. It was the moral quality of action he was interested in, not the sectarian paraphernalia.

6

The Persistence of Advaita

THE DOMINANCE OF ADVAITA

In his first public statement about religion in his Lectures on Hinduism in South Africa, Gandhi clearly indicated that his concept of the absolute was essentially the advaitic one of absolute non-dualism. He stated that the absolute was without qualities (*nirguna*), without form (*nirakar*), all-pervading and all-powerful; it was *Brahman*, who 'does not act, neither does he cause action'; and through him the whole creation is sustained. The soul (*atman*) is without beginning, and 'between its essential nature and *Brahman*, there is no difference'. When the spirit achieves deliverance it merges into *Brahman* and loses its individuality. This is a clear and simple statement of the advaitic concept of the absolute. The personal God (*Ishwar*) does not even rate a mention. Later, in a letter to Jamnadas, Gandhi declared that if any one could be called *Ishwar*, it was the *atman* that had actually reached *moksha*, a possibility open to every single spirit.[1]

Through his Indian period until the very end, Gandhi regularly reiterated this basic belief in a variety of ways. A few quotations chosen from some forty texts will suffice to make the point that he continued throughout his life to adhere to the basic tenets of Advaita Vedanta. (These are presented below as an amalgam, although the many sources are listed in the note.)

> *Brahma* alone is real; all else is non-existent. . . . Hindus, Muslims, Christians and others have employed innumerable epithets to describe God, but they are all products of our imagination. God is without attributes and beyond all qualifications. The reality which we call God is a mysterious, indescribable and unique power . . . So far as I know *Jivatma* is to *Paramatma* what a drop is to the ocean. And even as the properties of a drop are identical with those of the ocean, the properties of *Jivatma* are identical with those of *Paramatma* . . . In truth, there is no such being as Brahma or Shiva. The only reality is the neuter *Brahman* . . . The universal soul in which all the souls exist is

God. The living creature which does not know that Universal Soul
and looks upon itself as separate from other creatures is what we call
jiva. That Universal Soul, though dwelling in all, is not directly
experienced; that is its beauty, its miracle, its *maya*. The true end of
human effort consists in crossing that *maya* and knowing that Universal Soul, which is the one source of all . . . Mortal men can only
imagine the Unmanifest, the Impersonal, and as his language fails him
he often negatively describes It as 'Neti Neti' (Not That, Not That)
. . . I appreciate your argument. I am myself a follower of the
Advaita doctrine . . . For me God is formless and therefore my vision
of Him does not consist of any form . . . Then, what should God be
like? Passionless and Formless, He should be a repository of all
attributes and yet be wholly without attributes. Why should God
then be of masculine gender? This is purely a question of grammar.
The God of our conception, being formless, is neither male nor
female . . . The truth is that God is the force. He is the essence of
life. He is pure consciousness. He is omnipresent.[2]

His *Discourses on the Gita* were no doubt Gandhi's most deliberate
effort at religious instruction. It is striking that his commentary on this
theistic document contains many affirmations of his advaitic convictions.[3]
    Another very strong indication of Gandhi's belief in the advaitic
doctrine of the identity of *Brahman* and *atman* was that he used it as an
argument in one of the most passionate convictions he held, for which he
conducted crusade after crusade: his fight for the abolition of untouchability. He argued that it was totally irrational to believe in the inferiority by birth of the untouchables because it constituted a denial of the
advaitic doctrine of the essential identity of all spirits and of their
identity with *Brahman*:

> In my opinion there is no such thing as inherited or acquired superior-
> ity. I believe in the rock-bottom doctrine of Advaita and my interpre-
> tation of Advaita excludes totally any idea of superiority at any stage
> whatsoever. I believe implicitly that all men are born equal. Untouch-
> ability has to be rooted out completely, so that the fundamental
> principle of Advaita Hinduism may be realised in practical life.[4]

To Gandhi his ashram was the place where he expressed most forcefully his personal religious conceptions and its inhabitants were his most
important followers. It is significant that the very first verse of the
Bhajanavali, the collection of hymns compiled for the use of the Ashram

inmates in their daily prayers, was a strong affirmation of the doctrine of Advaita. Gandhi completed the translation of the Sanskrit version into English in Yeravda prison at the end of 1930, and sent it to Mirabehn. 'Early in the morning, I call to mind that being which is felt in the heart, which is *sat* (the eternal), *chit* (knowledge), *sukham* (bliss) which is the state reached by perfect men and which is the super-state. I am that immaculate Brahman . . .' He explained that it was 'a solemn declaration that we are not the changeful bodies . . . but deep down, are the Being'. He added that the description of it as *sat-chit-ananda*, being, intelligence and bliss, was the most apposite description of *Brahman*. In fact, it is the old, traditional concise definition of it.[5]

That text very boldly stated the advaitic tenet from the point of view of the individual spirit: it is identical with *Brahman* defined as *sat-chit-ananda*. This point of view is not Gandhi's most frequent approach to the heart of Advaita. However, there are quite a few texts that clearly state the position of the individual spirit. In answer to a question, he confirmed that he believed that the Trinity of Nature, Soul and God were 'separate in name but one in substance'. Elsewhere he wrote, 'the Upanishads and other scriptures teach us that an inward view will reveal only one soul pervading us all.'[6]

Stating that Gandhi remained a convinced advaitist does not imply that he was a philosopher who deeply studied the abstruse metaphysics of Shankara. He did no such thing, and had no inclination to do so. In fact he considered such interest in theorising to be, from the point of view of religion, a waste of time.[7] The fact that Gandhi often referred to a personal God has made some scholars consider him to have been not an advaitin, but a believer in a personal God, a Vaishnavite theist.[8] The following statement of Gandhi, written in answer to someone who wrote that he doubted Gandhi's advaitism, may seem to support the argument that he was in fact a theist.

I am an *advaitist* and yet I can support *dvaitism* (dualism). The world is changing every moment, and is therefore unreal, it has no permanent existence. But though it is constantly changing, it has something about it which persists and is therefore to that extent real. I have therefore no objection to calling it real and unreal.

I talk of God exactly as I believe Him to be . . . I believe God to be creative as well as non-creative. This too is the result of my acceptance of the doctrine of the manyness of reality. From the platform of the Jains I prove the non-creative aspect of God, and from that of Ramanuja the creative aspect. As a matter of fact, we are all thinking of the Unthinkable, describing the Undescribable, seeking to know the Unknown, and that is why our speech falters, is inadequate and even often contradictory. Then why do the Vedas describe *Brahman* as 'not this, not this'? But if He or It is not this, He or It *is* . . . He is *one* and yet many: He is smaller than an atom, and bigger than the Himalayas; He is contained even in a drop of the ocean, and yet not even the seven seas can compass Him. Reason is powerless to know Him. He is beyond the reach or grasp of reason.[9]

The most important part of this statement is the very first sentence: 'I am an advaitist and yet I can support *dvaitism*.' Gandhi affirmed clearly and definitely that his basic belief was in Advaita. Then he added a second clause starting with 'yet'; one could paraphrase this as follows: 'Notwithstanding my firm conviction in Advaita, I am able to support the doctrine that reality is more than one'; or one could rephrase it as follows: 'My support for dualism does not really negate my firm belief in Advaita.' In declaring that the advaitic view of the absolute allows the advaitin to also accept the dualism of theism, does Gandhi make a contradictory statement simply for the sake of not antagonising those who believe in theism, i.e. most Hindus and all Christians and Muslims? The answer must be a definite no. From the very early days of Gauda-pada, the first theoretician of Advaita, the system did accept a validity, be it limited, of the dualistic approach:

The advaita-darsana has no quarrel with any system of philosophy. While the pluralistic world-views are in conflict with one another, advaita is not opposed to any of them. It recognises that there is truth in each of them, but only that that truth is not the whole.[10]

Advaita accepts that there are various 'levels' of reality, and whereas *Brahman* is the one and only absolute reality, the world, the souls, and the theistic creator God have a level of 'relative reality'. This is for most people the sphere within which they consciously live all their lives. When the human being looks at the ground of being with his limited reason, 'through a mirror darkly', he mostly sees the creator-redeemer God. This God is not a pure illusion, an irrational fancy, but He is the absolute *Brahman* itself distorted by human perception. That this was Gandhi's conviction can be confirmed by the following statement. After a long enumeration of what God signified, he wrote 'He is a personal God to those who need His personal presence. He is embodied to those who need His touch.' In his Letters on the Gita he expressed that same idea as follows: 'But a full realisation of the Absolute is almost impossible for an embodied being. The Absolute is devoid of all attributes and thus difficult for men to imagine. Therefore they are all worshippers of a personal God, whether they are aware of it or not.' In a conversation about the meaning of prayer with the Buddhist Fabri, Gandhi tried to explain to him his own seeming inconsistency. He told him that he had the strong intellectual conviction of the truth of Advaita. But, on the other hand, his awareness of identity with the Absolute was imperfect, and made him feel so small, that he often felt that there was a 'Higher Power' that helped him.[11]

THE HINDU DIVINITIES

Speculation about God in a Hindu context necessarily needs to confront important concepts of the tradition, such as the Vedic Gods, *devas*, and the meaning of the great gods Shiva and Vishnu. Generally, Gandhi was not interested, and he subsumed all mythology under the formula that there are a thousand different names for God. It is only very occasionally, like in his *Discourses on the Gita*, that he faced those questions. He treated them there because he was writing a commentary, and he had in front of him a text to which he needed to respond. He came across the *devas* in verses 10–11 of chapter 3 of the *Gita*, and commented as follows:

> We should think carefully what the term god [*deva*], too, means. Who are god Indra and other gods? . . . Indra and others are not gods living in the heavens; they symbolise the forces of nature . . . The gods symbolise the different forms of energy, the forces which sustain the universe.[12]

A little further on he asked, 'but, then who is the Brahma mentioned in the first verse of this group? Who, again, are Vishnu and Shiva?' His answer was quite definite:

> I do not look upon them as distinct Beings. We may take them to represent aspects of God or His powers. They are represented in the *Puranas* as being different from other gods. All this is partly right and partly wrong. They imagined all these things because they wanted to teach people dharma somehow. In truth, there is no such Being as Brahma or Shiva. The only reality is the neuter *Brahman*. But as God

is conceived of as doing nothing, it was imagined that this universe comes into existence out of Brahma.[13]

GOD IS TRUTH

The definition of God as Truth was the next most frequent in Gandhi's work. We noticed the germ of the idea in the South African period, and it became an often repeated refrain for the rest of his life. Although there are repeated references to truth earlier,[14] they are rather fleeting. It seems that what really set him thinking seriously about the meaning of truth, was the writing of his autobiography, which he entitled 'The Story of My Experiments with Truth'. He tried in 1925 to sum up his thoughts in his Introduction to that work.

> But my purpose being to give an account of various practical applications of these principles, I have given the chapters I propose to write the title of *The Story of My Experiments With Truth*. These will of course include experiments with non-violence, celibacy and other principles of conduct believed to be distinct from truth. But for me, truth is the sovereign principle, which includes numerous other principles. This truth is not only truthfulness in word, but truthfulness in thought also, and not only the relative truth of our conception, but the Absolute Truth, the Eternal Principle that is God. There are innumerable definitions of God, because his manifestations are innumerable. They overwhelm me with wonder and awe and for a moment stun me. But I worship God as Truth only. I have not yet found Him, but I am seeking after Him . . . But as long as I have not realised this Absolute Truth, so long must I hold by the relative truth as I have conceived it . . . Often in my progress I have had faint glimpses of the Absolute Truth, God, and daily the conviction is growing upon me that he alone is real and all else is unreal.[15]

For Gandhi truth was 'the sovereign principle' of morality, which included numerous others, and it was also the Absolute Truth, the Eternal Principle, the Absolute whereas all else is unreal. Truth is, therefore, both the definition of the most central moral dimension, and the very essence of the Absolute. Gandhi was aware of the derivation of the word *satya* (truth) from the root *sat* (to be). *Brahman* is *sat* in its fullness (He alone is the real), and therefore also the fullness of *satya* (truth). Truth, therefore, was the central value of morality, which constitutes the essence of religion and also the most appropriate name of God: God is Truth.[16]

About seven years later Gandhi declared that he had now gone 'a step further' by saying that 'Truth is God', and he proceeded to explain 'the fine distinction between the two statements':

> It is difficult to understand 'God is love' (because of a variety of meanings of love) but I never found a double meaning in connection with Truth and not even atheists denied the necessity of Truth. Not only so. In their passion for discovering Truth, they have not hesitated, even to deny the very existence of God – from their point of view rightly. And it was because of their reasoning that I saw that I was not going to say 'God is Truth', but 'Truth is God'.[17]

What Gandhi did here was to replace the statement 'God is Truth', which is meant to give a description of the nature of the Absolute, by the statement 'Truth is God', which affirms that wherever there is truth-in-action, *that* is where God is found. This is clearly confirmed by Gandhi's answer in the same speech to the next question, 'what is Truth?':

> A difficult question, but I have solved it for myself by saying that it is what the voice within tells one . . . It follows that what may be truth for one may be untruth for another . . . And since everybody says it is his inner voice which speaks, you must listen to the voice, and you will then find out your limitations as you go along the path. Therefore, we have the belief based upon uninterrupted experience that those who would make diligent search after Truth-God, must go through these vows: the vow of truth-speaking and thinking of truth, the vow of brahmacharya, of non-violence, poverty and non-possession. [18]

Gandhi left no doubt about what truth, which is God, meant to him: the genuine morality of action here and now. T. K. Mahadevan put it very well: 'the Gandhian truth is essentially the existential truth of everyday life. It is the truth of a given situation fully within the confines of space and time. It is the truth which, in its given contexts, is indubitable and self-evident and, therefore, absolute.'[19] Truth is, Gandhi held, where we touch the absolute: in the absolute morality of the concrete deed. Gandhi firmly held to this insight and re-explained it several times in the following years.[20]

GOD IS LAWGIVER AND LAW

The vision of Advaita and the concept of truth thus became the dominating aspects of Gandhi's idea of the absolute. In his later years two additional ideas emerged: God as Law, and God as Power. The idea that God is Law first emerged in the *Discourses on the Gita*, as a commentary on verse eleven of the fourth chapter, which translates as: 'In whatever way any may resort to me, in that same way do I grant them my love. Men follow my path in every way, O Krishna.' Gandhi commented as follows:

> In the second line, therefore, the Lord says that men are governed by His Law. He means that law, the law of karma, which rules the world. We can truly say that God is law . . . God is not a ruler; He is all-pervasive, He is life, He is unconditioned and devoid of form. His rule consists in the rule of His law.[21]

This was reiterated in 1928 – 'That Law then which governs all life is God. Law and the law-giver are one' – in the wider context of an article about God, and again in 1940 in answer to a missionary.[22] Obviously it was not high on Gandhi's agenda. It is mentioned twice more in correspondents' specific questions. 'God is not a person. He transcends description. He is the Law-maker, the Law and the Executor.'[23]

Towards the end of his life, Gandhi had an upsurge of his belief that Nature Cure Treatment in connection with Ramanama constituted an infallible remedy for all illness. In this context, he explained the efficacy of Nature Cure by reference to God's identity with His law, as follows: 'All illness is the result of the violation of the laws of nature, in other words, the penalty of sin against Him, since He and His laws are one.' Consequently, if one eliminated all sin, one eliminated all illness: 'Disease is impossible where there is purity of thought.'[24]

GOD IS POWER

The equation 'God is power' appeared only very rarely in Gandhi's writings. In *Young India* of 2 March 1925, he wrote one of his longest descriptions or eulogies of God, and the word power did not even get a mention. A year later he finished a letter with the observation, 'The Reality which we call God is a mysterious, indescribable and unique power.'[25] Another couple of years later, in answer to the letter of a youth who found it difficult to believe in a God who allowed so much evil in this world, Gandhi, for the first time, developed his idea of God as power:

There is an indefinable mysterious Power that pervades everything. I feel it, though I do not see it. It is this unseen Power which makes Itself felt and yet defies all proof, because It is so unlike all that I perceive though my senses . . . I do dimly perceive that whilst everything around me is ever changing, ever dying, there is underlying all that change a living Power that is changeless, that holds all together, that creates, dissolves and recreates. That informing Power or Spirit is God. And since nothing else I see merely through the senses can or will persist, He alone is.[26]

This was very much a restatement of his belief in *Brahman*, but he looked at the absolute here specifically from the point of view of power. After this, in the thirties, he referred to the power-aspect only twice, each time in specific answers to questions, and once during a general discussion in 1942.[27]

It is striking therefore, to find that towards the very end of his life, Gandhi wrote two articles dealing specifically with God as Power, which appeared both in English in *Harijan* and in Gujarati in *Harijanbandhu*. The first was published in August 1946:

In my view, whether called Rama, Rahman, Ormuzd, God or Krishna, He is that Supreme Power that man is ever trying to find a name for. . . . Man however can describe this Infinite Power only with his imperfect means . . . One ought always to remember, while dwelling on Him, that one is but a drop, the tiniest of creatures of the ocean that is God. One may experience Him by being in Him, but one can never describe Him . . . So it is immaterial if some worship God as a Person and some other as a Great Power . . . All the other forces are static, while God is the Life Force, immanent and at the same time transcendent.[28]

It is evident that the idea of God as power had come to the forefront of Gandhi's conception of the absolute. Why had this idea taken such a hold on his mind in these last months of his life? The second article, published in June 1947, gave the answer. It reminds us that Gandhi considered idle theological speculation as a waste of time. Religion was

to him about practice, action. This article made the connection of his
view of God as Power with his religious action quite clear:

> The truth is that God is the force. He is the essence of life. He is pure
> consciousness. He is omnipresent. In spite of that all do not get
> benefit from or shelter in Him or say everyone is not able to secure
> shelter under Him. Electricity is a great force but all cannot benefit
> from it. There are certain laws for generating it and therefore we can
> get electricity only if we abide by those laws. Electricity is a lifeless
> force. Men, the living beings, have to labour hard to acquire the
> knowledge of its laws.
>
> Similarly there are laws for knowing the great living force which
> we call God. But it is self-evident that it requires hard labour to find
> out those laws. That law in short is called *brahmacharya*. I can say
> from my experience that the simplest way to cultivate *brahmacharya*
> is Ramanama. Devotees and sages like Tulsidas have shown us this
> path . . .
>
> There are numerous aids to *brahmacharya*. But the true and eternal
> one is Ramanama. Only when Rama descends from the lips into the
> heart can one know His real power.[29]

What Gandhi said here is that just like man can tap the power of electri-
city if he knows and applies its laws, so can he tap the Great Cosmic
Power that underlies the cosmos, if he applies the basic law of access,
which is chastity. This chastity is to be understood in that fullest sense
it had acquired for Gandhi of total renunciation of body, pleasure, and
self, and of total dedication of all action to *Brahman*.[30] One should
remember that the time Gandhi wrote this was the time of his deepest
darkness and depression on account of the brutal Hindu–Muslim conflict
that was engulfing the continent. He felt that he needed all the spiritual
power possible to stem that flood. That is why he now concentrated on
God as Power, and on the method of tapping that power.

GOD AS AVATAR

The consideration of Gandhi's concept of the absolute needs to consider
his idea of avatar, which is a very important part of Hindu theology. The
most striking aspect of Gandhi's concept of avatar, is that it remains
totally the same from the first time he formulated it up to the very end of
his life. The first time Gandhi stated his own view of avatar was in the

letters he wrote from South Africa between May and August 1913 to Jamnadas Gandhi, who had left for India. An *atman* about to attain *moksha*, in other words somebody who has achieved extraordinary moral greatness, is called an avatar. Avatarhood, therefore, is not the descent of God into a human form, but the recognition of the spiritual achievement, of a particular spirit, which is in fact a possibility for every spirit.[31] Jamnadas had difficulties in understanding the stories told about Krishna in the scriptures, some of which seemed to involve immorality. Gandhi's answer was that there were two different ways of looking at Krishna. One could look upon him as an historical figure: in that case there was no harm in admitting that he was imperfect, because as long as one is in the body, perfection is impossible. On the other hand, if one looked upon Krishna as 'the Supreme Being', then one had to read the exploits described in the scriptures in a different way; one had to interpret them 'symbolically'.[32]

After his return to India, the first time that Gandhi treated the question of avatar specifically and at length was in his *Discourses on the Gita*, where he commented on the classical statement of the *Gita* on avatarhood in chapter 4, where Krishna says to Arjuna: 'Though unborn and inexhaustible in My Essence, though Lord of all beings, yet assuming control over my nature, I come into being by my mysterious power' (Bh.G. 4,6). Gandhi proceeded to explain this text which seemed to claim that the Lord of all beings, by using the full mysterious power of his own nature, assumed a human form. He said that this could not be taken as literal truth, because Krishna was not making a philosophical statement, but he was using 'the idiom of common speech'. Avatar does not mean that 'God comes down from above'. To show that this could not be so, Gandhi appealed to the advaitic doctrine that in fact there is only one *atman*, since 'in our awakened state all are one, though in our ignorant state we may seem separate existences'. Therefore, God does not 'incarnate himself as an *atman* and is never born as a human being, he is ever the same'. Calling someone an avatar proceeded from the limited point of view: 'We see special excellence in some individual, we look upon him as an avatar.' But in 'God's language', there is no such word as avatar.[33]

A statement written by Gandhi six months before his death shows clearly how his ideas at that time were identical with those he put forward 35 years earlier in South Africa, and 20 years earlier in India.

> God is not a human being. Therefore to say that He incarnates himself in the form of a human being is also not the whole truth. We can only

say that God incarnated in the form of a man only means that *that* man has more godliness in him than other men. As God is omnipresent, he is everywhere and dwells within every human being and all may therefore be said to be incarnations of him. But this leads us nowhere. We call Rama and Krishna incarnations because people saw divinity in them. In truth Krishna and others exist in men's imagination – they are creations of his imagination. Whether they were historical figures or not has nothing to do with men's imagination. Sometimes we tread a dangerous path in believing that Rama and Krishna were historical entities and we are compelled to take recourse to all manner of arguments to prove that.[34]

During his Indian period Gandhi repeatedly returned to that distinction between history and imagination. In his introduction to his translation of the *Gita* he wrote:

Krishna of the *Gita* is perfection and right knowledge personified; but the picture is imaginary. That does not mean that Krishna, the adored of his people, never lived. But perfection is imagined. The idea of a perfect incarnation is an aftergrowth.[35]

He often repeated this same theme of the distinction between the historical figure and the divinised perfect avatar, which was the creation of human imagination.[36] Similarly, he reiterated his idea that the elevation of some figure to avatarhood was caused by the special extraordinary God-like qualities exhibited by that person.[37]

Gandhi's view of avatar was one that easily fitted in with his overall advaitic concept of the absolute. Every *atman* is fundamentally identical with *Brahman,* and, therefore, every *atman* has the potential of a total merger with the absolute in *moksha.* Avatarhood is not a supernatural, miraculous intrusion of the divine into the historical sphere, but the attribution by men of a title on someone of exceptional spiritual accomplishment. When that person is viewed from the historical point of view, he remains imperfect, however great his virtues. But the imagination of man sometimes divinised the figure, and thus created the magnificent Krishna of divine resplendence, the perfect God-man.

ADVAITA AND *BHAKTI*

Because of the intimate connection of *bhakti* with the theistic approach, it seems apt to treat in this chapter Gandhi's conception of *bhakti.* He was brought up in the *bhakti* of the Vallabhacharya sect, and he knew it intimately. Since *bhakti* means love or devotion to the Lord, it is not surprising that its cult contains a strong dose of sentimental effusiveness, and that it makes ample use of representational forms. Idol-worship, temple attendance, and guru worship are prevalent devotions, as are rosaries, readings, and hymn singing. This can be contrasted with the much soberer approach of Advaita Vedanta.

Of all the Hindu sacred books, Gandhi chose the *Gita* as his favourite. He came to know it in London, and read and studied it throughout his life. He constantly referred to it as his 'spiritual dictionary', 'the mother who never let him down', or his *kamadhenu* (the cow that grants all wishes). It is the only Hindu text he wrote about, and that at great length: his three works on it present us with no less than 360 pages of text. The *Gita* was the first major Hindu text on *bhakti*, composed probably around 200 BC, and, although it was not part of *shruti*, revelation in the strict sense, but of *smriti*, 'tradition', it has been given by the Hindu tradition a pre-eminent status among all the sacred texts.

The *Gita* came after the ancient *Upanishads*. It was in the latter that the Advaita approach had emerged. They held that liberation meant absorption into the impersonal absolute, *Brahman*, which could be achieved by the cultivation of knowledge of a philosophical and mystical kind. This knowledge was difficult to cultivate, and could be realised only by the full-time specialist, the *sannyasi*, who renounced the world and devoted his whole life to the task. The message of the *Gita* opened up a new avenue of spiritual endeavour: *bhakti*. This devotional love of the Lord, incarnated as Krishna, was within the reach of everybody, and opened up the gates of liberation to all. The *Gita* did not deny the teachings of the *Upanishads*, but incorporated and transcended them. It accepted the existence of *Brahman*, but held that this was but a lower aspect of the Personal God. It accepted the importance of knowledge, but subordinated it to the path of *bhakti*. Much of the *Gita* is about the relationships of the three basic methods of spiritual endeavour: *karma*, renunciation of all attachment in action, *jnana*, pursuit of knowlege, and *bhakti*, love of the Lord. The whole development of the *Gita* presents the superior rank of the *bhakti* approach, just as it presents the superiority of the Personality of God over its *Brahman* aspect.

It has been shown that Gandhi considered *Brahman* as the most fundamental and eternal aspect of reality. How did he deal with the three paths, *karma, jnana*, and *bhakti*, described in his favourite scripture? He did not consider *bhakti* as of great importance in the trilogy. This is evident first of all from his choice of the most important chapter in the

Gita: 'The theme of the *Gita* is contained in the second chapter'; 'from the last verse of chapter two, it would seem that Sri Krishna had nothing further to add'; 'with chapter two the *Gita* ends. It need not have been followed by anything more.'[38] The second chapter concentrates on the following themes: the spirit is immortal, and the body is mortal; a Kshatriya's duty is to fight; concentrate on two methods: the method of *karma*, being dedicated to action and remaining indifferent to its results, and the method of *jnana*, the acquisition of wisdom. The word *bhakti*, or the idea, are not mentioned even once in the text Gandhi considered to be the key text of the *Gita*.

In his three commentaries on the *Gita* Gandhi occasionally referred to the *bhakti* method and its relationship to the other two, and in each case *bhakti* came a poor third to the others. *Bhakti* was a relatively easy way to acquire knowledge: 'But he who lovingly cultivates devotion . . . gets knowledge without any special effort.' 'Therefore, says the *Gita*: Have devotion and knowledge will follow.' In the paragraphs where he says that the three methods are necessary, he mostly ends up by dismissing *bhakti* quickly, and concentrating on the other two.[39] Just like the Creator-God is really a creature of the imagination, so is the 'grace' of God, and 'The word grace is a poetic term. *Bhakti* itself is poetry.' In this context poetry is contrasted with the logical presentation of truth. Gandhi acknowledged that the twelfth chapter of the *Gita* described the characteristics of someone filled with *bhakti*. He went on to point out that these were essentially the same as those of the man of self-control, described in the second chapter. He remarked that whereas the description of the second chapter was 'rigorous', that of the twelfth was cast 'in ordinary language, with a touch of poetry'.[40]

In his two long descriptions of the characteristics of the ideal devotee, we have an accumulation of moral excellences and ascetic qualities, but devotion to Krishna is not specifically mentioned. Wherever one turns in Gandhi's writings, *bhakti* is always downgraded in comparison with *karma* and *jnana*. In fact, he expressed this most aptly and succinctly already in his South African period, when he wrote: 'The true meaning of *bhakti* is a search for the *atman*. When the *atman* realises itself, *bhakti* is transformed into *jnana*'. This is the clear opinion of an advaitin to whom the empty sentimentality and ritualism of many *bhakti* practices were definitely inferior, and could at most be a handmaiden to help the dawning of knowledge, the full realisation of perfection. He expressed this suspicion of *bhakti* most clearly as follows:

The popular notion of *bhakti* is soft-heartedness, telling beads and the like, and disdaining to do even a loving service, lest the telling of beads, etc., might be interrupted. This *bhakti*, therefore, leaves the rosary only for eating, drinking and the like, never for grinding corn or nursing patients.[41]

At this point, it is very instructive to remember Raychand's answer to Gandhi's questions in his early South African career. Gandhi's questions were: 'Can an illiterate person attain *moksha* through *bhakti* alone?' And, 'Can we attain salvation through faith in the avatars?' Raychand answered that *bhakti* had the power of purifying knowledge, but that it was knowledge that was the cause of *moksha*, whereas *bhakti* only played a subsidiary role. Faith in Krishna and devotional worship could not cause *moksha*, but they could help us to gain the means for attaining it. Till the end of his days Gandhi held on to that belief.[42]

CONCLUSION

Right through his life Gandhi personally held on to the basic advaitic approach he adopted in South Africa. He expressed it forcefully whenever he spoke about God, and that same Advaita permeated his conception of avatars. The ultimate identity of all spirits with *Brahman* became a potent argument against the injustices pervading the practice of untouchability. This conviction of the fundamental truth of Advaita went hand in hand with the tolerant acceptance of the many names given to the Absolute, whom from South African times he often referred to as 'Khuda or Ishvar', addressing both Muslims and Hindus. He found the theoretical explanation of the multiplicity of names and descriptions of God in the Jain doctrines of relativity.

The idea that 'Truth is God', as we explained it, forcefully expressed one of his most fundamental ideas about religion, namely, that religion is primarily not about mythologies, theologies, and ritual systems, but about the moral action of the individual. 'Truth is God' means that God is essentially to be found in the truthful, moral act performed here and now.

The upsurge towards the end of his life, of the idea that 'God is Power', gave voice to his desperate feeling of impotence in face of the slaughter of Hindus and Muslims. It was a cry for help.

7

Scriptural Authority and 'the Voice Within'

Within the religious universe of Gandhi the question of authority is of crucial importance. Most religions accept several sources of authority. There is, first of all, the authority of the divine revelation that may be contained in sacred books, or in an oral tradition. Secondly, there is a 'human' authority that interprets revelation, and pronounces on contemporary issues. This authority, which claims that it has received this right and function from above, is sometimes referred to as the establishment, and frequently involves a priesthood. Besides this establishment there exists a floating charismatic authority of small groups or individuals claiming authority on the basis of religious, often mystical, experiences. And finally, there is the authority of the individual. Individuals mostly have a choice of options within their religious allegiance, be they options of belief or of action. The religions, sects, or denominations, recognise this personal authority in various degrees: it is very restricted in some institutions and very broad in others.

For religious people who do not belong to any organised or community-based religion, there is no problem of authority, because they will be convinced that all authority rests with their own intelligence and conscience. There is no need for them to assess various sources of authority. Although Gandhi may appear to be such an individualist, he did persistently claim that he was a *sanatani* Hindu, a Hindu with roots in ancient traditions. It is precisely because he claimed to be such that he needed to clarify his conceptions of the various forms of authorities that have traditionally been a part of Hinduism. He had to face questions such as: which are the authoritative Hindu scriptures; are they divine compositions; are they limited by the time and the place of their composition; who has the right to interpret them; what is the authority of a pandit, of a *shastri*, of a Shankaracharya, of the head of a great sect; what authority does the individual have?

By the end of the South African period Gandhi had consolidated some convictions, but they were still basic and undeveloped. As for the Vedas being God-given, Gandhi considered the Jain idea that they were the result of human authorship, a much more logical stance. Being man-made, they were not infallible, and the validity of their contents had to be judged by the yardstick of morality. He realised that the scriptures contained interpolations, another imperfection. But sifting out these interpolations was a waste of time that the religious aspirant should leave to the pandits. Gandhi suggested that mythological Krishna stories allowed two levels of interpretation. If they were taken as historical accounts, then one should not be disturbed by the fact that Krishna was not perfect, because he was embodied. If, on the other hand, one read the text as referring to Krishna as Supreme Being, then a symbolical interpretation was appropriate. This is the sum total of Gandhi's pronouncements on scripture and revelation on the eve of his return to India. Actually, he had little knowledge of the Hindu scriptures: he had only read a few *Upanishads*, and the *Bhagavadgita*.[1]

THE NATURE OF SCRIPTURE

A striking aspect of Gandhi's conception of scripture and revelation is that it developed within the context of the study of his favourite text, the *Gita*. This is a rather small text interpolated into the great epic, the *Mahabharata*. It does actually not form part of what the Hindus call *shruti*, revelation proper, which comprises the enormous collection of Vedas, *Brahmanas*, and *Upanishads*. Strictly speaking it belongs to the derived collection of holy books called the *smriti*, the tradition. Gandhi's theory of revelation developed from his reflections on a small work which could not be called representative of the works of revelation, but was in fact very different from all of them in language, style, and content, and post-dated them by many centuries. The Hindu tradition has now for a long time looked upon the *Gita* as one of its most sacred texts, and in his preference for it, Gandhi was acting well within the tradition. It is, however, significant that Gandhi's theory of scripture and revelation is built upon the study of that one text. It is as if a Christian evolved a theory of Christian revelation by concentrating exclusively on, for instance, the Epistles of Paul or the *Imitation of Christ* of Thomas à Kempis. One may object that in fact Gandhi did read widely in the Hindu tradition. Certainly, he read much in Yeravda Jail in 1922, but his theories as he stated them first in full in 1925, appear little influenced by that reading, and though referring directly to the *Gita* only, were obviously meant to have validity for scripture in general.

Gandhi's first public statement on the meaning of the *Gita* appeared in his 'Satyagraha Leaflet no. 18' of 8 May 1919. In this call for a national strike he suggested that people should observe a fast and read the *Gita*. Right away some Hindus disputed the appropriateness of the *Gita* for a non-violent agitation, since they were convinced that the text promoted fighting. Gandhi's answer was:

[the *Gita*] is not a historical work, it is a great religious book, summing up the teaching of all religions. The poet has seized the occasion of the war between the Pandavas and the Kauravas . . . for drawing attention to the war going on in our bodies between the forces of Good and the forces of Evil.[2]

The *Gita* was not a history, but a religious allegory. Over the next few years Gandhi touched on various other aspects, but his first comprehensive statement was published in 1925 in *Navajivan* under the title 'Meaning of the *Gita*'.[3]

This document primarily deals with the interpretation of the *Gita*: how one should interpret, who has the right to interpret, and what is the basic meaning of the text. The need for interpretation stems from the very nature of the *Shastras*: Gandhi had long since acknowledged that they were man-made, and were full of later interpolations. But there was even more than textual imperfection; already in 1921 Gandhi had clearly stated that the *Shastras* were quoted by Hindus in order to justify sinful behaviour:

What do we not do in the name of the Shastras? In their name, mendicants consume bhang and smoke *ganja*; in the name of the Shastras some devotees of a goddess consume mutton and wine and numberless people indulge in immoral practices; in the name of the Shastras, in the Madras Presidency, girls of tender age are forced to become prostitutes.[4]

A friend of Gandhi put to him what he called the dilemma of morality and shastric injunctions as follows:

You are against the marriage of girls under fifteen, but the Shastras enjoin us to get girls married before they attain puberty. Even those who are against child-marriage follow this injunction of the Shastras. How does one solve this dilemma? [And Gandhi answered:] I see no dilemma here. Anyone who claims that whatever is found in the books known as the Shastras is true and that no departure from it is permissible will find himself in such dilemmas at every step. A given verse may be interpreted in many ways, and these meanings may even be mutually contradictory. Moreover, the Shastras lay down some principles which are immutable, while some others related to conditions at a particular time and place and applied only to those circumstances.[5]

In summary, the *Shastras* are man-made, limited by history and geography, often ambiguous, on occasion advocate sinful action, and were interfered with by interpolators over the centuries. Proper interpretation was, therefore, of the greatest importance.

THE QUALIFIED INTERPRETER

Before considering the principles of interpretation, the question had to be asked who had the *right* of interpretation. In Hinduism the traditional authorities were the shastris or pandits, specialists in the study of the *Shastras*. In more recent times there had been a tendency to look for authoritative statements from the Shankaracharyas, heads of the great monastic orders founded by Shankara. Gandhi had already made his opinion clear in that matter. 'I do most emphatically repudiate the claim [if they advance any such] of the present Shankaracharyas and Shastris to give a correct interpretation of the Hindu scriptures.'[6] If the specialists assigned by the Hindu tradition had no right to claim they were the true interpreters of the Shastras, who then had such a right? His article on the 'Meaning of the Gita' emphatically repeated his answer three times:

For understanding the meaning of the Shastras, one must have a well-cultivated moral sensibility and experience in the practice of their truths . . . Anyone who offers to interpret the Shastras must have observed the prescribed disciplines in his life . . . Learned men may please themselves and draw seemingly profound meanings from the Shastras, but what they offer is not the real sense of these. Only those who have experience in the practice of their truths can explain the real meaning of the Shastras.[7]

'Experience' is the key word here, offering a clear statement of the conviction that was in Gandhi's mind from at least early 1919. He then wrote that his own interpretation of the *Gita* had 'stood the test of experience', which is 'something more powerful than argument', and added, 'you will readily admit, I am sure, that learned commentaries are of much less value than the experience of one limited intelligence'.[8] The only legitimate interpreters of the *Shastras* are, therefore, those who have put their injunctions into practice, not the learned specialists. Gandhi held that opinion in 1922 during his stay in Yeravda jail before he read the commentaries of Shankara, Jnaneshwar, Tilak, and Aurobindo.[9] This reading did not change his conception of scriptural interpretation; to the very end Gandhi held on to his conviction that only experience entitled one to interpret the *Shastras*.[10] He not only claimed that right, but he amply exercised it by writing no less than three books of interpretation of the *Gita*.

THE SUPREME TEST OF AUTHENTICITY

The next question is how the interpreter should sift the pure grain from the chaff in the *Shastras*; what criteria should be used? In the 'Meaning of the *Gita*' Gandhi proposed two basic principles for testing shastric texts: truth and non-violence. He had already stated them earlier with expressive vigour:

> Every religious principle claiming authority from the Shastras should be tested on the anvil of truth with the hammer of compassion. If it is found hard enough and does not break, it should be accepted as correct, else we should say 'Not this, not this.' to a thousand experts in the Shastras.[11]

Truth and non-violence remained the fundamental tests throughout, though he sometimes formulated them differently. 'That which is opposed to trained reason, cannot be claimed as Shastra no matter how ancient it may be.'[12] Although Gandhi often mentioned the test of reason, questions of rationality were rare, except for his occasional affirmation of disbelief in miracles, and his objection to logical inconsistencies. This is not surprising given Gandhi's disinterest in the theoretical side of religion. He put this most forcefully when he wrote: 'It is a misuse of our intellectual energy and a waste of time to go on reading what we cannot put into practice.'[13]

The paramount test of scripture for Gandhi was the moral test. 'From my youth upwards, I learnt the art of estimating the value of scriptures on the basis of their ethical teaching.'[14] Gandhi repeated this conviction with increasing force. 'Any conduct that is contrary to truth and ahimsa is to be eschewed and any book that violates these principles is not a shastra'; and 'Nothing that is inconsistent with the universally accepted first principles of morality has for me the authority of the shastras.'[15] This test became crucial in his battle with orthodox Hindus about untouchability. These orthodox tried to show that untouchability was sanctioned by the Hindu *Shastras*. Gandhi made the most definitive affirmation of the supremacy of ethics when he stated with passionate assurance and certainty the depth of his conviction. He declared that if it were proven that the Vedas, the *Upanishads*, the *Gita* and the books of Hindu law claimed divine authority for the practice of untouchability, then he would have no choice: he would have to follow the dictate of his own conscience and reject Hinduism like a 'rotten apple'.[16]

THE PRE-EMINENCE OF THE *GITA*

Gandhi realised very well the great extent of what Hindus called *shruti*, revelation, and the enormous volume of later writings such as the *Puranas*, which were subsumed under the broad appellation *shastra*. He recognised that they had authority: 'I do accept the shastras as authoritative; the sum total of these books is certainly inspired; I believe in the Puranas as sacred books.'[17] This, however, did not mean that he made a deep study of them although he had read a fair amount. He stated clearly that from his first encounter with the *Gita* in London he became convinced that it contained 'the essence of dharma . . . the highest knowledge'.[18] That conviction remained firm throughout his life, and he often repeated it: the *Gita* 'is the essence of dharma; a synthesis of the Hindu religion; the key to a knowledge of the Shastras'. He has stated 'whatever is contrary to its main theme I reject as un-Hindu', and 'if all the other scriptures were reduced to ashes, the seven hundred verses of this imperishable booklet are quite enough to tell me what Hinduism is and how one can live up to it'.[19] Since the *Gita* represented to Gandhi the very essence of religion itself, it is not strange to hear him say that 'The *Gita* has become for me the key to the scriptures of the world. It unravels for me the deepest mysteries to be found in them.'[20]

Gandhi made a point of reading the Vedas, the *Puranas*, and the major *Smritis* such as the *Manusmriti*, but none of them ever became a focus for further study. From the very beginning of his spiritual development in London the *Gita* was the centre of attention, and remained so throughout his life. From the start it was part of his household devotions, became the central element of the ritual of his ashrams, and was constantly referred to in his correspondence. Between 1926 and 1932 he wrote no less than 360 pages of translation and commentary.[21]

His choice of the *Gita* as the supreme norm of all Hindu scriptures, with neglect of other Hindu texts, was accepted within the Hindu tradition. Apart from the injunction that the devout Brahmin should include the reading of the Vedas in his daily observances, a duty fulfilled by only few Brahmins, there is no real obligation on a Hindu to study, or choose as his guide any particular *shastra* as long as he believes that the Vedas have a special relation to the divine. In fact the four Vedas are of very little interest to the great majority of Hindus. Only one modern reformer, Swami Dayananda Sarasvati, made the Vedas the central focus of the doctrine and practice he bequeathed to his Arya Samaj.[22]

Gandhi offered various reasons why he chose the *Gita*. He was attracted to it because of its pan-Hindu universality: 'It is accepted by all Hindu sects as authoritative.'[23] This certainly distinguishes the work from many sectarian books that appeal to only small groups of Hindus. Although the Vedas enjoy a similar pan-Hindu recognition, their antiquarian, cryptic language puts them effectively out of reach of most except a handful of Vedic specialists. The *Gita*, on the contrary, was cast in 'incredibly simple Sanskrit', and was thus accessible in the original to anyone with even a rudimentary knowledge of that language. Gandhi also distinguished the *Gita* from many sectarian scriptures claiming the exclusive faith and love of the devotee for their favoured God or their divinised guru. He asserted that the *Gita* was free from dogma, and excluded 'no faith and no teacher', thus becoming acceptable to everybody.[24]

However, there was another reason for this selection of the *Gita*, that put all the other reasons in the shadows: its concentration on action, on ethics. Most sacred Hindu texts do include ethical teachings, but these tend to be dispersed among dogmatic elaborations, analyses of mythical cycles, formalistic ritual discourses, sectarian disputations, and descriptions of meditation practices. All these topics were for Gandhi mostly without deep religious value, and it required scholarship and lots of time to sift the pure gold of ethics from the dross of ritual, mythical and dogmatic paraphernalia. The *Gita* was different: 'a pure religious discourse without any embellishment. It simply describes the progress of the pilgrim soul towards the supreme goal.' He repeatedly came back to that idea to justify his love of the *Gita*: 'in a short compass it gives a complete reasoned moral code', and it provides 'in a nutshell the secret art of living'. The *Gita* is supreme among the *Shastras* because, in a clear, direct, and succinct fashion, 'it enunciates the principles on which all conduct must be based'.[25]

There is no doubt that the *Gita* is intensely concerned with action, and most serious commentators, ancient and modern, consider the theme of 'renunciation-in-action' as one of its main messages. However, most would also agree that two other major themes connect with and enlarge it. These themes are the revelation of Krishna as avatar and as identical with the Universal Godhead, and the dominant injunction that all action should be inspired by *bhakti*, loving devotion to Lord Krishna. In fact, the principal message of the work is that *moksha* is not reserved for the philosopher saints or mystics as the more ancient *Upanishads* proclaimed, but attainable by all, provided they performed their duties without egotism and dedicated all their actions with love to Krishna. The first chapters of the *Gita* concentrate on the way in which one should make one's actions free from all selfishness by being indifferent to their consequences. Later chapters concentrate more on the revelation of Krishna and the description of *bhakti*.

Gandhi chose the *Gita* as his principal and only scripture, but his selection did not end there. In his favourite text he selected the second chapter, and even more narrowly, the last nineteen verses of that chapter, as its central message. 'These stanzas are the key to the understanding of the *Gita*. I would even go so far as to advise people to reject statements in the poem which bear a meaning contrary to that of these nineteen stanzas' – thus he wrote in 1925 in his 'Meaning of the *Gita*', before his main commentaries and translations of the text. He wrote that ever since he read the *Gita* as a youth in London, those verses had 'ever remained engraved in my heart', although he never asserted as much at that time.[26] He often reiterated that conviction: 'The theme of the Gita is contained in the second chapter; from the last verse of chapter two, it would seem that Sri Krishna had nothing further to add; with chapter two the Gita ends. It need not have been followed by anything more.' These assertions by Gandhi are completely confirmed by his own writings on the *Gita*: nearly half his commentary is devoted to chapters 2, 3, and 4. The remaining fourteen chapters average less than ten pages each.[27]

In order to understand why Gandhi chose the last nineteen verses of chapter two as the core of the *Gita*, one has to look at their content. These lines basically constitute Krishna's answer to a very specific request of Arjuna for a description of the *sthita-prajna*, the person whose

mind is stabilised, who has, in other words, achieved perfect control of
his inner self. These verses describe someone who has gained a complete
mastery over feelings of attachment, aversion, love, lust, and hate, who
cannot be swayed by his outer senses or his imagination, who has an
attitude of total indifference to all that may please or displease him. Such
a person is at peace and has achieved an indifference which reflects the
very important moral message of renunciation in the *Gita*. Most commentators would agree that the passage is important, because it summa-
rises beautifully the basic principles of the early chapters, which are
concerned with the self-control, non-attachment, and mental equilibrium
necessary for religious achievement. They would also agree that this
moral achievement is but the first step, important and essential, on the
path to liberation. Anyone who has achieved that state of mind is well-
prepared for a life of selfless performance of duty, and for the cultivation
of *bhakti* by which all actions are dedicated to Krishna. That *bhakti* is
generally accepted as the culminating doctrine of the *Gita*. Gandhi,
however, chose the second chapter as the central part, thus affirming that
in his judgement the control and non-attachment described there are not
only mental and moral preparations for the fullness of religious endeavour and achievement in *bhakti*, but they are the very essence of religion
and consequently the very essence of the *Gita*.

> There can be no doubt that non-attachment is the central core of the
> *Gita*. I am certain that there is no other inspiration behind the com-
> position of the *Gita*. And I know from my own experience that
> observance of truth or even ahimsa is impossible without non-attach-
> ment.[28]

THE SHORTEST SUMMARY: THE *ISHOPANISHAD*

Only one other sacred text was given by Gandhi the priority he gave the
Gita: the *Isha Upanishad*. He had read and liked it in jail, but in 1934 he
began giving it a special place; he wrote in a letter to Vallabbhai Patel:

> So long as Death remains unconquerable, nothing that Man does will
> avail him. Hence the first verse of the *Ishopanishad*. Do you remem-
> ber it? I used to recite that Upanishad everyday in jail . . . The author
> has compressed all knowledge within that short compass. There is no
> difference between its teaching and the *Gita*'s. What is present in it in
> the form of a seed has become a beautiful tree in the *Gita*.[29]

In 1937, during his tour of South India, he eulogised the *Isha* in four successive speeches.[30] He had been asked by people what the essence of Hinduism was, and he was pondering which short formula from the scriptures he could present as a synthesis which would answer the needs of pandits as well as of simple people. He considered the *Gayatri mantra*, and the *Gita*, but thought that both required a lot of prayerful study before they yielded their fruit.

> But I have fixed upon the mantra that I am going to recite to you as containing the whole essence of Hinduism. Many of you, I think, know the *Ishopanishad*. I read it years ago with translation and commentary. I learnt it by heart in Yeravda jail. But it did not then captivate me as it has done during the past few months, and I have now come to the final conclusion that if all the Upanishads, and all other scriptures happened all of a sudden to be reduced to ashes and if only the first verse of the *Ishopanishad* were left intact in the memory of Hindus, Hinduism would live forever.[31]

Gandhi then proceeded to comment in detail on that first verse: 'Everything in the universe is pervaded by God; therefore nothing really belongs to anybody. Renounce everything and God will look after your essential needs. Do not covet anybody's possession.' It is quite clear that the fundamental message of the text for Gandhi was the message of renunciation – and that was to his mind also the essential message of the *Gita*, and of Hinduism and all religions:

> The whole of Hinduism could be summed up in the first verse of the *Ishopanishad*. . . . The whole of philosophy or religion found in any part of the world is contained in this *mantra*. I venture to suggest to my Christian and Mussulman friends that they will find nothing more in their scriptures if they will search them.[32]

SCRIPTURAL INTERPRETATION

As we have shown, Gandhi claimed the right of the interpretation of scripture on the basis of having spent many years practising its councils. Some basic laws of interpretation lie scattered in his writings. First of all, Gandhi rejected the way the specialist in the *Shastras* used the texts, as he clearly explained in his letter to Pandit V. S. R. Shastri:

The texts you have quoted are not unfamiliar to me nor the meanings that you have given. The difference arises from the application. I observe that there is a fundamental difference between you and me . . . That difference is in the interpretation. I look at the Shastras as one organic whole. You take isolated texts and prove your point. That method is as ancient as the human race, but I hold it to be altogether erroneous . . . May it not be just possible that those who have the Shastras and the different interpretations of everyone of the texts by heart may miss the central point, and those who neither know them by heart nor understand the meaning of various texts may realise that central truth?[33]

Secondly, Gandhi rejected the claim that the task of the interpreter was limited to discovering the exact meaning of the text: 'A literal interpretation lands one in a sea of contradictions. The letter killeth, the spirit giveth life.' In the search for the meaning of a text, 'one should not stick to its letter, but try to understand its spirit, its meaning in the total context.' In other words, interpretation is not a process of establishing the literal meaning of the text, although we should take note of the rules of grammar, but interpretation by its very nature means 'new' interpretation, expansion of the literal meaning, application to new circumstances. That was, according to Gandhi, exactly what the author of the *Gita* had done, 'extending the meaning of words':[34]

[The *Gita* itself] has given a new meaning to karma, sannyasa, yajna, etc. It has breathed new life into Hinduism. It has given an original rule of conduct. Not that what the *Gita* has given was not implied in the previous writings but the *Gita* put these implications in a concrete shape.[35]

Since the author of the *Gita* himself had thus expanded the meanings of the concepts he inherited, 'There is no harm in our expanding the meaning of the word "yajna", even if the new meaning we attach to the term was never in Vyasa's mind . . . Sons should enrich the legacy of their fathers.'[36]

Naturally, this enrichment or re-interpretation is not a function of discovering a new speculative framework, but it concerns ethical principles and their practical applications, because 'The *Gita* was not composed as a learned treatise.' So, the voluminous commentaries written by great scholars were evaluated as follows by Gandhi:

I have read Lokamanya Tilak's and Shankaracharya's commentaries and tried to understand them as well as I could. I am not qualified to pronounce judgement on their learning. If we accept the point of view I have suggested, the question of expressing an opinion on their learning does not arise.[37]

The scholarship of the treatises, however profound, is in last instance quite irrelevant to the real task of interpretation as Gandhi conceived it.

THE INTERPRETATION OF THE *GITA*

In his 'Satyagraha Leaflet no. 18' Gandhi formulated for the first time his global interpretation of the *Gita:*

Now the *Bhagavad Gita* is not a historical work, it is a great religious book, summing up the teaching of all religions. The poet has seized the occasion of the war between the Pandavas and the Kauravas . . . for drawing attention to the war going on in our bodies between the forces of Good (Pandavas) and the forces of Evil (Kauravas) and has shown that the latter should be destroyed.[38]

This was a firmly established conviction of Gandhi, which he reiterated regularly. In fact, the struggle between good and evil is also, according to Gandhi, the fundamental meaning of the *Mahabharata* and the *Ramayana*.[39]

This global interpretation was the leading light in the hundreds of pages of Gandhi's commentaries. In one particular procedure Gandhi followed a traditional process, that of identifying in a text the *mahavakya*, the great saying, that is held to summarise the central message of the text. The tradition thus considers expressions such as *tat-tvam-asi, aham brahma asmi* as *mahavakyas* of the oldest *Upanishads*. Gandhi chose the last verses of chapter 2 of the *Gita* as its *mahavakya*. This text describes the *sthitaprajna*, the person in whom the war between the forces of good and the forces of evil has resulted in the rout of the latter. This decision about what is the core of the *Gita* allowed Gandhi to devalue certain aspects of the work which most scholars accept to be central. The whole self-revelation of Krishna as avatar became a product of the imagination. Krishna was not even mentioned in the passage which Gandhi considered to represent the essence of the *Gita*. The work

proclaims the practices of *jnana* and *bhakti* to be built upon and tran-
scending the way of renunciation. Gandhi turned this upside-down and
made renunciation the supreme practice.[40]

THE *PURANAS*

Gandhi did try to read the Vedas, but found them practically incompre-
hensible and offered no suggestions as to their interpretation. He read,
and enjoyed some of the *Puranas*, but rarely referred to them. At one
time he was asked by a teacher how he could approach these works in
the classroom. Gandhi tried to give some direction towards an acceptable
method of interpreting these works, and he published his answer in
Navajivan to make it available to other teachers who had similar problems, and may 'find guidance from my ideas on this subject'. First
Gandhi affirmed that he believed in the *Puranas* as sacred books, and
also in gods and goddesses, but not in the conventional way. He did not
believe that the divine creatures that featured in these books were
separate individuals. They only represented various powers of nature,
and the stories and descriptions were 'sheer poetry'. They had to be
understood as such and as long as the interpretations increased faith in
God, and good conduct, they were acceptable. If they did not have that
effect, they should be shunned. Whereas the saint Eknath could read the
Bhagavata Purana with a pure mind, contemplating the *atman*, for others
the reading of that book replete with sexual symbolism, only engendered
impure thoughts, and should therefore be avoided.[41]

SUPREME RIGHT OF RE-INTERPRETATION

The right of re-interpretation of the *Gita* on the basis of his 'enforcing
the meaning in my own conduct for an unbroken period of forty years',
was so firm in Gandhi that it even entitled him to prefer his own version
over that of the traditional author, Vyasa:

> Let it be granted that according to the letter of the *Gita* it is possible
> to say that warfare is consistent with renunciation of fruit. But after
> forty years' unremitting endeavour fully to enforce the teaching of the
> *Gita* in my own life, I have, in all humility, felt that perfect renuncia-
> tion is impossible without perfect observance of ahimsa in every
> shape and form.[42]

Elsewhere he repeated that conviction even more strongly: 'I believe that the teaching of the *Gita* does not justify War, even if the author of the *Gita* had intended otherwise'.[43] Gandhi was prepared to contradict all learned commentators, even the saintly author himself, because his conviction of the rightness of his own interpretation was unshakeable. In fact, even if he were wrong, he would still be right:

> My philosophy represents the true meaning of the *Gita*. I may be mistaken. Such a mistake can do no harm either to me or to anybody. For the source of my inspiration is of no consequence if what I stand for be unadulterated truth.[44]

One could not imagine a stronger affirmation of his conviction that in the final instance the supreme authority in matters religious is vested in the individual conscience. This primacy has been given the name of 'the inner voice' by Gandhi.

THE INNER VOICE

Gandhi claimed in 1932 that he learned to recognise his inner voice in 1906, at the time of the Zulu Rebellion, when he decided on his vow of chastity, the time when he 'started praying regularly'.[45] However, there is no evidence of this until after his return to India, when the first references to the inner voice appear in his writings. The first two references occurred in 1920. The first was an explanation, or perhaps rather a non-explanation of an action certain collaborators did not approve of. 'There are moments in your life when you must act, even though you cannot carry your best friends with you. The "still, small voice" within you must always be the final arbiter when there is a conflict of duties.'[46] The second reference had a similar context. In an article on the caste system, he radically condemned untouchability as 'a heinous crime against humanity', although many Hindus believed it was supported by scriptural authority:

> Indeed I would reject all authority if it is in conflict with sober reason or the dictates of the heart. Authority sustains and ennobles the weak when it is the handiwork of reason but it degrades them when it supplants reason sanctified by the still small voice within.[47]

On both occasions Gandhi was faced by a moral dilemma, in which many people would not accept his choice of alternative. He declared that the 'still, small voice within' had to be the final arbiter for everybody in such a situation.

It is not until the early 1930s that the idea resurfaced. At first the statements were still general in the sense that they applied to everyone. But a new persistent concern appeared now. Anyone could assert at any time that his inner voice prompted this action. But when could one be sure that this was a genuine claim? Some people used this concern to cast doubt on Gandhi's own claim of being directed by the voice within. In order to counteract this objection, Gandhi stressed in his next four statements that there were certain conditions that needed to be fulfilled before the claim of correctly hearing the inner voice could be sustained.

> We should listen to everybody's advice, but do only what our conscience tells us. And in order that our conscience may speak, we should observe the *yama-niyamas* [rules and regulations for the spiritual aspirant similar to the Ten Commandments]. Everybody cannot hear the inner voice. We need divine ears to hear it.[48]

Elsewhere Gandhi expressed the condition as 'keeping the five vows' (truth, chastity, non-violence, poverty, non-possession); on another occasion he wrote 'only that person will be fit to recognise it who possesses the characteristics of the *sthitaprajna* of the *Gita*'. All these statements so far are general statements in that they tend to give a general rule about how anybody can be judged to be in a position to recognise the inner voice.[49]

In 1933, at the height of his intense agitation against untouchability, Gandhi took the unprecedented step of claiming in very concrete terms that the 'inner voice' actually spoke to him and told him in so many words to start a 21-day fast. He wrote as follows on a piece of paper he gave to his companions in the morning.

> At about twelve o'clock in the night something wakes me up suddenly, and some voice – within or without, I can not say – whispers, 'Thou must go on a fast.' 'How many days?' I ask. The voice again says, 'Twenty-one days.' 'When does it begin?' I asked. It says, 'You begin tomorrow.' I went off to sleep after making the decision.[50]

In the public statement he issued on 30 April, he referred to the 'voice', and again in his long article in *Harijan* on 5 May. Many people

were rather sceptical about his account of the voice, and Gandhi treated
the subject in both *Harijan* and *Harijanbandhu* in a long article entitled
'All about the Fast'.

The first question that puzzled many is about the Voice of God. What
is it? What did I hear? Was there any person I saw? If not, how was
the Voice conveyed to me? These are pertinent questions. For me the
Voice of God, of Conscience, of Truth or the Inner Voice, or 'the
still small Voice' mean one and the same thing. I saw no form. I have
never tried, for I have always believed God to be without form.[51]

Gandhi then proceeded to eliminate an answer that may occur to
some. He admitted that 'one who had realised God' was totally free from
all evil, and all that person did was perfect, because of being completely
merged in God; in fact, it was God within who did everything. That,
said Gandhi, was something he did believe in, but he knew that he
himself was still very far from that condition. The voice was, therefore,
not God speaking through him, but rather some kind of 'inspiration'
which can come to anybody who has made the necessary spiritual effort.
He then went on to describe the experience:

The inspiration I got was this: The night I got the inspiration, I had a
terrible inner struggle. My mind was restless. I could see no way. The
burden of my responsibility was crushing me. But what I did hear was
like a Voice from far and yet quite near. It was as unmistakable as
some human voice definitely speaking to me and irresistible. I was not
dreaming at the time I heard the Voice. The hearing of the Voice was
preceded by a terrific struggle within me. Suddenly the Voice came
upon me. I listened, made certain it was the Voice, and the struggle
ceased. I was calm. The determination was made accordingly, the date
and the hour of the fast were fixed. Joy came over me.[52]

Obviously Gandhi realised that he had made a very unusual claim,
which many people, even friends and followers, did not understand and
preferred to interpret in a symbolic fashion. Actually, we may throw
some light on this subject by looking back to Gandhi's previous fasts and
see how the decision to fast was made in those instances.[53]

His very first Indian fast at Ahmedabad started with a kind of 'inspiration', a light that came 'unbidden' at a time when he was lost as to what
he should be doing next.[54] In fact, three more of his pre-1933 fasts
started in a similar fashion. There was a time of intense agony and

prayer, and sleeplessness, and suddenly, 'in a flash', usually in the middle of the night, the decision to fast was taken and he felt totally at peace. This is the pattern repeated in the 1921 Bombay fast, the 1924 Delhi fast, and the 1932 Yeravda fast.[55] So, of the first eight fasts in India, five showed that pattern. But whereas previously Gandhi did not refer to God, but rather to a decision that came to him 'in a flash', in his 1933 Poona fast he stated that he heard a voice within that told him exactly what to do. He actually repeated this and tried to explain it in the paragraph quoted earlier. He tried to describe the voice, which he spelled throughout with a capital letter, and a little further he declared that he could not offer any tangible proof to the sceptic who thought that it was all self-delusion or hallucination, but 'I can say this – that not the unanimous verdict of the whole world against me could shake me from the belief that what I heard was the true voice of God.' He then went on to philosophise about the very notion of God in an interesting way, in view of his personal advaitic view of the Absolute, which looks upon the conception of the personal God as a preliminary and imperfect one that is clouded by a human intellect still under the influence of illusion.

> But some think that God himself is a creation of our own imagination. If that view holds good, then nothing is real, everything is of our own imagination. Even so, whilst my imagination dominates me, I can only act under its spell. Realest things are only relatively so. For me the Voice was more real than my own existence. It has never failed me, and for that matter, anyone else. And everyone who will can hear the Voice. It is within everyone. But like everything else, it requires previous and definite preparation.[56]

Gandhi here admitted that the 'reality' of the Voice of which he was thoroughly convinced, was probably not 'ultimate' reality, just like God is not ultimate reality. Both are the result of a view influenced by the imagination. But admitting that much as a convinced Advaitist, did not in any way undermine his personal certitude about 'the event'.

It is interesting to note that between 1933 and 1947 Gandhi did not again claim that kind of intense experience. From time to time he repeated his general statement how anybody could hear the voice provided they cultivated an intense spiritual life.[57] Twice he recalled his special 1933 experience, and each time he gave the same account of it as he did originally. His belief in what then happened had not been shaken.[58]

It was on 12 January 1948, shortly before his death, that Gandhi made another clear claim that the Inner Voice had called him to start what was to be his last fast to death.

> Though the voice within has been beckoning for a long time, I have been shutting my ears to it lest it might be the voice of Satan, otherwise called my weakness. My impotence has been gnawing at me of late. It will go immediately the fast is undertaken. I have been brooding over it for the last three days. The final conclusion has flashed upon me and it makes me happy . . . With God as my supreme and sole counsellor, I felt that I must take the decision without any other adviser. If I have made a mistake and discover it, I shall have no hesitation in proclaiming it from the house-top and retracing my faulty step. There is little chance of my making this discovery. If there is a clear indication, as I claim there is, of the Inner Voice, it will not be gainsaid.[59]

Gandhi affirmed all along that in matters of morality, the inner voice of conscience had to have the decisive final word, not the text of the *Shastras* or the pronouncements of the *shastris*. He stressed that only the true aspirant of religious life was able to properly recognise that voice. Practically always he put these ideas forward as general ideas applicable to everyone. Only twice in his life did he claim that he actually heard a voice clearly, and at these two times he spelled it with capitals, the Inner Voice. Both were times of most acute crisis. The first was when he decided, at the most critical time of his fight against untouchability in 1933, to go on a dangerous unconditional 21-day fast. The second occasion was shortly before his death, when the intensity of Hindu–Muslim violence drove him to decide on a fast to death, the conditions of which seemed unfulfillable. In both cases the Inner Voice drove him to desperate measures in a time of desperation.

CONCLUSION

Was Gandhi right when he claimed to be a *sanatani Hindu*? There are a good number of reasons why one would have to give an affirmative answer. He always acknowledged the validity and authority of the Hindu sacred books. He made a deep study of the *Gita* and made it the guide of his life. The advaitic structure of his essential belief was thoroughly Hindu. He accepted that, within limits, the Hindu pantheon and the Puranic myths had their genuine place in religion. Similarly he acknowl-

edged the value of idol-worship and temple rituals. He recognised the
worth of the Hindu social system, even if it had degenerated in modern
times. One could not doubt it, when he claimed that he loved Hinduism
as he loved his own mother.

But many of the strictly orthodox Hindu establishment did not accept
his claim, because he did not accept a cardinal law of Hindu orthodoxy:
that the primacy of proof is always based on scriptural truth, the very
text of revelation, *shruti*. Gandhi consistently, and adamantly, refused to
accept that *a priori* primacy of the text. According to him, the text had
always to be submitted to two tests, the test of reason, and the test of
morality. He refused to accept the authority of the pandits in the interpretation of those texts; only the person who had practised the teaching,
and then forced it on his life, was entitled to interpret it. Thus Gandhi
claimed the right to interpret the *Gita* because he had lived it all his life.
As we have seen, he was convinced that the final authority in matters of
religion was the individual conscience, the voice within. No single text
or pandit was entitled to override that voice.

There is no doubt that Gandhi could not pass that test of strict orthodoxy: to acknowledge the absolute primacy of the text of revelation. This
claim of primacy was founded on the dogma that *shruti* was *a-puru-
shaya*, of non-human origin. As T. K. Mahadevan succinctly put it:

> The essence of the Hindu philosophical tradition . . . consists in the
> primacy not of reason but of scriptural truth. What the text says is
> final and inarguable. It is beyond the pale of reason. It is a priori.
> Neither perception nor inference can dare challenge what the text
> says. It is often the trump card in Indian philosophical disquisition.
> 'For the text says so' is the final clinching argument. It can be
> refuted, if at all, only by another text, equally authentic.[60]

It is only in the very high, rarefied atmosphere of Hindu scriptural
theology that the claim of heresy could be held against Gandhi. And it is
a futile claim, simply because Gandhi never pretended that he was active
at that level of speculation. He was a deeply believing Hindu, with no
ambition of building a metaphysical system, or of becoming a theologian
of note. He was extremely intelligent, well-read, and aware of the
profound obscurantism and moral ambivalence of much that claimed the
umbrella of *shastra*, as he was aware of the ignorance and insincerity of
many pandits. He was much too busy to spend time on scriptural analysis or discussions with pandits about the niceties of obscure texts. He
had a deep conviction about the total immorality of untouchability and

the desperate need for Hindu-Muslim peace, and no text or pandit was allowed to shake these convictions. Even if one does not accept that the epithet 'heretic' can be properly applied to Gandhi, one has to admit that he was a fierce individualist, whose fanatical belief in the rightness of his own judgement never wavered, and who thus remained an irritating thorn in the side of Hindu pandits trying to defend what they considered their rightful territory.

8

Religious Pluralism

From the time of his definitive return to India in 1914, Gandhi repeatedly made statements about religious pluralism. The reason for this was that he was frequently asked, even challenged, to clarify his ideas about Hinduism in relation to other religions. These questions came from different quarters. Many Hindus were uneasy about what they considered Gandhi's radical and unorthodox stance on untouchability and Hindu–Muslim relations, and disliked what they considered his open flirtation with Christianity and Islam. On the other hand, Christian missionaries kept asking Gandhi questions about his attitude to Christianity, whereas Gandhi regularly took them to task for their conversion work, which he considered a misdirection of effort. All these issues touched upon the basic problem of religious pluralism.

The household in which Mohandas Gandhi grew up was one in which a young mind could experience religious pluralism in action. His parents belonged to different sects. Moreover, the Gandhi home was frequently visited by Jain monks, who provided religious counselling, and by Muslim friends. It was open to people of all faiths, and religious issues were often discussed in these gatherings. Religious pluralism was a living reality in Mohandas' life: it was simply taken for granted. There was nothing disturbing about it, except for the proselytising methods of the local Christian missionaries, including vilification of Hinduism, which fostered in the young boy a deep revulsion against Christianity.[1]

SOUTH AFRICA: RELIGIOUS PLURALISM BECOMES AN ISSUE

During his period in England Gandhi began his search for the meaning of Hinduism, and he met some Christians, but this did not produce any anxiety. It was in South Africa that religious pluralism became a pressing personal problem. Some of his closest friends and collaborators were fervent Christians, whom Gandhi admired and loved as much as they admired and loved him. These friends started to put great moral pressure on Gandhi to become a convert to Christianity. They claimed that it was the one true religion, that it was as such revealed by God in the Bible, and that the very content of the Bible proved its unique divine origin. This was a challenge of absolute superiority which Gandhi could not ignore.

We have detailed in Chapter 2 the answers to his doubts from various sources: Raychand's letters, Advaita Vedanta texts, and the two Christian thinkers Maitland and Tolstoy. Here we simply summarise what these sources told Gandhi about religious pluralism. They held that there existed from hoary antiquity a set of truths and values of divine character, which constituted the essence of religion. That original religion came to mankind via a number of 'scriptures'. These were human attempts to formulate that original religion, fallible, imperfect, and deeply influenced by the cultures from which they sprang. All scriptures basically shared two things – first, they had drunk from the common divine fountain, and, therefore, shared fundamental truths. Secondly, as human creations, influenced by time and place, they had their share of imperfection, confusion, and even error. The acceptance of those conceptions made for tolerance of many different interpretations and practices. But the claim of any religion to be the only source of divine truth, and to be the only way leading to salvation, was unacceptable within that framework of religious pluralism. And it was precisely that claim that had been asserted strongly by Gandhi's Christian friends.[2]

Raychand's idea of religious pluralism, however, did not hold that all religions were equal; he affirmed that there was a great difference in value and depth between them. He considered the teachings of the Jain sages infinitely more profound than those contained in the Vedas, and he had a very low opinion of the doctrines of Christianity as compared with those which originated in India. He accepted that it was useful to compare the various scriptures, not in order to find out which elements were true or false, but to ascertain which system 'had more power-truth'. In fact, he indicated how this comparison should proceed: 'Only the test of proof can show what is the best and what is not. That religion alone is the best and is truly strong, which is most helpful in destroying the bondage of worldly life and can establish us in the state which is our essence.' In other words, the comparative test consists of putting the counsels of various religions into practice, and a religion proves its worth and truth by the degree of its effectiveness in producing a totally free spirit.[3]

Although, as a scholarly Jain, Raychand knew the subtle Jain doctrine of the relativity of all propositions, he did not present Gandhi with a discourse on that. But he was also a poet and writer of religious pamphlets, where he expressed these doctrines in a practical, simple, and pithy fashion. Gandhi read those works, and was influenced by them. Here are a few examples of Raychand's sayings, which could well have been uttered by the mature Gandhi himself:

> In essential reality there is no difference whatsoever; the difference is only in the eye of the beholder. Believe that, grasp the essence, and you will make progress in religion. Whatever religion you profess, I do not take sides for or against. Only this is worth saying: by whatever method, devotion, or dharma the contamination of the soul by this world is destroyed, that is the dharma, that is the discipline you should follow . . . This world has been unable to discover the truth because it is shackled by the chain of doctrinal disputes.[4]

Gandhi acknowledged Raychand's influence, and later he summarised his friend's religion as follows: 'Dharma does not mean any particular creed or dogma. Dharma is a quality of the soul.' He praised Raychand's respect for other faiths and he presented his own view of religious tolerance as one 'that followed Raychandbhai's point of view'.[5]

The effect of Gandhi's reading of Raychand and others like Maitland in 1894, effectively pacified him, and his anxiety about the claims of Christianity and his doubts about Hinduism disappeared. During the remainder of his stay in South Africa religious pluralism was no more raised as a problem. In a New Year message to his Hindu readers in 1907, he advocated Religious tolerance in *Indian Opinion* as follows:

> If the people of different religions grasp the real significance of their own religion, they will never hate the people of any religion other than their own. As Jalaluddin Rumi has said, or as Shri Krishna said to Arjun, there are many rivers, and they appear different from one another, but they all meet in the ocean. In the same manner there may be many religions, but the true aim of all is the same . . . Hence, if we look at the aim, there is no difference among religions.[6]

TOLERANCE: 'THEY ARE RIVERS MEETING IN THE SAME OCEAN' (1914–30)

We will now consider Gandhi's conception of religious pluralism during the Indian period, which we divide into two segments, before and after 1930. But, before analysing what the 'religious tolerance' of the first segment meant to Gandhi, we need to remind ourselves that his concept of Hinduism was wider than that adopted by most Indians: to him the term Hinduism always included both Jainism and Buddhism under its wide umbrella.[7]

The attitude of tolerance was mostly described by Gandhi in the context of his description of Hinduism. Hinduism is non-exclusive, or all-inclusive, accepts truth and revelation in all religions, gives room to the worship of all prophets, and admits that all religions are both perfect and imperfect and are able to lead to the final goal, *moksha*, liberation from the cycle of transmigration and merger with the Absolute. Hinduism is 'as broad as the Universe and takes in its fold all that is good in this world', and 'what of substance is contained in any other religion is always to be found in it'. Not being exclusive, 'it enables the followers of that faith not merely to respect all other religions, but also to admire and assimilate whatever may be good in them.' However, Gandhi did not mean to say that Hinduism was but an eclectic amalgam: no, its inclusiveness stemmed from its very nature, from the fact that it was 'a faith based on the broadest possible toleration'.[8]

A couple of times Gandhi indicated how that principle of toleration was formulated as a logical axiom in the tradition: he referred to the doctrines of *anekantavada* and *syadvada*, well-known categories of Jain philosophy. This is not surprising since to him they were part and parcel of the broad Hindu tradition, and since he believed that Jainism had most rationally expressed the essence of religion, he considered it to be 'the most logical of all faiths'. He stated: 'I am an *anekantavadi*. This is the most important thing that I have learned from Jain philosophy. It is implicit in Vedanta philosophy, while in Jain philosophy it is explicitly stated.' Elsewhere he declared that with the help of the *syadvada* he 'had established long ago the unity of all religions'.[9]

The *anekantavada* doctrine of Jainism is the doctrine that reality is not uniform, but manyfold; it is so complex that many acceptable propositions about it may be very different, and even contradictory, depending on the point of view of the observer. From there follows the *syadvada* principle of logic: since all propositions about reality can only present partial views, they should all be qualified by *syad* (possibly), or be prefaced by 'from one point of view', thus leaving the door open for different statements which are equally true from other points of view.

It has been my experience that I am always right from my point of view and often wrong from the point of view of my honest critics. I know that we are both right from our respective points of view. And

this knowledge prevents me from attributing motives to my opponents
or critics . . . I very much like this doctrine of the manyness of
reality. It is this doctrine that has taught me to judge a Mussalman
from his own standpoint and a Christian from his.[10]

However, for Gandhi there was beyond those ontological and logical
categories an even deeper specifically religious justification why tolerance is of the very essence of Hinduism: 'tolerance is also at the root of
the dharma of truth'. Gandhi never tired of asserting that truth and non-
violence constituted the essence of Hinduism:

> My correspondent accuses me of using the ambiguous middle in that
> I have confused truth and non-violence with the Hindu creed. The
> crime is deliberate. It is the good fortune or misfortune of Hinduism
> that it has no official creed. In order, therefore, to protect myself
> against any misunderstanding, I have said that truth and non-violence
> is my creed. If I were asked to define the Hindu creed, I should
> simply say: search for truth through non-violent means.

It is evident that a search for truth that respects non-violence must be
based on tolerance: tolerance therefore, is 'at the very root of the dharma
of truth'.[11]

Thus Gandhi linked tolerance with the very essence of Hinduism.
However, it is important to note that in defining the essence of Hinduism, Gandhi also intended to indicate what he considered to be the
essence of religion in general. Whenever he specifically referred to the
comparison of religions, or asked the question how one can detect the
essence and root of all religions, his answer was the same as the one he
gave when he spoke about the essence of Hinduism. For example, in
answer to Dr Crane's question, 'But when you say that all religions are
true, what do you do when there are conflicting counsels?', Gandhi
answered:

> I have no difficulty in hitting upon the truth because I go by certain
> fundamental maxims. Truth is superior to everything and I reject what
> conflicts with it. Similarly that which is in conflict with non-violence
> should be rejected. And on matters which can be reasoned out, that
> which conflicts with Reason must also be rejected.[12]

Tolerance, therefore, was the proper attitude to all religions because
of its intimate connection with the essence of Hinduism and of all

religion, namely truth and non-violence. On the other hand, Gandhi repeatedly stated that Hinduism was 'the most tolerant of all religions'. Since Hinduism was the most tolerant of all religions, and since tolerance was of the very essence of religion, Gandhi drew the conclusion that it was pre-eminent among them, superior to them: 'Hinduism is the most tolerant of all religions. Its creed is all-embracing. But to claim that is to claim superiority for the Hindu creed over all the other creeds of the world.'[13] That same idea is clearly implied in the following statements:

> What of substance is contained in any other religion is always to be contained in Hinduism. And what is not contained in it is insubstantial or unnecessary . . . I do not want you to become a Hindu. But I do want you to become a better Christian by absorbing all that may be good in Hinduism and that you may not find in the same measure or not at all in the Christian teaching.[14]

He expressed that combination of tolerance of all religions and the preeminence of Hinduism most clearly in an answer to the question 'Why are you a Hindu?', in an article entitled 'Why I am a Hindu', published in *Young India*:

> Believing as I do in the influence of heredity, being born in a Hindu family, I have remained a Hindu. I should reject it, if I found it inconsistent with my moral sense or my spiritual growth. On examination, I have found it to be the most tolerant of all religions known to me. Its freedom from dogma makes a forcible appeal to me inasmuch as it gives the votary the largest scope of self-expression. Not being an exclusive religion, it enables the followers of that faith not merely to respect all the other religions, but it also enables them to admire and assimilate whatever may be good in the other faiths. Non-violence is common to all religions, but it has found the highest expression and application in Hinduism.[15]

EQUALITY: 'THEY ARE ALL BRANCHES OF THE SAME TREE' (1930–48)

It was precisely the realisation that his doctrine of tolerance implied a suggestion of the superiority of Hinduism that made Gandhi change his teaching. This deliberate change can be accurately dated: on 23 September 1930, he wrote to Narandas Gandhi as follows:

Equality of Religions. This is the new name we have given to the Ashram observance which we know as 'Tolerance'. *Sahishnuta* is a translation of the English word Tolerance. I did not like that word but could not think of a better one. Kakasaheb, too, did not like that word. He suggested 'Respect for all religions'. I did not like that phrase either. Tolerance may imply a gratuitous assumption of the inferiority of other faiths to one's own, and respect suggests a sense of patronising, whereas ahimsa teaches us to entertain the same respect for the religious faiths of others as we accord to our own, thus admitting the imperfection of the latter.[16]

This was for Gandhi a deliberate and important change to which he referred several times in later years. In a discussion with Krzenski on 2 January 1937, he answered, as follows, the latter's observation that he had great respect for Gandhi's religion:

Not enough. I had that feeling myself one day, but I found that it was not enough. Unless I accept the position that all religions are equal, and I have as much regard for other religions as I have for my own, I would not be able to live in the boiling war around me.[17]

In answer to a question about his attitude to conversion, in a discussion with Sarat Chandra Bose and others he said: 'I have, of course, always believed in the principle of religious tolerance. But I have gone even further. I have advanced from tolerance to equal respect for all religions.'[18] That this change was decisive for Gandhi is clearly demonstrated by the fact that in his writings after 1930 no single statement can be found affirming, or even suggesting, the superiority of Hinduism, which he had repeatedly referred to before that date.

Another way in which the deliberate change of Gandhi's ideas is clearly indicated, is the use of a new metaphor, which emerged in that most important letter to Narandas Gandhi previously referred to: 'Even as a tree has a single trunk, but many branches and leaves, so is there one true and perfect religion, but it becomes many as it passes through the human medium.'[19] Previously Gandhi's metaphor was that 'religions are all rivers that meet in the same ocean'. That image stressed the similarity of the final goal to which by their individual meandering ways all religions eventually lead. However, it did not suggest the equality of religions: although they all ended up in the ocean, some may be majestic, fast-flowing rivers, others may be brackish, stagnating creeks. The new metaphor concentrated on the sameness of essence: religions are equal because at the root, at the trunk, they are really one: there is one true and perfect Religion, and the various branches equally share its wood and its sap. Gandhi never went back to the metaphor of the river, but from 1930 onwards he repeatedly used the one of the tree.[20]

Although on the one hand this change from tolerance to equality was presented by Gandhi as a change of attitude and a new insight, on the other hand it does not seem to have been precipitated by a new discovery. In fact, Gandhi believed that he was simply drawing a conclusion that had always been implicit in his doctrine of tolerance, that he was making explicit what he had really believed and practised before. He tried to explain this to Narandas Gandhi by recalling his experiences in South Africa:

> When I was turning over the pages of the sacred books of different faiths for my own satisfaction, I became sufficiently familiar for my purpose with Christianity, Islam, Zoroastrianism, Judaism and Hinduism. In reading these texts, I can say that I felt the same regard for all these faiths although, perhaps, I was not then conscious of it. Reviewing my memory of those days I do not find I ever had the slightest desire to criticise any of these religions merely because they were not my own, but read each sacred book in a spirit of reverence and found the same fundamental morality in each.[21]

If all religions are in final instance the same, only different branches of one tree, then the question arises what exactly that fundamental essence they shared consisted of. 'The fact is that there are no irreconcilable differences between religions. If you were to probe the surface, you will find one and the same thing at the bottom.'[22] Gandhi was pressed to explain how this could be reconciled with the fact that there were so many conflicting doctrines and counsels between the great religions. He held that the underlying unity could be discovered in the following manner:

> After a study of those religions to the extent that it was possible for me, I have come to the conclusion that, if it is proper and necessary to discover an underlying unity among all religions, a master-key is needed. That master-key is that of truth and non-violence. When I unlock the chest of a religion with this master-key, I do not find it difficult to discover its likeness with other religions.[23]

Truth and non-violence, therefore, were for Gandhi the supreme tests which in final instance decided what in any religion was fundamental and everlasting, what constituted the one Religion, the truth, from which all branches grew. He wrote, 'that one Religion was beyond all speech. Imperfect men throughout the ages put it into such language as they could command, and their words continued to be interpreted by other men equally imperfect in scriptures and *shastras'*. Whose interpretation was to be held to be right? Everybody was right from his own standpoint, but 'it is not impossible that everybody may be wrong'.[24] All scriptures, dogmatic structures, theological interpretations and moral codes are essentially imperfect, because they proceed from imperfect men: none should be considered to articulate ultimate answers. Gandhi's generous acceptance of the equal truth of all religions, including Hinduism, was based on the conviction that all their scriptures, teachings, and counsels were essentially of a relative nature. The rare pure gold of ultimacy could only be detected by the application of the acid test of truth and non-violence; that universal Religion was one that 'transcended Hinduism, – the basic truth that underlies all the religions of the world'. In fact, when accused of confusing truth and non-violence with the Hindu creed, Gandhi retorted, 'the crime is deliberate'.[25]

Gandhi was, indeed, prepared to stand by his judgement, even if all Hindus rejected it: 'my religion is a matter solely between my Maker and myself. If I am a Hindu, I cannot cease to be one even though I may be disowned by the whole of the Hindu population.' Elsewhere he wrote: 'It has been whispered that by being so much with Mussulman friends I make myself unfit to know the Hindu mind. The Hindu mind is myself.'[26] Gandhi was unrepentantly individualistic in his conception of Hinduism and of the essential Religion. In fact, his ultimate criteria of truth and non-violence were not really criteria for sifting the true and the false propositions of scripture and dogma: the latter were by definition imperfect, relative and ultimately unimportant. His criteria were criteria for deciding the right *action*, because for Gandhi ultimately religion was not about credal or conceptual systems, but about moral action, right action to be undertaken by the individual here and now: 'what cannot be followed out in day-to-day practice cannot be called religion.'[27] That was the very essence of Gandhi's concept of religion, and that was the norm by which all had to be judged.

CONCLUSION

In fact, that concept of religion as self-purification in action, as the liberation of the individual spirit from the bonds of matter, was the stance Gandhi took from very early days, and from which he never moved away. His explanation of Hinduism, his doctrine of tolerance, his doctrine of the equality of religions, his pronouncements about the one Religion, the trunk of which all religions were but branches, all these statements find their deepest explanation and justification in that fundamental Gandhian concept. To him religion was about self-realisation, about the constant fight of spirit to conquer matter. Scripture, faith, dogmas and rituals were only imperfect human creations that may be a help or a hindrance in that struggle; as such they were all non-essential, interchangeable, dispensable, and therefore not worth quarrelling over. Religion is essentially the individual's perpetual effort to realise perfect self-control in all his action, and it is precisely in that area of individual moral decision-making that the absolute criteria of truth and non-violence come into operation.

It is reasonably clear what the criterion of non-violence means in the sphere of moral action, but what does the criterion of truth mean in that context? Gandhi does not specifically answer that question at any one time, but one finds scattered fragments of the answer all along: truth-in-action means principles of conduct such as sexual abstinence, frugality, service, selflessness, fasting. Perhaps a more comprehensive answer may be indicated in the following way. According to Gandhi the *Gita* contained the essence of *dharma*, and the essence of the *Gita* was expressed in the last twenty stanzas of chapter 2.[28] What exactly is said in that vital passage? It spells out Krishna's definition of the *sthita-prajna*, the person who has achieved complete mastery over inner and outer senses, over desires and dislikes, and has reached an attitude of total indifference to all that may please or displease: that total inner and outer control makes for peace. To Gandhi that constituted the supreme religious achievement: such a person's every action has been and continues to be governed by 'truth'. That is the comprehensive answer to the meaning of truth as a criterion of action. In that context one understands why Gandhi, whose ideal was the *sthitaprajna*, called his autobiography 'The Story of My Experiments with Truth'.

In the final analysis Gandhi's attitude to the multiplicity of religions stemmed from a basic normative stance: his own definition of religion which was a very individualistic one, and which could not really be challenged because it was, to quote Gandhi himself, 'a matter solely between him and his Maker'. That is the normative dogmatism that lies at the root of his tolerance. Gandhi was able to accept the value of all the creeds, dogmatic structures, ritual systems, and ethical codes, because he considered none of them as ultimate, but all of them as having only relative and pragmatic value: they were imperfect means by which various cultures attempted to achieve the essential purpose of Religion: to shape the spiritual man who controls all this thoughts and actions by truth and non-violence.

How many Christians, Muslims, or even Hindus would be prepared to accept the religious 'tolerance' or 'equality' proposed by Gandhi with its full implications? Admittedly, Gandhi did not exalt Hinduism above any other religions in the last eighteen years of his life, a fact of which many Hindus were acutely and painfully aware. But what he did exalt above all religions including Hinduism, was his own individual concept of the essence of religion: a religion of naked truth and non-violence, totally stripped of all its cultural, historical, sociological, ritual, and theological vestments. No doubt, as we have indicated at the beginning, the influence of Jain ideas was very important in the emergence of the Gandhian concept of religion, and he did consider Jainism the most rational exposition of religion, but even the Jain believer would find it difficult to subscribe to Gandhi's radical relativism. In the final instance, Gandhi's attitude of tolerance and equality towards religious pluralism was based on such an individualistic normative concept of the essence of religion, that it is difficult to see how it could be accepted or countered outside that narrow framework.

Part III
India: Religion in Action

9

The Ashram-dweller

In South Africa the founding of the Phoenix Settlement and Tolstoy Farm were not primarily inspired by religious concerns. Those communes were started basically for economic reasons. They first looked after the publication of *Indian Opinion*, and later cared for the Satyagraha workers and their families. Although religion did play some part, it was not a major one. Moreover, both institutions housed quite a diversity of people, some of whom were very transient.[1]

SATYAGRAHA ASHRAM

When Gandhi arrived back in India, one of his first preoccupations was to arrange for the establishment of a commune, as decided before leaving South Africa, and this time to be properly called an Ashram.[2] More than twenty relatives and colleagues from Phoenix had come to India before the arrival of Gandhi, who had been delayed in London; they needed a home and wanted to continue sharing Gandhi's. Eighteen boys were temporarily housed at Rabindranath Tagore's Shantiniketan near Calcutta and the Gurukul of Mahatma Munshiram (later Swami Shraddhananda) near Hardwar.[3] Gandhi chose Ahmedabad for the site of his new ashram, because he was a Gujarati speaker, because this city was an ancient centre of handloom weaving, and also because he expected that the wealthy people of the area would help him financially. In May 1915 the community settled in a hired bungalow, but later moved to a large area on the banks of the river Sabarmati on the outskirts of Ahmedabad. They decided to call their new settlement Satyagraha Ashram.[4]

Gandhi had given a lot of thought to this venture, and he drafted with his co-workers a detailed constitution during 1915. This document clearly shows that the Satyagraha Ashram was to be a new beginning, a creation drawing on the South African experience, but also radically new. The continuation is expressed in the very first sentence of the Constitution: 'The object of the Ashram is to learn how to serve the motherland one's whole life and to serve it.' The radical innovation was succinctly and strikingly expressed by a sentence in the middle of the document: 'The Ashram inmates will be in the stage of *sannyasis.*' This was not a fleeting thought; Gandhi repeated it several times.[5] The immediate purpose of the statement was to justify the vow against untouchability. This vow meant that they would not observe the rules of *varnashrama dharma*, the laws of caste and ritual pollution, although they accepted the validity of such rules for ordinary Hindus. Traditional Hindu law accepted that the *sannyasis*, those who had entered the fourth stage of life, were not subject to those social and ritual laws. By declaring the ashramites to be *sannyasis*, Gandhi justified their disregard of ritual caste rules in their own behaviour in the ashram.

However, calling the ashramites *sannyasis* has another deeper meaning, not expressed directly, but certainly implied in the constitution. The reason why the *sannyasi* was absolved from following caste and ritual rules, was because he was supposed to totally dedicate himself to the single-minded pursuit of liberation. If one looks over the Ashram constitution from this point of view, much of its laws become more comprehensible. This was not to be an ordinary ashram for a temporary dip in the waters of spirituality, or for retirement in old age. Here vows were required that reached far beyond the piety of even the most pious of Hindus. One had to take a vow of total truthfulness, and of non-violence of an heroically high order. The vow of chastity was equally absolute. In his speech on the Ashram vows Gandhi said: 'Those who want to perform national service, or those who want to have a glimpse of the real religious life, must lead a celibate life, no matter if married or unmarried.'[6] Chastity was supported by the vow of 'control of the palate', which intended to eliminate all possible enjoyment from eating. The vows of non-stealing and non-possession demanded more than the most stringent monastic vows of poverty do. To be in possession of anything that was not absolutely necessary for the basic nourishment and protection of the body (e.g., a chair), would constitute an infringement of those vows. He put it thus to the students in Madras: 'In India we got three millions of people having to be satisfied with one meal a day . . . consisting of a chapati . . . You and I have no right to anything that we really have until these three million are clothed and fed better.' This ashram was obviously destined to be much more than an economic way of running a newspaper by a commune, or a staging post for the coming and going of freedom fighters. This was more like a monastery of a very strict order of monks.[7]

The constitution made the ashram totally different from the usual kind of monastery. The inmates were expected to take a number of subsidiary vows. The vow of *svadeshi* barred the use of articles which 'involve violation of truth in their manufacture or on the part of their manufacturers'. In the case of cloth, for example, this would exclude all foreign cloth and cloth made by machinery. The vow of fearlessness urged the inmates 'to endeavour to be free from the fear of kings or society, one's caste or family . . . ferocious animals, and even of death'. They also vowed to use the mother tongue, to do manual labour, to promote spinning, and to learn about and work in the fields of 'politics, economics, social reform, etc., in a religious spirit'. These various vows obviously had to do with the service of the country and of one's countrymen, which service was said in the very first sentence of the constitution to be the object of the existence of the ashram. This service envisaged involvement in political and social action without fear, and also promotion of national languages and national manufacture. It also endorsed Gandhi's condemnation of western civilization, so forcefully expressed in his book *Hind Svaraj*, which condemned large-scale machinery, the exultation of all kinds of work over manual labour, and the pursuit of riches and luxury.[8]

This new Satyagraha Ashram was intended to nurture and train a new kind of person, a *satyagrahi*. This would be a person totally dedicated to the good and the freedom of the country, and prepared to put his life on the line. This person would believe in the values scorned by western civilization such as simplicity, manual labour, frugality, self-sufficiency. And it would also be a person practising the basic virtues of truthfulness, chastity, and personal poverty to an heroic degree. It would be a *sannyasi*, a social reformer and a political activist all in one. The Satyagraha Ashram was meant to be the sacred place where people would grow into *satyagrahis* inspired by religion and totally dedicated to the service of India. No single piece of writing of Gandhi demonstrates better than this Constitution of the Satyagraha Ashram, the central concept of Gandhi's political action: that politics and religion cannot be separated. If you want to be a fighter for India's freedom, and dedicate your life to the service of your country, you must totally renounce your ego, your comfort, and live the life of a *sannyasi*.

The new emphasis on the the spiritual basis of ashram life was clearly demonstrated by the place of prayer in its routine. 'If insistence on truth constitutes the root of the ashram, prayer is the principal feeder of that root. The social activities of the Ashram commenced every day with the congregational morning worship at 4.15 to 4.45 a.m. and closed with the evening prayer at 7 to 7.30 p.m.' Whereas in South Africa only hymns were sung on these occasions, the new ashram prayer was carefully constructed, consisting of four distinct parts: a recitation of ancient verses in Sanskrit, a hymn, the repetition of Ramanama, and a reading from the *Gita*. Gandhi spoke and wrote often about the necessity of communal prayer, and increasingly incorporated such prayer in his public addresses.[9]

It seems quite clear that Gandhi intended his new Ashram to become the training ground whence would go forth the real 'servants of India'. He saw it as 'his best and only creation'.[10] Probably the occasion when this ideal seemed to start to be fulfilled, was when the first band of *satyagrahis* to accompany Gandhi on his Salt March to Dandi in 1930 were chosen mainly from among the inhabitants of Sabarmati Ashram; they were no less than 80 in number.[11]

By that time the Ashram had expanded significantly from its humble beginnings. The sum total of its inhabitants was 277 in 1928. This included a good number of teachers and other professionals who were not considered to be full ashramites. In fact, the teachers had their own quarters, where the rule of *brahmacharya* did not apply.[12] The differences between the initial Ashram and the later one are clearly discernible in the revised constitution that was promulgated in 1928. To cope with this Ashram that had become a village, a new Managing Committee was formed. The most striking development was the expansion and organisation of small industry sections: Spinning, Agriculture, Dairy, and Tannery had become efficient units of production. The high religious ideals of the original ashram were reaffirmed, but one notices some flexibility: the arrangement of special quarters for teachers, and the new provision in the daily timetable of no less than three and a half hours of recreation in the evening.[13]

However, with the ideals of ashram virtues set at an heroic high, the realities of ashram life fell generally far short of that target, particularly as the community kept growing in size. Shortly after the foundation, Gandhi faced a very serious revolt when he accepted an untouchable couple and their child into the Ashram. Kasturbai was furious, and it took her a couple of months to calm down and accept the situation. Maganlal, Gandhi's closest collaborator, actually left with his family, and spent six months in Madras. Others left for good. Gandhi was devastated.[14] Throughout the years of the existence of Sabarmati Ashram, the attendance at morning prayers was erratic, as Gandhi himself admitted, as was the performance of the daily duty of spinning.[15]

There seems always to have been some who had problems with the radical demands of *brahmacharya*, some even putting forth 'a great effort without making any progress'. In 1925 Gandhi fasted for a week because of some minor sex-related incident amongst youngsters in the Ashram. In 1926 a widow living in the Ashram was seduced by a young man also living there, and they carried on a clandestine affair. Gandhi realised that the ashramites lived on a considerably more comfortable level than the really poor, and it must have pained him that even in 1927 he had to urge the women not to long for jewellery and fine clothes. To be totally free from the desire for private property was a high ideal. Gandhi's cousin Chhaganlal was found to have been engaged in a series of petty larcenies over a number of years. Even Kasturbai was found to have kept money given to her for her own personal use despite the Ashram rule against it. 'Her action,' wrote Gandhi, 'amounted to theft.' Right at the end there was still trouble about families having their own kitchen, and about the possession and use of personal money.[16]

The Ashram was rife with personality clashes, and petty fights. Everything was referred to Gandhi, be he present or absent, and his correspondence is full of allusions to these incidents. In fact, Gandhi felt that the running of the Ashram was his most taxing task, a task greatly increased after the death of his trusted lieutenant Maganlal in 1928. His faithful secretary, Mahadev Desai, wrote the following comment in his diary on the constant flow of Gandhi's letters to the Ashram: 'Bapu's spiritual ambition knows no bounds. He is introducing one reform after another at Sabarmati . . . How long will all the Ashramites be able to bear all this strain?'[17]

The reason for these flaws was not just human nature, it was also Gandhi's absence – especially after Maganlal's death. His absences were frequent and prolonged. 'He had received many complaints from members of the Satyagraha Ashram . . . that the 'soul' went out of ashram activities in his absence, and that inmates often bickered amongst themselves during these periods.'[18] Gandhi admitted in 1929 that his Ashram had been 'imperfect and full of corruption', but these flaws did not shake his faith in it:

This may be a gross delusion on my part. If so I can say with the immortal Tulsidas that even as one sees silver in the mother of pearl or water in the mirage till his ignorance is dispelled, so will my delusion be a reality to me till the eyes of my understanding are opened.[19]

Was it the opening of 'the eyes of his understanding' that motivated Gandhi in 1933 to close Sabarmati Ashram? The reasons given publicly and privately in mid-1933 were rather different. In a letter to Jamnalal Bajaj he wrote:

> The reason for handing over control of the Ashram is that it is better to hand over ourselves what the Government is sure to take by force in due course. Instead of carrying away our belongings one after another against land revenue, let them take the entire land. Moreover, when thousands of people have been ruined forcibly, it seems desirable, and even necessary from the point of view of dharma, that an Ashram which bears the name of Satyagraha Ashram should voluntarily sacrifice itself.[20]

The situation of the Ashram had become impossible: its large constructive programmes of agriculture, weaving, and education could not be carried on unless the Ashram ceased its involvement in the anti-government campaign. This involvement had caused the incarceration of the inmates and the confiscation of property by the government on account of the non-payment of land taxes. But to Gandhi the very existence of the Satyagraha Ashram was for the training of Satyagrahis dedicated and able to carry out that kind of anti-government campaign. To him the constructive programme and the civil disobedience campaign were both essential ingredients of the existence of the Ashram. In fact all the ashramites agreed that the sacrifice had to be made.[21]

No doubt these were compelling reasons, but when asked if he was closing the Ashram because of disappointment he answered:

> I am not only not seriously disappointed, but I am convinced that the majority of the inmates have made all endeavours humanly possible to come up to the ideal. This much, however, is true that though the inmates, including myself, have made an honest endeavour to come up to the principles, we have all failed. But that is no cause for disappointment. It is a cause for greater effort.[22]

The institution had become unwieldy, and Gandhi must have realised that his prolonged absences were not good. He was already thinking about his long Harijan tour that was to last eight months, starting in early November that same year. His disappointment is also evidenced by the fact that he did not even attempt to found a new ashram to replace Sabarmati. He expressed that feeling openly at the time of suspending the Civil Disobedience Movement:

This statement owes its inspiration to a personal chat with the inmates and associates of Satyagraha Ashram. More especially it is due to a revealing information I got in the course of conversations about a valued companion of long standing who was found reluctant to perform the full prison task, preferring his private studies to the allotted task. This was undoubtedly contrary to the rules of Satyagraha.[23]

This lapse of one of his closest companions showed clearly that his teaching of Satyagraha had been very defective. Satyagraha was to be suspended, and he himself had 'for the time being to remain the sole representative of civil resistance in action'. Because 'Satyagraha was a spiritual weapon, it was henceforth to be confined to one qualified person – himself'. There seems to be no doubt that the dissolution of Sabarmati Ashram was not only motivated by financial and political difficulties, but also by a sense of failure.[24]

SEVAGRAM

In June 1934, after finishing his Harijan tour, Gandhi went to Wardha in central north India. There Vinoba Bhave had been managing since 1921 a branch of the Sabarmati Ashram. For the past ten years he had, with Jamnalal Bajaj, been engaged in constructive village work. In October 1934 Gandhi announced his retirement from politics, and declared his intention to concentrate on village development. Congress authorised the formation of the All India Village Industries Association to be guided by him, and Jamnalal Bajaj donated his Wardha house and twenty acres of orchard to be the headquarters of the Association.[25]

From the 1920s Gandhi had connected the creation of an ideal *sarvodaya* society with the struggle for independence and had given it concrete shape in his constructive village work programme. This programme had suffered, according to Thomson, from two major problems. First, there was the 'overpowering lethargy' of the people in greatest need in the impoverished villages. The second was that the very people who were able to promote the reforms, were not willing to put their energy into it for various egotistical reasons. As time went on it became clear that the programme was largely ineffective.[26] In Wardha too Gandhi did not seem to be achieving much. His own experience in Sindhi village, where he went every morning for several months with his co-workers to clean the place, was very frustrating. 'At first the people were apathetic. Gradually they became resistant, and even resentful of the reform.'[27] The programme did not seem to be having much impact on the villages:

> There existed a growing body of people, including village workers, who voiced dissatisfaction with Gandhi's concern for quality of work, purity of spirit and the duty of bread labour. Much of this discontent was patently valid in terms of the village worker who was expected to work for his livelihood for eight hours a day and then find time and energy to attend to the other multifarious concerns of the programme.[28]

In the midst of this frustration Gandhi, to the consternation of his friends and collaborators, decided to settle down alone nearby in a backward little village Sevagram, which had nothing to recommend it according to Nanda:

> It was not even connected by road to Wardha; it did not even have a post-office; it was infected with snakes; it was situated in a low-lying area inaccessible during the rains, and its stagnant pools of water made it seriously malarial. There were even stories of robberies and murders in the neighbourhood.[29]

It was clearly Gandhi's intention to live alone in the village:

> I needed the solitude of Sevagram. It has been my experience that I can draw my inspiration only from my natural setting – the surroundings in which I live. Since the discovery of Satyagraha I have been fixing up my abode in what are called *ashrams* and pursuing my *sadhana* [vocation] there. But Sevagram I have hesitated to call by the name of *ashram*. I had originally thought of living and working there in solitude.[30]

Elsewhere he wrote, 'Why am I at Sevagram? Because I believe that my message will have a better chance of penetrating the masses of India, and maybe through them to the world.'[31]

But Gandhi was not alone for long. Gradually some of his Wardha collaborators moved to Sevagram, and on top of that a number of strange and eccentric individuals such as the undescribable ex-professor and ex-*sannaysi* Bhansali, a Japanese monk, a leper who was a profound Sanskrit scholar, and the mechanical genius Maurice Frydman. Gandhi referred to the growing Sevagram settlement as 'a hospital', or a 'lunatic asylum', and Sardar Valabbhai Patel called it 'a menagerie'. In July 1936 Gandhi wrote to Mirabehn, 'This has become a confused household instead of a hermitage it was expected to be. Such has been my fate: I must find my hermitage from within.'[32]

It was often referred to as 'Sevagram Ashram', but it was very different from Sabarmati Ashram. Whereas that was perfectly planned, this one grew haphazardly with the sprawling household: the over-supply of sick people created a small hospital, and the need for milk demanded a dairy. Sabarmati Ashram was regulated by vows and strict time-tables, but Sevagram never attempted to enforce such a regime.[33] When Gandhi, on occasion, wrote guidelines for Ashram behaviour they were only guidelines and did not take the form of vows or rules. He himself admitted, 'The Ashram at Sevagram is only so called . . . The Ashram is a medley of people come together for different purposes. There are hardly half a dozen permanent residents having a common ideal.'[34] Pyarelal summed it up beautifully:

> Gandhi had not come to Sevagram with any cut-and-dried plan. He did not even wish to found an Ashram. The whole village henceforth should be our Ashram, he said. The name Ashram, however, stuck to it in spite of him. And a strange kind of Ashram it was, without any constitution or even set rules and regulations except such as grew out of the day-to-day experience of community living. The whole idea was that he with his co-workers should live there as a villager of his dreams ought to live, associate the villagers with the community life of the Ashram in as many ways as possible and let the leaven of his example permeate their life.[35]

Just as Gandhi was not able to become a recluse, and allowed another Ashram to haphazardly shoot up around him, similarly he was not able to stay much more at Sevagram than he had been able to reside at Sabarmati. His duties called him away for long stretches of time, and between August 1942 and May 1944 he was in prison for nearly two years. His letters testify to the personal problems that seemed endemic in his ashrams.[36] During the last two years of his life he did not set foot in Sevagram: after he left in March 1946 and his death in January 1948. He always kept caring for his people in his Ashrams, but statements he made in the very last weeks of his life clearly show that he knew that the Sevagram Ashram was disintegrating:

> About Sevagram I have come to the conclusion that it should either become self-supporting or it should be closed down. The Ashram has

become a *pinjrapole* [a shelter for old and sick cattle] . . . You should give up the craving to live in the Ashram. I have told the few people who are still there to stay there only if they can stand on their own feet.[37]

What, then, did Gandhi want to achieve spiritually by the Sevagram Ashram? First of all, he was looking for a new method of village development, having become disappointed by the way community workers failed to integrate with the villagers. By personally sharing the village life with the villagers, he hoped to refine a method by which the villagers themselves would gradually become their own community workers.[38] He was convinced that the key to svaraj was 'not in the cities but in the villages'.[39] One village, he thought, may give him the method that would transform India:

> If I can be one with its six hundred souls, if I can engage them in constructive work and in the necessary work of reform, and if I can easily make a satyagrahi army of them, I should discover the key to do the same work in the whole of India.[40]

That is why the new Ashram was to be an 'open' ashram, co-extensive as much as possible with the village itself, so that the spirit of the Ashram could permeate the village. That is why he 'expected from the ashramites that they would exemplify the principle of non-violence in their daily lives through selfless service.' It is difficult to assess in how far his dream was realised; all one can say is that in some aspects a small start was made, for instance in the treatment of untouchables.[41]

But there was another spiritual side to Gandhi's expectations of Sevagram, to which he only occasionally referred. 'I am here to serve no one but myself, to find my own self-realisation through the service of these village folk.' In another letter from Simla he wrote:

> My window opens on the Himalayas . . . on a clear day the hills are covered with snow. For a spectacle better than this, one must go to Shiva's Kailas [heavenly abode]! My Kailas, however, is Sevagram. The life-giving waters of my Ganga flow from there.[42]

In these significant statements Gandhi directly connected his stay in Sevagram with his own self-realisation. The Ashram allowed him to be continually involved in nursing and service, of both the body and the spirit. Gandhi needed the Ashram to be able to get away from his many political and official duties, and immerse himself in that demanding yet soothing and invigorating pond of service.

Thus ashram life had over his lifespan gradually taken a different function in Gandhi's spiritual endeavour. In South Africa the spiritual aspect was not pronounced but hidden as an inner ferment. Sabarmati had a very strong spiritual focus, and the accent was on the spiritual, social, and political training of the ideal *satagrahi-sannyasi*. This endeavour, however, did not produce a plentiful harvest, and had to be discontinued when it ran out of steam. Sevagram Ashram haphazardly grew around the lonely hut in a backward village, where Gandhi had sought the blessings of being a recluse. But that was not his lot or vocation. This last ashram became the locus where Gandhi's spiritual life and aspiration could become intensely focused upon himself, in order that he may make himself become the real man of self-realisation, who could work wonders at a time when India needed no less than that.

10

Calling on the Divine Power

This chapter examines the various ways in which Gandhi tried to sanctify his life by referring it to the divine. He did this by what is mostly called 'prayer', and also by taking vows, which linked a series of actions, or abstentions, to the divine presence. Gandhi was not attracted to, and never engaged in, any form of mysticism, the search for an intense psychological experience of the divine by meditation and concentration. In this field the Hindu tradition was always very vigorous, but to Gandhi, the activist, it never had any attraction.

VOWS

The threefold vow Gandhi took before leaving for England was no doubt the first important religious act in his life. These vows were not to touch wine, women, and meat. There were two circumstances that made these vows of great weight to Mohandas: first, they were solemnly taken as an act of religion before a Jain monk, and secondly they constituted a solemn promise to his mother. She had always been the greatest example of religious dedication, a dedication that constantly expressed itself in the taking of vows. The connection of the vow with his mother made it doubly sacred for Mohandas, who at that time was not really interested in religion. An Indian friend in London tried to convince him to be sensible in his diet, and called into doubt 'the value of a vow made before an illiterate mother'. Gandhi's reaction was uncompromising and adamant. Later on, when he started his experiments in dietetics, he once decided to live on cheese, milk, and eggs, which many considered all part of a true vegetarian diet. Gandhi soon gave this up, because he realised that his mother's definition of meat included eggs. 'As soon as I saw the true import of the vow I gave up eggs and the experiment alike.'[1]

In South Africa Gandhi took the vow of chastity, but at that time he does not seem to have reflected much on the meaning of vows. This reflection started at the time of the Satyagraha struggle, when he wrote an article in *Indian Opinion* entitled 'Importance of Vows'. There he gave a simple definition:

> If we resolve to do a thing, and are ready even to sacrifice our lives in the process, we are said to have taken a vow . . . one can strengthen one's power of will by doing so and fit oneself for greater tasks. One may take easy and simple vows to start with and follow them with more difficult ones . . . To embrace satyagraha amounts to taking a great vow. Having taken it one must die rather than forsake it.[2]

It is interesting to note here that God or religion is not explicitly mentioned in this article. A vow is portrayed as a promise one makes to oneself, a promise that must be kept at all costs.

Chapter 9 describes the vows Gandhi demanded of the inmates of his Ashram. In a long address about the Ashram vows, he stressed the need for the Ashram, and for the vows of its inmates, because of the need of the country: 'What we perhaps of all the nations of the world need just now, is nothing else and nothing less than character-building.' And that was exactly what the vows were intended to achieve.[3]

That same year, on a visit to Hardwar, he took a vow that had a different purpose. This is how Nanda tells the story:

> At Hardwar he saw the corruption and hypocrisy practised in the name of Hinduism: the swarms of 'sadhus' who sponged on the community, and the frauds practised by the priests to extract the last copper from the pilgrims. As an atonement for the iniquity he saw around him, he vowed never to eat more than five articles of food in twenty-four hours and never to eat after dark. Here he was expiating for the sins of others.[4]

This was the vow for expiation, which was mostly a vow of fasting. The public vow of fasting was practised by Gandhi very often during his life. This practice is described in detail in Chapter 11.

One of Gandhi's first attempts at defining vows occurred in a letter he wrote to Esther Fearing, who had asked a list of probing questions about the deeper meaning of the vow.

> A vow is nothing but a fixed resolution to do or abstain from doing a particular thing . . . In each case, the result expected is the same, viz. purification and expression of the soul. By these resolutions, you bring the body under subjection. Body is matter, soul is spirit, and

there is internal conflict between matter and spirit. Triumph of matter
over the spirit means destruction of the latter . . . We . . . must by
making fixed resolutions bring our bodies under such control that
finally we may be able to use them for the fullest service of the soul.[5]

Thus he put vow-taking squarely in the very centre of the drama of
religion: the struggle between spirit and matter. He continued to give
glimpses of his concept in his letters. Vows purify the mind. They are by
definition always difficult, and therefore falls are to be expected; but the
'success lies in the very struggle. If you fall, do atonement, and get up.'[6]

In 1929 Gandhi wrote a lengthy article on 'The Efficacy of Vows' in
answer to a correspondent who was very troubled by the anticipated
contradiction between the seemingly absolute character of the vow and
his expectation of circumstances in which observance of the vow would
become practically impossible. In his answer Gandhi first explained why
vows had to be strict; because they 'impart stability, ballast and firmness
to one's character'. The entire social fabric was founded upon the
sanctity of the pledged word, just like the earth itself and the solar
system were firmly stabilised by permanent laws. 'A person unbound by
vows can never be absolutely relied upon', he wrote. He said that a vow
is like a right angle: 'An insignificant right angle will make all the
difference between ugliness and elegance, solidity and shakiness of a
gigantic structure.' It was precisely because of the absoluteness of the
vow that vow-taking had to be done with 'moderation and sobriety',
taking into account one's personal capacities. Moreover, a vow could be
made conditional without losing its efficacy or virtue. 'For instance,
there would be nothing wrong about taking a vow to spin for at least one
hour every day . . . except when one is travelling or one is sick.' It was
not of the essence of a vow to be exceedingly difficult, but the determination to adhere to it in all difficulty was what made it into a tower of
strength.[7]

Gandhi's flexibility within the framework of his philosophy of vows
expressed itself most clearly in the way in which he was prepared to
adapt dietary rules when health required it, and when the purse of the
poor could not afford the ideal diet. The most striking example of this
adaptability was recounted by M. Chatterjee as follows:

In spite of his vegetarianism, when he found that the health of some
of his Bengali volunteers in Noakholi was suffering because of a fish-
less diet, he laughingly advised that they should go back to their

natural food, after all, since the fish flourished in the water of the flooded paddy fields there could be no great harm in eating them![8]

In a letter to his Ashram from Yeravda jail he dealt with the necessity of vows. He declared that 'the universal experience of humanity supports the view that progress is impossible without inflexible determination.' This kind of resolve could only be achieved by vows.

> God is the very image of the vow. God will cease to be God if He swerved from His laws even by a hair's breadth. The sun is a great keeper of observances; hence the possibility of measuring time and publishing almanacs . . . We thus see that keeping a vow is a universal practise. Are such promises less necessary in character building or self-realisation? We should, therefore, never doubt the necessity of vows for the purpose of self-purification and self-realisation.[9]

Two of Gandhi's closest admirers disagreed with him on his attitude to vows: C. F. Andrews and J. C. Kumarappa.[10] They did not directly criticise Gandhi's personal use of vows, but they did not believe that it was a universal way to religious development, as to their mind Gandhi seemed to present it. They argued that different people have different needs at different times, and that lifelong commitments were unwise, and even dangerous for some, especially young people. Vows stifled originality and new initiatives, they tended to become so rigid that their observance became a routine in which the original ideal was forgotten. Rather than being a vital stimulus to determination, they tended to be a substitute for it: Kumarappa wrote that a vow was no more than a helpful crutch or a protective hedge. Gandhi thought that they had somehow misunderstood him. He, therefore, tried in his letter to Kumarappa to clearly explain what he really meant:

> You seem to think of vows publicly administered to audiences. This may or may not be good. The 'vow' I am thinking of is a promise made by one to oneself. We have to deal with two dwellers within, Rama and Ravana, God and Satan, Ormuzd and Ahriman. The one binds us to make us really free, the other only appears to free us so as to bind us tight within his grip. A vow is a promise made to Rama to do or not to do a certain thing which, if good, we want to do, but have not the strength unless we are tied down, and which, if bad, we would avoid, but have not the strength to avoid unless similarly tied down. This I hold to be a condition indispensable to growth . . . A

life of vows is like marriage, a sacrament. It is marriage with God indissoluble for all time.[11]

In his two most thoughtful explanations about vows, the above one and his letter to Esther Fearing previously quoted, Gandhi referred to the role of vows in the basic struggle of the religious life: between spirit and matter. This approach to vows links Gandhi's concept very closely to that of Jainism. In Hinduism there is a wide gap between the religious duties of the *sannyasi* and those of the lay people, a gap which is bridged in one leap at the time of taking up *sannyasa* with its strict vows. The gap between the two is differently bridged in Jainism. There lay religiosity involves a gradual and continuous change in life which leads to the smooth transition from the lay status to that of the monk. This gradual change is systematically set out as the climbing of a ladder, the steps of which constitute progressively more and more demanding vows. Vow-taking, ever accelerating, is of the essence of the religious development of the Jain lay person. One cannot but conclude that Gandhi's concept of vows had been strongly influenced by Jain spirituality.[12]

COMMUNAL PRAYERS

Gandhi started to organise communal prayers in South Africa, and they remained a constant feature of his life. He began the practice in his home, and then made it a regular feature at the Phoenix Settlement and the Tolstoy Farm. Whereas in South Africa the singing of hymns was the only item, at Sabarmati Ashram the prayer developed to contain four parts: a recitation of Sanskrit verses, a hymn, the recitation of *Ramdhun* (repetition of the name of Rama), and the reading of some verses of the *Gita*. Over the years, a few small items were added: the first verse of the *Isha Upanishad* after his Harijan tour, and later a passage from the Koran, and one from the Zoroastrian Avesta. The great difficulty Gandhi had to get the ashramites to regularly attend these prayers, has been referred to earlier.[13]

To Gandhi communal prayers were simply a consequence of man being a social creature. Their purpose was not to list a number of common requests, but it was primarily meant for daily purification: 'It is to the heart what a daily bath is to the body.' This cleansing process for the whole congregation helped it to be in tune with the Infinite. If anything was asked, it was 'a prayer for God to make them better men and women'. When Gandhi was asked if it would not be better to give the time spent in worship to the service of the poor, and thus make worship unnecessary, he answered:

> I sense mental laziness and unbelief in the question. The biggest of *karmayogis* [action-saints] never give up devotional singing and worship. Of course as a general principle it can be said that selfless service itself is worship and those who engage in it do not need any other kind of worship. But in truth *bhajans* [devotional hymns], etc., are a help in the work of service and keep the awareness of God ever fresh.[14]

Gandhi spent a lot of time, even protracted periods, outside his ashrams. He tended to always have some communal prayers with his staff and friends. Gradually a new custom developed of having Prayers at Public Meetings. The first reference we found was that, 'After the meeting was the prayer which had become an institution during our stay at Kumara Park (in Bangalore).'[15] This was noted at the end of August 1927, during Gandhi's extensive tour for the promotion of spinning. Ten years later the custom had been firmly established. On his famous pilgrimage to Travancore he had enormous pleasure in conducting these public prayer meetings in the courtyards of the great temples of Travancore.[16] During his last years, in his pilgrimages through Noakholi and Bihar, and whenever he stayed in Allahabad, Calcutta, or Delhi, every evening he conducted a Public Prayer Meeting, usually followed by a speech. His assassination took place at such a meeting.

PRIVATE PRAYERS

In most monastic establishments, Christian, Buddhist, and others, specific times are daily set aside for private prayer or meditation, in addition to the times for community worship. Gandhi never had such a regime in his ashrams or in his personal life, and he only seldom spoke about private prayers. He considered prayer to be 'the very soul and essence of religion', and that, therefore, 'it must be the very core of the life of man'. He explained how it was intrinsically linked to the very essence of religion:

> We are born to serve our fellow men, and we cannot properly do so unless we are wide awake. There is an eternal struggle raging in man's breast between the powers of darkness and of light, and he who

has not the sheet-anchor of prayer to rely upon will be a victim to the powers of darkness.[17]

Gandhi recommended that one should pray immediately on waking up and before falling asleep. But the whole day should be prayerful: 'During the rest of the day, every man and woman who is spiritually awake will think of God when doing anything and do that with Him as a witness.'[18] Such prayer consumes no time; all it requires is wakefulness.

In a long discussion with Dr Charles Fabri, a Hungarian archaeologist who had become a Buddhist, Gandhi tried to explain what exactly he did when he prayed. Fabri did not believe in a personal god 'sitting on the great white throne listening to our prayers', and was puzzled by any form of prayer, which to him necessarily implied 'to beg or to demand'. The first step of Gandhi's answer was to explain his intellectual conviction that 'Divinity is in everyone and everything . . . and the meaning of prayer is that I want to invoke that Divinity within me'. So, yes, he did beg when he prayed: 'You may say I beg it of myself, of my Higher Self, the Real Self.' Thus Gandhi reaffirmed his intellectual conviction of the truth of Advaita. But then he went on to the second part of his answer:

> I am part of that Infinite, and yet such an infinitesimal part that I feel outside it . . . I feel that I am so small that I am nothing . . . I feel my unworthiness and nothingness, and feel that someone else, some Higher Power has to help me.

This was because the intellectual conviction of oneness with the Absolute was not always experienced by him as an actuality. 'What is present is the intensity of faith whereby I lose myself in an Invisible Power.'

> And so it is far truer to say that God has done a thing for me than that I did it. So many things had happened in my life for which I had intense longing, but which I could never have achieved myself. And I have always said to my co-workers that it was in answer to my prayer. I did not say to them that it was in answer to my intellectual effort to lose myself in the Divinity in me! The easiest and the correct thing for me was to say, 'God has seen me through my difficulty'. [19]

Another facet of private prayer was his response to what Gandhi called 'the voice within', the voice of conscience, or 'the voice of God'. This is studied in detail in Chapter 7.

RAMANAMA

In his article about individual prayer cited earlier, Gandhi stated that the spiritually awake person would think of God at all times, and do all his actions with God as witness. He added: 'This will be a state in which one will have reduced oneself to a cypher. Such a person, who lives constantly in the sight of God, will every moment feel Rama dwelling in his heart.'[20] Gandhi's practice of Ramanama, the repetition of the name of Rama, was a very important spiritual exercise to him, but its character changed over time.

Gandhi recalled that he learned the practice in childhood from his nurse Rambha, who told him that it would chase away the ghosts that frightened him. He also wrote that Ramanama saved him three times in his young days from having sexual contact with prostitutes. He described these occurrences in his autobiography, and later related them together in *Navajivan*. Although Gandhi wrote that he was saved from falling thanks to the power of Ramanama, it was quite clear that at that time the recitation was not a habit of his. 'His name was not on my lips at that hour, but he ruled in my heart.' It seems that in his younger days, and even till the end of his South African period, Gandhi did not really practise Ramanama. He wrote in his Autobiography, 'I had not then [towards the end of his stay in South Africa] completely understood the wonderful efficacy of Ramanama.'[21] The first time the practice was mentioned in the *Collected Works* was in a letter to Raojibhai Patel, written in March 1914 shortly before Gandhi's return to India. He recommended the practice to Raojibhai but he did not put it forward as his own personal recommendation, but rather as a council from Tulsidas.[22]

In fact, it is not until ten years after his return to India, in 1924, that Ramanama resurfaced in Gandhi's letters. In a letter to Malji he first acknowledged that actually as a youth he soon 'ceased to take the name of Rama'. He went on to explain that it was the intense reading of Tulsidas' *Ramcharitmanas* in Yeravda Jail that led him to seriously take up the recitation of Rama's name.[23] From then on we find the topic of Ramanama recurring regularly in Gandhi's correspondence, professing his own dedication to the practice and recommending it to his friends and followers. The time of the resurgence of Ramanama was also the period when he devoted much time to the study of the *Gita*, which became his favourite sacred text.

It was in May 1924 that he wrote his first public statement about Ramanama in an article about *brahmacharya* in *Navajivan*. Over the following four years, until mid-1928, there was a regular succession of such articles, some of which were quite long, for example, the six pages long article entitled 'Power of Ramanama' in *Navajivan* of 17 May 1925. After the middle of 1928, public statements or articles about Ramanama practically disappeared. The recitation of Ramanama, however, had become second nature to Gandhi, and he continued recommending it in his private letters. [24]

Gandhi's references to Ramanama over those twenty years from 1924 to 1945 draw a uniform picture. He repeatedly praised the salutary effects of the practice and warmly recommended it. He declared that the effect of regular recitation was the acquisition of peace of mind, mental equilibrium and composure, which were essential characteristics the *sthitaprajna* of the *Gita*, one who has his mind and heart totally under control. This was a recurring theme primarily in his letters to followers and friends. [25] Another way in which Ramanama contributed to that equanimity was by cleansing the mind of impure thoughts and desires, achieving *brahmacharya* in thought and deed. [26]

Gandhi also considered the recitation a powerful help in the establishment of mental health: 'Ramanama is an invaluable remedy for mental illness'. [27] It also had a positive effect by strengthening the mind in its moral resolutions, so that it helped closely adhering to vows. [28] Gandhi warned against superstitious belief in the magical effectiveness of mechanical recitation, condemning 'sinners who . . . chant the *mantra* of Ramanama in order to nourish their sins . . . , who believe that by sitting in company and loudly repeating the Name they can wash away all their past, present and future sins'. [29] In order to be effective, Ramanama had to be accompanied by positive moral action, which basically meant by 'service' to mankind and the nation. [30] Gandhi also liked Ramanama because it made the sacred syllable OM, which was a privileged mantra available only to Brahmins and learned pandits, accessible in a popular form to the poor and the illiterate. He acknowledged that there were other great mantras in Hinduism, which gave religious support to many, but to him 'Ramanama was supreme'. [31]

During these twenty years between 1924 and 1945, Gandhi's presentation of Ramanama remained basically unchanged. His claims for the practice's mental and religious efficacy remained moderate. Anybody understanding its practice as taught by Gandhi, would have to accept that, if properly executed, it would mostly have positive effects on the practitioner. He did not recommend it with burning fervour, nor did he claim for it extraordinary powers or effects. In fact, his advocacy of the practice was, from 1928 onwards, after the enthusiasm of its discovery, mostly restricted to personal letters to close collaborators.

This changed suddenly in early 1946. There was a revival of the public propaganda for the Ramanama practice, which remained strong during the remaining two years of his life. This revival was closely connected with an upsurge in his advocacy of Nature Cure Centres at Poona and at Uruli Kancham.[32] Ramanama reappeared in a short article in *Harijan* of 3 March 1946 entitled 'Nature Cure Treatment', in which Gandhi made a vital connection between Nature Cure and Ramanama as follows:

> Nature cure treatment means that treatment which befits man . . . both mind and soul. For such a being, Ramanama is the truest nature cure treatment. It is an unfailing remedy . . . No matter what the ailment . . . recitation of Ramanama from the heart is the sure cure . . . But the recitation must not be parrot-like, it must be born of faith . . . Man should seek out and be content to confine the means of cure to the five elements of which the body is composed, i.e. earth, water, akash [ether], sun and air. Of course Ramanama must be the invariable accompaniment. If, in spite of this, death super- venes, we may not mind. On the contrary, it should be welcomed. Science has not so far discovered any recipe for making the body immortal. Immortality is an attribute of the soul. [33]

The totally new idea in this statement is that Ramanama 'is an unfailing remedy'. This was not a casual claim; it was repeated many times. Ramanama was 'a cure for all ailments', an 'infallible remedy', 'a cure for all diseases'.[34] This sweeping claim for Ramanama's power of healing was not only a theoretical stance of Gandhi or a poetic hyperbole. He proved his firm belief in it by his actions. He refused to take penicillin for a persistent and severe attack of coughing and flu because Ramanama coupled with nature cure was his medicine.[35] The firmness of his belief showed itself most forcefully in his dealings with his young great-niece Manu, who was at that time his constant compan- ion, and who was then chronically ill with intestinal problems. 'She will not have frequent bouts of fever, if she had Ramanama firmly enshrined in her heart. . . . Still I am convinced that if she only has Ramanama inscribed in her heart she will suffer no physical enfeeblement.'[36]

His own practice of Ramanama, he was convinced, had an immediate effect on her health:

> Her health should improve to the extent she and I are able to enshrine Ramanama in our hearts. This girl is my partner in this *yajna*. I have

not a shadow of a doubt that whatever her thought, word and deed,
they are bound to interact on my actions and the purity or impurity of
my thought, word and deed will have a bearing on her actions.
Therefore the more sincere I am in reciting Ramanama the greater
will be her improvement.[37]

When Manu finally had to be operated upon for appendicitis, Gandhi was
mortified; he saw it as a clear indication that his practice of Ramanama
was ineffective because it was still imperfect. 'Though I have no longer
the desire to live for 125 years as I have said again and again of late, my
striving to meet death unafraid with Ramanama on my lips continues. I
know my striving is incomplete; your operation is a proof.'[38]

Gandhi resolutely denied that his practice of Ramanama had anything
to do with faith healing, and he was incensed when it was suggested that
it looked rather like the mumbo-jumbo of superstitious incantations: 'I
can, therefore, categorically say that incantations have no connections
whatsoever with my Ramanama'. This suspicion about his Ramanama
was never raised by anybody during the long period when his claims
were 'moderate'.[39]

It is quite clear that the Ramanama of the earlier period (1924–45) had
changed profoundly. Now it had become 'a sovereign remedy for all our
ailments', 'a most powerful remedy', with 'miraculous powers', 'a
panacea for all our ills'; 'when Ramanama holds sway, all illness
vanishes'.[40] He even wrote, 'Remember that Ramanama is the unfailing
remedy for eradicating malaria.' Gandhi explained the rationale of his
conviction in the following way. 'All illness is the result of the violation
of the laws of nature, in other words, the penalty of sin against Him,
since He and His laws are one.'[41] God and his laws, including the
physical laws, are identical; all illness results from some violence done
to these laws of nature, which is violence against the divine order, in
other words, sin. When one succeeds in eliminating all sin, all forms of
violence against God and his laws, then one eliminates also all illness,
which is a consequence of sin. 'Where there is absolute purity, inner and
outer, illness becomes impossible.'[42] Gandhi reiterated that firm conviction in various ways:

If one is knowingly filled with the presence of God within, one is that
moment free from all ailments, physical, mental or moral . . . Disease is impossible where there is purity of thought . . . Conscious
belief in God and a knowledge of His law make perfect cure possible
without any further aid.[43]

Ramanama, according to Gandhi, played a vital part in that process of purification: 'I know no other way than Ramanama of achieving purity.' It was the most effective way of gaining self-control which would make it impossible to commit, or even to think of sin. By reciting Ramanama one taps into the very source of spiritual force, which is, 'like any other force at the service of man'. 'The conservation of the vital energy has been likened to accumulated wealth, but it is in the power of Ramanama alone to make it a running stream of ever-increasing spiritual strength ultimately making a fall impossible.'[44] Gandhi deplored that people did not understand what he was saying, but he was totally determined to discover for himself and conquer that power:

> People have no idea of the full potency of Ramanama. I am out to demonstrate it. I must wish to live only to serve Him and live, therefore, through His grace only. I have plunged into this fire to discover the science of Ramanama just as a doctor or a scientist rushes into an area where an epidemic is raging in order to discover the laws of physical science. I must discover it or perish in the attempt.[45]

It is essentially this fascination with the power of Ramanama that made Gandhi's concept and practice of it so strikingly different from the earlier years. The following statements make that quite clear:

> I have said that to utter Ramanama or any other name of God from the heart is to seek succour from the supreme power. What that Power can do no other power can. The atom bomb is as nothing compared with it. . . . It is the highest thing in life . . . God is filling me with strength and I am sustained by Ramanama. Just as men derive vigour and vitality from the daily nourishment and sleep I derive my strength from Rama.[46]

After his last desperate fast, the day before his death, he once more affirmed his faith in Ramanama, and his consciousness of his own shortcomings: 'I am regaining strength fairly well. This time both the kidneys and the liver have been affected. According to me, it indicates that my faith in Ramanama is not complete.'[47]

CONCLUSION

The vow was to Gandhi an unbreakable promise to oneself, to the inherent divinity, to perform or abstain from certain actions. He considered that vows were necessary for the religious life, which essentially meant the battle between matter and spirit. Its primary aim was to purify the self and give spiritual life the necessary stability: this strongly reflected the Jain way of lay spirituality. Such vows were Gandhi's own vow of chastity, and the various Ashram vows. Vows could also have another aim: expiation for sins and omissions by oneself and others. Gandhi's long series of public fasts were often directed towards that goal.

Gandhi's life of prayer started with the communal prayers in South Africa, which remained a rule throughout his life. Their essential purpose was the purification of the community, and the fostering of the awareness of the divine presence within that community. The concern with private prayer came to the fore after his first period in Yeravda jail. Apart from the time of waking up and going to bed, Gandhi did not set specific times aside for private prayer. This prayer was not about asking favours of God, but about ensuring the awareness of the divine in all actions: it was supposed to permeate all the day. Gandhi's 'voice within' belonged to this sphere of private prayer. It was the answer of the divinity within to the doubts assailing the spirit. It was not the external answer of a distinct God, but the illumination of an uncertain mind by the growing inner spirit.

Of all the possible forms private prayer could take, to Gandhi Ramanama was the best. It was only in the mid-1920s that he started practising it in earnest, inspired by his reading of Tulsidas' *Ramcharitmanas*. The prayer's effect was inner control, peace and steadfastness, and the penetration of all actions by the divine purpose. At the very end of his life Gandhi became desperate to stem the Hindu–Muslim blood bath. Ramanama took on a new meaning: it was the practice which, above all, could activate within his spirit the immense spiritual power needed for that task.

11

The Potency of Perfect Chastity

Towards the end of the South African period Gandhi's ideas about *brahmacharya* took shape, and he summarised them in his essay in the series 'General Knowledge about Health' under the title 'An Intimate Chapter'. Nature has bestowed upon man a mysterious power, the generative fluid, which is a source of great physical and mental strength. *Brahmacharya* is the means of conserving that treasure by keeping the body and the mind free from all carnal enjoyment. The violation of chastity gradually leads to a decline of the body, the loss of mental capacity, and is the basic cause of all kinds of moral evil. Everyone should aspire to that virtue: those who are married should only have sexual relations when they desire progeny. *Brahmacharya* meant great physical, mental, and moral power.[1] Gandhi became convinced that 'Those who want to become passive resisters for the service of the country have to observe perfect chastity.'[2]

BRAHMACHARYA AND MARRIAGE

Two years after his return to India, in a speech on Ashram Vows delivered in Madras, Gandhi said, 'Those who want to perform national service, or those who want to have a glimpse of the real religious life, must lead a celibate life, no matter if married or unmarried.' This conviction remained to the end, and was reiterated from time to time: 'For realisation of God is impossible without complete renunciation of the sexual desire.' 'As faith in God is essential in a satyagrahi, even so is *brahmacharya*. Without *brahmacharya* the satyagrahi will have no lustre, no inner strength to stand unarmed against the whole world.' Although that basic conviction remained firm, over the years one can detect changes in emphasis and application.[3]

In the early years in India we notice a strong downgrading, even denigration, of the married state, accompanied by a further exultation of *brahmacharya*. In a letter to C. F. Andrews in 1920, Gandhi still put it mildly: 'From the highest standpoint it [marriage] is a status lower than that of celibacy.'[4] But soon his comments became very negative.

> Take it from me that there is no happiness in marriage . . . I cannot imagine a thing as ugly as the intercourse of man and woman. That it leads to the birth of children is due to God's inscrutable way . . . The occasion of marriage should remind us of self-restraint. If desires cannot be conquered, they should be harnassed, that is, they should be directed to one object. Such a restriction is better than promiscuity . . . I refuse to believe that the sensual affinity [between man and woman] referred to here can at all be regarded as natural. No, I must declare with all the power I can command that sensual attraction even between husband and wife is unnatural.[5]

This fanatical negativity also found expression in other ways. If the situation arose between a married couple that one of the partners wanted to abstain from sex, but the other did not, Gandhi decreed that 'In my opinion husband and wife do not have to obtain each other's consent for practising *brahmacharya* . . . Mutual consent is essential for intercourse, but no consent is necessary for abstention.' One partner's desire to abstain did in fact override the marriage contract.[6]

As for married people, there was only one way in which they could possibly achieve *brahmacharya*. 'There is a way out for them. They can behave as if they were not married.' In other words, even the sex act engaged in for the express purpose of procreation is not free from lust, and is an infringement of chastity. It also violates *ahimsa* because 'procreation involves violence'. The only way married people could achieve dedication to the service of humanity was by the total suppression of sexual activity.[7]

So, there obviously was a contradiction between living in Gandhi's Ashram and the celebration of marriage:

> How can marriage be solemnised in the Ashram when the aim is to encourage everyone in the observance of *brahmacharya*? It happens sometimes that marriages cannot be avoided. In order to pacify my mind I took the one way out. The ceremonial should be performed outside . . . the Ashram.[8]

Therefore the first three marriages were conducted outside the Ashram. However, Gandhi changed his mind and had the marriages performed inside the Ashram. This had several advantages. It allowed him to control the ceremony and the festivities. The latter were practically totally eliminated and the former was reduced to its bare Vedic essentials. But even more importantly, the Ashram ceremony gave Gandhi a good opportunity for preaching his message of *brahmacharya*:

> I perform the ceremonies in the hope that self-control can be strengthened thus . . . Let us pray to God that we may attain our ideals and we may bring up men and women here who do not think about marriage and procreation, but who regard all children as their own, and who spend their lives in serving children who have no sunshine in their lives.[9]

Gandhi devised his own rite of the Vedic *Saptapadi*, the seven steps, for those occasions. The bridegroom and the bride vowed mutual support, supportive friendship, service of the people, a life according to moral rules, and promised not to leave one another. At no stage was there any mention of sex or offspring.[10]

In early 1936 Gandhi slightly modified and softened his adamantine concept of *brahmacharya* for the first time. A long conversation with Margaret Sanger, a zealous advocate of birth control, and of the positive aspects of sexual relations, had stirred his mind.[11] A discussion with Vinoba Bhave on a shastric text made him see things differently. Gandhi explained it to a meeting of the Seva Sangh. For a long time he had believed 'that those who procreate cannot be called *brahmacharis* . . . I was under the impression that *brahmacharya* and procreation were contradictory.' But after his discussion with Vinoba his heart was filled with a new light:

> An avowed *brahmachari* is one who has practised it since birth, who has not lost his semen even in a dream. But I did not know why a person who cohabits for the sake of procreation was considered a *brahmachari*. Yesterday this great truth flashed on my mind. The couple which, in a state of marriage, withdraw into privacy and cohabit for the purpose of procreation are *brahmacharis* in the right sense of the word . . . That is to say, procreation ought to be looked upon as duty and sexual union resorted to for that purpose only. Apart from this they should never engage in the sex act. Nor should they allow themselves privacy. If a man controls his semen except on the occasion of such purposeful cohabitation, he is as good as an avowed *brahmachari*.[12]

Gandhi was very happy with this new insight and reiterated it several times.[13] He felt it gave a new meaning to marriage, and the following statements stressed the positive aspect of this new insight:

> Marriage is a natural thing in life, and to consider it derogatory in any sense is wholly wrong . . . The ideal is to look upon marriage as a sacrament and therefore to lead a life of self-restraint in the married state . . . Sex urge is a fine and a noble thing. There is nothing to be ashamed of in it. But it is only meant for the act of creation.[14]

There is another matter in which Gandhi changed his previous stance. His principle, often reiterated, was that 'mutual consent is essential for intercourse, but no consent is necessary for abstention'.[15] In mid-1937 he reversed his opinion on the latter. In answer to a question of a married man wishing to observe *brahmacharya* against the wishes of his wife, Gandhi wrote:

> A husband or wife can strive for any aim which was not present in the minds of both at the time of marriage, only with the consent of the other party. In other words, a husband cannot take the vow of *brahmacharya* without the consent of his wife.[16]

In other words, Gandhi here recognised the lasting value of the marriage vows which were now considered binding even if one of the partners wished to pursue the highest ideal.

WIDOW REMARRIAGE

There is one aspect in the case of marriage versus *brahmacharya* where Gandhi took from the start a humane and liberal stance, which became even more liberal as time went on, and that is the case of the child-widows. As early as 1918, Gandhi clearly stated his opinion about widows and widowers:

> My view about remarriage is that it would be proper for a man or a woman not to marry again after the death of the partner. The basis of Hinduism is self-control . . . In such a religion, remarriage can be only an exception. These views of mine notwithstanding, so long as the practice of child-marriage continues and so long as men are free to marry as often as they choose, we should not stop a girl, who has

become a widow while yet a child, from remarrying if she so desires, but should respect her wishes.[17]

Gandhi often expressed his profound admiration for the state of Hindu widowhood:

> The ideal of widowhood is one of the glories of the Hindu religion. If the vow of unswerving devotion to the husband has any meaning, it is that once a woman has, with full knowledge, accepted and looked upon a man as her husband, even when he has died she should cherish his memory and rest in it, nay, find joy in it.[18]

He contrasted it with the behaviour of men:

> The nobility of an Indian husband, however, does not last beyond the cremation ground and, at times, in the very precincts of the crematorium, even as the body of his holy wife is being consumed to ashes on the pyre, his relatives do not hesitate to propose to him remarriage and the widowed man feels no shame in lending his ear to such talk.

The greatness of the widow is the perfection of self-control, self-denial, and service.[19]

The basic argument used by Gandhi to justify his opinion that a child-widow should be allowed to remarry was that she was not really a widow:

> The definition of a widow can have no reference to child marriages. A widow means a woman who, at the proper age, married a person of her choice or was married to him with her consent, who has had relations with her husband, and who has then lost her husband. A wife who has not known consummation of marriage or a girl of tender age sacrificed by her parents cannot and must not be included in this definition.[20]

Such an invalid marriage does not force widowhood on the woman. Evidently in the case of child-widows there was neither consent nor consummation.[21]

The logic of Gandhi's position was strengthened by his enormous compassion for the plight of the child-widows. It is interesting to indicate that this compassion led him to open the door to widow remarriage even wider than his strict definitions seemed to allow. In his important article

on widowhood in *Navajivan* of 4 May 1924, he enunciated the following
rules, the third of which widened the possibilities:

1 No father should get a daughter under the age of 15 married.
2 If a girl below this age has already been married and has become a
   widow, it is the father's duty to get her married again.
3 If a 15-year-old girl becomes a widow within a year of her marriage,
   her parents should encourage her to marry again.[22]

Later Gandhi went even further in widening the admissibility of widow
remarriage. In June 1929 he wrote in the *Hindi Navajivan* in response to
the question how the problems of the widows should be dealt with. The
questioner excluded remarriage, which he thought 'lowers the banner of
chastity', and looked for a way which would 'safeguard their virtue'.
Gandhi's answer was broad-ranging and clear:

> To say that widow remarriage leads to loss of chastity is wrong. To
> forcibly prevent a widow from remarrying when she wishes to do so
> would be harming chastity and dharma as well. Only by marrying a
> child-widow can we safeguard dharma and chastity. We can safeguard
> brahmacharya only by respecting the widows, by providing them
> means of education, and by granting them full freedom to remarry.[23]

Later on he explained that,

> The rights or latitude allowed to widowers should also be allowed to
> widows. Otherwise widows become victims of coercion and coercion
> is violence, out of which only harm can come . . . It can only be
> because laws applying to women have been framed by men . . . No
> obstacles should be placed in the way of those [of all widows] who
> wish to remarry.[24]

In early days Gandhi wanted to extend the ban on remarriage from
widows to widowers too. He came to totally reverse his position by
giving widows the same rights as widowers.
    There is a final astonishing example of the latitude Gandhi was
capable of towards the end of his life. In a conversation with a woman
whose husband had remarried after tricking her into signing the divorce
papers, Gandhi faced the question of what she should do in the circumstances. He felt that she should 'devote herself to any work of service'.
But he acknowledged an alternative: 'If you are not able to restrain

yourself, you should find an eligible partner and marry him'. This woman was not a widow, only a divorcée, yet Gandhi advised her to marry again if she felt she needed the intimacy of marriage.[25]

MARRIAGE AND CASTE

Towards the end of his life Gandhi introduced a totally new idea about marriage. From early days he had held that marriages should be within the caste of the partners. The purpose was:

> to put disciplinary restraints upon the choice of men and women. Just as it would be improper for a brother to marry his sister, I would make it improper for a person to marry outside his or her group which may be called caste. I would thereby make the other men or women free from the attention of that person.

It was a measure meant to impose restrictions and self-restraint, and to narrow the circle of physical attraction. He went on to write, 'If Manilal [his son] fell in love with a pariah girl, I would not quarrel with his choice but I would certainly consider that he had failed to imbibe my teachings.'[26] This was written in 1925. Twenty years later Gandhi totally reversed this teaching:

> Your views about mixed marriages are not expressed clearly. Since I believe that we cannot have too many such marriages, I do not at all approve of marriages within the same caste . . . You accept inter-marriages only as exceptions. I would encourage them and they ought to be encouraged. Reformists, being indifferent to religion, may do that, but their example will have no effect. We, however, who keep religion in the forefront should make up our minds how far we are prepared to go. If . . . castes and sub-castes as we know them disappear – as they should – we should unhesitatingly accord the highest importance to marriages between Ati-shudras and caste-Hindus . . . Where parents are wise, there should be no difficulty even about marriages between persons of different religions.[27]

The reason why Gandhi now advocated intermarriage between caste Hindus and untouchables was the following. After many frustrating years of fighting the cancer of untouchability with little success, Gandhi became convinced that the only way in which untouchability could be eradicated was by making all Hindus belong to one single caste, that of the Harijans:

> You must be aware that ordinary marriages no longer have any interest for me. I am interested, if at all, in a caste Hindu marrying a Harijan. For, if we wish to observe *Varnashrama* dharma, we should all belong to one caste, i.e. of Harijans. And how else can we prove that we have really become Harijans?[28]

This new attitude shows how much Gandhi's values had shifted over the years. In the 1920s he proposed to use the caste system to more easily enforce the values of *brahmacharya* by restricting marriages in scope, and also in quantity. Towards the end of his life he saw the cancer of untouchability as the greatest threat to Hinduism. Since he had found that working within the caste system was ineffective, he decided that untouchability could only be eradicated by demolishing the caste structure itself. And now he proposed to use a form of marriage, that between caste Hindus and Harijans, as one of the main methods to achieve that end.

BRAHMACHARYA AND BRAHMAN

From about 1920 Gandhi specifically said about the *brahmacharin* that 'He alone is a seeker after truth. He alone becomes capable of knowing God.' But in the mid-1920s he broadened the very concept of *brahmacharya*: 'A full and correct meaning of *brahmacharya* is search for the *brahman*.'[29] In other words, the concept of *brahmacharya* broke its previous limiting connection with sensual and sexual restraint, and began to refer to the very essence of spiritual endeavour and to the ultimate religious achievement: 'it is the royal road to self-realisation or attainment of *brahman*', and 'achieving *brahmacharya* means realising God'.[30] This is a very important development in Gandhi's thought, or rather a clearer articulation of its fundamental approach. To say that the achievement of chastity, not in its narrow meaning of sexual control, but in its extended meaning of total control of all desires and passions, means the realisation of God, or the attainment of *Brahman*, which is the ultimate goal of religious life, clearly signals that the essence of religion according to Gandhi is to be found in self-control and total abnegation of all desires and passions. This seems to suggest that only the perfect ascetic is the authentic saint. We will have to look elsewhere in the Gandhi legacy for different approaches that will flesh out that rather harsh and meagre skeleton of asceticism.

There is another aspect of the concept of *brahmacharya* that developed considerably from the mid-1920s onwards, and that is the aspect of 'power'. From his South African days Gandhi had referred to his conviction that chastity as the conservation of the vital fluid engendered physical, mental, and moral strength. He stressed that a man of 'inviolate *brahmacharya*' would never fall ill or even have a headache. He declared how, if he himself violated chastity, he would instantly lose 'in a twinkling all that power which would enable one to achieve svaraj'.[31] But the following quotation clearly shows a shift in his conception:

> The real value of *brahmacharya* lies in the expenditure of the great energy required for mastering the senses: when, through such expenditure, the senses become *atman*-oriented, the power which is generated by the effort can pervade the entire universe.[32]

The power generated referred to here is clearly of a different kind from that referred to earlier. Whereas previously the power was an individual one, this power transcends the individual and has a cosmic quality. It would not be wrong to say that there is here a hint of a divine, absolute power, as confirmed by Gandhi: 'We should remember that the soul's power is unlimited. He whose desires have totally perished is practically fit to be God.' He now referred to chastity as 'spiritual energy', 'celestial passion', 'creative energy of the highest order', 'unfailing power', 'the richest capital man can ever posses'.[33]

In the following statement Gandhi made the divinity of the power of *brahmacharya* quite clear:

> I have defined *brahmacharya* as the way of life which leads to *Brahman*. The knowledge that *Brahman* is God does not help us to know what his real nature is. So if we have true knowledge of God we can know the correct path that leads to Him. God is not a human being . . . the truth is that God is the force. He is the essence of life. He is pure consciousness. He is omnipresent . . . Electricity is a great force but all cannot benefit from it. There are certain laws for generating it and therefore we can get electricity only if we abide by these laws . . . Similarly there are laws for knowing the great living force which we call God but it is self-evident that it requires hard labour to find out those laws. That law in short is termed *brahmacharya*.[34]

Brahmacharya is the method of tapping into the power that is *Brahman*, the very essence of life, the energy that sustains the universe.

THE LAST EXPERIMENT

It is from that standpoint, the concept of *brahmacharya* as access to the cosmic power of *Brahman*, that we should look at Gandhi's last controversial experiment in mustering that power. We are referring here to his practice between 1945 and 1947 of having some of the women of the Ashram at times share his bed in a state of nakedness. First of all we should recall some basic aspects of the situation. Gandhi was at that time 76 years old, and his health was very poor, giving often rise to uncontrollable shivering during the night. Secondly, Gandhi lived in an ashram environment where his room was a very public place where inmates and visitors were continually present. Doctor Sushila Nayar, for instance, used to give Gandhi massage and medicated baths during which he transacted a lot of business with his co-workers and secretaries.[35] The sleeping arrangements were similarly non-private, as N. K. Bose described them. When Gandhi suffered these fits of shivering the women attendants used to clasp him tightly 'so as to restore warmth to his shivering frame'.[36] Probably this was the way in which it all started. 'She [Prabhavati] often used to sleep with me to keep me warm even before I was conscious that I was making an experiment.'[37] But soon there was more to it. Gandhi started to refer to the practice of sharing his bed as an 'experiment', and later when he practised it only with his grand-niece Manu, he called it a *yajna*, a sacrifice.

We have no intention here to do psycho-history; that is an endeavour that should be left to scholars qualified in that field, such as Erik Erikson.[38] We want to find out, from Gandhi's own writings, what exactly the experiment meant to him, and how it fits in with the gradual development of his own conception of *brahmacharya*.

This close contact of Gandhi with women was not a sudden development: he never believed in a chastity that could only survive by avoidance of all contact. He expressed this most forcefully in an article entitled 'How Non-Violence Works', published in *Harijan* in 1938. After having stated that a very high degree of chastity is absolutely necessary for one 'who has to organise vast masses of mankind for non-violent action', he went on as follows:

It has been said that such *brahmacharya*, if it is at all attainable, can be so only by cave-dwellers. A *brahmachari*, it is said, should never see, much less touch a woman. Doubtless a *brahmachari* may not think of, speak of, see or touch a woman lustfully. But the prohibition one finds in books on *brahmacharya* is mentioned without the important adverb . . . Difficult though, therefore, *brahmacharya* is of observance when one freely mixes with the world, it is not of much value if it is attainable only by retirement from the world.

He then explained how throughout his career he had not followed the prescribed restrictions, but freely mixed with women, who were to him like sisters and daughters. He did not look upon them as sources of evil and temptation, but with the veneration due to his own mother, to whom 'he owed all the good that may be in him'.

Gandhi's next paragraph shows that the thoughts that would lead to the experiments in later life, were already stirring in his mind:

But recently a doubt has seized me as to the nature of the limitation that a *brahmachari* or a *brahmacharini* should put upon himself or herself regarding contacts with the opposite sex. I have set limitations which do not satisfy me. What they should be I do not know. I am experimenting. I have never claimed to have been a perfect *brahmachari* of my definition . . . I must acquire greater control over my thoughts.

And next, Gandhi put into context the worry expressed above: 'There is perhaps a flaw somewhere which accounts for the apparent failure of leadership adverted to in the opening sentence of this writing.' In other words, he thought he may be failing as a leader because he lacked power. And his lack of power and influence he felt, may derive from the fact that his *brahmacharya*, a source of unlimited power, was deficient. Hence his desire to 'experiment' in order to enhance that power.[39]

There were two periods when Gandhi was actively pursuing the particular practice of sleeping with Ashram women. The first was in the beginning of 1945. Gandhi lived at Sevagram, and was in very bad health on account of overdoing some Ayurvedic practices. The Congress Working Committee members were still in captivity. There was famine in Bengal and nothing much was happening on the political scene. Gandhi was heavily involved in Ashram matters and his letters of the period suggest lots of tension in Sevagram. It seems clear that occasionally some of the women attendants slept with Gandhi in order to bring

some warmth to his shivering frame. Gandhi 'saw an opportunity and
seized it', or, as he wrote elsewhere, 'I was not out for an experiment,
but when the situation presented itself before me I did what I felt was
necessary.' In other words, Gandhi decided to transform these occasions
into an experiment in *brahmacharya*.[40]

He had always held that proper chastity was not one that protected
itself by avoiding as much as possible all contact with women, but rather
a state of mind where even in the closest contact with women the
awareness of sexual difference did not even arise.[41] He wanted to feel
about women, not as a male, but as a woman, and wanted to be accepted
by them not as a male, but as a sister or a mother. He saw now that the
situation of sleeping with a woman in the same bed was a supreme
experiment in which to test if his chastity was indeed genuine. 'I deliberately want to become a eunuch mentally. If I succeed in this then I
become one physically also. That alone is true *brahmacharya*.' 'The
experiment was designed to make of myself a perfect *brahmachari* and
if God so wills it will lead to perfection'.[42]

That is how a casual, unusual, but innocent situation, was transformed
into a deliberate experiment, in which some four women were involved.
It did not last long, because some of the inmates of the Ashram became
very worried about it, and could not approve of that extraordinary
behaviour. Gandhi discontinued the experiment. The reason was not that
he felt that he had done something wrong, 'I claim that whatever I have
done I have done in the name of God. I go to bed reciting his name.' 'If
it is satyagraha it can never cause physical harm, nor even moral harm.
If my conduct is trusted there can be no harm, whoever may be my
associate.' Gandhi made it clear that his aim was to achieve perfect
brahmacharya, and that in achieving this he would be able to increase
his power of service: 'If I can become a perfect *brahmachari* thereby [by
the experiment], would I not be able to contribute more to the welfare of
the world?' Because of the pressure of the ashramites Gandhi discontinued his experiment, and it looks as if it took a couple of years to surface
again in the beginning of 1947.[43]

The second phase of Gandhi's last experiment in *brahmacharya*
started at the end of 1946. On 6 November 1946 Gandhi had left for
Noakholi in Bengal, where the Hindu–Muslim disturbances were very
bad, and many Hindus had been killed by Muslims.[44] Manu Gandhi was
the Mahatma's grand-niece. During her final illness in the Aga Khan
Palace Detention Camp, Kasturbai had asked if Manu could be transferred from another prison in order to come and nurse her. Manu's own
mother had died in her childhood. On her death bed Kasturbai entrusted

the young girl to Gandhi, who became 'her mother' after Kasturbai. In fact, Manu herself wrote a book entitled *Bapu, My Mother*. Manu had not been close to Gandhi for some time, but at the end of 1946 she wrote to him in Noakholi asking if she could come back and serve him. Gandhi accepted, provided she became totally truthful with him, and submitted to his discipline. She gladly accepted the conditions.[45]

Manu arrived in Srirampur on 19 December 1946. It seems that shortly after her arrival she started sharing Gandhi's bed, and there was no secret about it. This 'provoked quite a storm' among Gandhi's followers, some leaving their service.[46] On 25 February, after Gandhi had a long discussion about the matter with Thakur Bapa, Manu asked Gandhi if he would agree to suspend the experiment. Gandhi readily agreed. The experiment was resumed three months later, after Gandhi had settled down in Delhi on 27 May 1947, and it continued till his death.[47]

This last year was the most tragic of Gandhi's long life. During this year all he had fought for seemed to be destroyed in chaos. The country for the freedom of which he had offered his all was breaking into two. The Hindu–Muslim peace and understanding he had agitated for in the last 25 years was disintegrating into an orgy of hatred and killing. Gandhi felt as if he were engulfed in darkness:

> Have been awake since two a.m. God's grace alone is sustaining me. I can see there is some grave defect in me somewhere which is the cause of all this. All around me is utter darkness. When will God take me out of this darkness into His light? . . . I am still surrounded by darkness. I have no doubt whatever that it indicates a flaw somewhere in my method . . . I am groping for light. I am surrounded by darkness – but I must act or refrain as guided by truth. I find that I have not the patience and the technique needed in these tragic circumstances. Suffering and evil often overwhelm me and I stew in my own juice.[48]

Gandhi had never in his life experienced the darkness and the impotence as he felt them now strangling him. At the same time he was convinced that somehow the very cause of the persistence of that situation had to be found in his own deficiency, in his own lack of spiritual power.

Gandhi's 'experiment' with Manu was part of a personal spiritual offensive which was to him not an experiment as it had previously been, but a duty, a sacred duty, a matter of *dharma*, imposed upon him by God himself.[49] He specifically called it a great *yajna*.[50] Gandhi's use of this

term is significant. *Yajna* refers to the sacrificial rituals of the early
Vedic times, and they are speculated upon in the *Brahmanas*. In the
latter they became the carriers of cosmic powers, which were brought to
bear whenever the *yajna* was properly executed according to the rules.
Gandhi was convinced that if he succeeded in completing his great *yajna*,
then the darkness and violence that surrounded him and had engulfed
India, would be dissipated. He wrote to Satis Chandra Mukherji, 'If I
attain the state [of total equanimity and purification] or even come near
enough to it (and probably that is all that a human being can reach), this
problem of Noakholi will be easily solved.' Elsewhere he wrote, 'I
believe that if even only one brahmachari of my conception comes into
being the world will be redeemed.' And in his last days in Delhi he still
clung to that conviction:

> I must achieve something or die in the attempt. I cannot say what will
> happen. I seek light. I can glimpse some rays in the darkness. Only
> when I attain enlightenment in full, shall heart-unity in Delhi be
> enduring.[51]

Sleeping with Manu was seen by him as an integral part of that *yajna*,
the aim of which he expressed in different ways:

> I am engaged in achieving self-purification, utmost self-purification
> . . . What is choking the action of my ahimsa? May it not be because
> I have temporised in the matter of brahmacharya? . . . I am launched
> on a sacrifice which consists of the full practice of truth . . . In this
> *yajna* I got a glimpse of the ideal of truth and purity for which I had
> been aspiring . . . I wish to reach the stage of a perfect *sthitaprajna*
> and attain perfect non-attachment.[52]

Gandhi's relationship with Manu in this great *yajna* was conceived by
him as an integral part of his search for perfection, a search that became
frantic and desperate in that last year of his life. He wanted total truthfulness, total non-violence, total chastity, total self-effacement, total
equanimity. He was convinced that his spiritual power would increase a
thousand fold if he could approximate that ideal. That power would
radiate and dissipate the darkness around him. It is only in that context
of the desperate situation of India and the deepest convictions of Gandhi
that we can begin to understand why he persisted in a practice which he
saw as his supreme *yajna* of purification, but which many of his closest
collaborators rejected as a sorry aberration, if not as a demeaning of the
traditional values of *brahmacharya*.

12

The Power of Fasting

Gandhi, who had experimented with diets for some years, finally discovered the religious value of fasting late in his stay in South Africa. From time to time he reminded his readers in India of the religious importance of fasting for everybody. In 1919, commenting on the Moslem Conference of Lucknow's proclamation of Friday 7 October as a day of fasting and prayer, he welcomed their action and wrote: 'Prayer expresses the soul's longing and fasting sets the soul free for efficacious prayer.' Shortly afterwards he elaborated in an article entitled 'Fasting and Prayer' as follows: 'There is nothing as purifying as a fast, but fasting without prayer is barren . . . it is only a prayerful fast undertaken by way of penance to produce some effect on oneself which can be called a religious fast.' A year later Gandhi considered himself 'a specialist *par excellence*' in fasting: 'I do not know any contemporary of mine who has reduced fasting and prayer to an exact science and who has reaped a harvest so abundant as I have.' He rephrased his previous definition: 'Fasting then is crucifixion of the flesh with a corresponding freedom of the spirit and prayer is a definite conscious longing of the soul to be utterly pure.' However, the discussion of the religious value of fasting in general as an accompaniment of prayer never became a major theme for Gandhi. The hundreds of pages on fasting that lie scattered in his writings do not deal with fasting in general, but with the many public fasts of the Mahatma himself. The first of these had occurred in South Africa, in the Phoenix Settlement, and fourteen more were staged by Gandhi after his return to India.[1]

THE TWO PROTOTYPES OF PUBLIC FASTS

As we have seen, the Phoenix fast was a fast of penance and purification. Some young ashram inmates had acted against the rules. Punishing was not practised; Gandhi considered himself, as the leader of the ashram, responsible. Therefore, he decided that he would fast for seven days as penance for the sins committed, and as a means of purification both for himself and the culprits. Gandhi's seventh fast in India, the Satyagraha Ashram fast of 1925, was practically identical. It was in response to misbehaviour among the youngsters of the ashram and it lasted seven days. As Gandhi wrote, 'the reasons for the fast were purely private and personal, and for ashram purification'.[2]

Gandhi's first public fast in India was very different. In early 1918 he was asked to go to Ahmedabad to participate in the arbitration of a dispute between weavers and mill-owners. The city had been visited by a virulent plague the year before, and the mill-owners had given their weavers a bonus above their normal wages. When the plague was over, the mill-owners wanted to discontinue the bonus, but the weavers objected. The dispute was referred to an arbitration committee, in which Gandhi was on the panel that represented the weavers. Before arbitration could start, the mill-owners declared a lockout on 22 February which they continued for three weeks. When they then re-opened the mill, the weavers went on strike. They put in their ambit claim of a 50 per cent wage increase, the mill-owners offered 20 per cent. Gandhi carefully studied the situation, proposed that 35 per cent was a reasonable increase, and got the weavers to accept his assessment. However, the mill-owners refused to budge.[3]

Gandhi now took on the leadership of the weavers' struggle. He laid down a number of rules for the strikers: no violence, no molesting of blacklegs, no dependence on alms, and earning a basic living by honest labour. The workers took a pledge not to resume work until either their terms were accepted or the mill-owners agreed to arbitration. After a couple of weeks work was getting scarce, and some workers started flagging; attendance at the daily meeting began to drop, and despair started taking hold of many. Then the mill-owners ended their lockout, re-opened the mills, and invited back all the workers who were prepared to accept their 20 per cent offer. By mid-March many strikers were obviously at the end of their tether, and ready to give up.[4] Some started to grumble against Gandhi. Gandhi was at a loss; he recounted as follows in his autobiography the next development:

> One morning – it was at a mill-hands' meeting – while I was still groping and unable to see my way clearly, the light came to me. Unbidden and all by themselves the words came to my lips: 'Unless the strikers rally,' I declared to the meeting, 'and continue the strike till a settlement is reached or till they leave the mills altogether, I will not touch any food.'[5]

Within three days all agreed to arbitration, and Gandhi broke his fast.

There are some characteristics that clearly distinguish this fast from the Phoenix fast. First of all, the decision to fast was preceded by a period of uncertainty and confusion on the part of Gandhi. This was followed, unexpectedly on his part, by his declaration that he would immediately take up a fast. In other words, the decision did not seem to Gandhi to have been the end-point of clear reason and argument, but rather something spontaneous, like an inspiration. Secondly, whereas the Phoenix fast set a clear limited target of seven days, this fast would only end when certain conditions were fulfilled. If these conditions were not fulfilled the fast would not end, and would of necessity lead to death. This was a conditional fast to death, although Gandhi did not specifically name it as such. Thirdly, and this follows from the previous characteristic, this fast was meant to bring certain people into action, and quick action, because how long can life continue without food? Whereas the Phoenix fast was an exercise in penance and inner purification, this fast was directed to a specific group of people (the weavers primarily but also the mill-owners) who were the only ones able to take the steps that would cause the condition for the stoppage of the fast to be fulfilled. All those involved obviously understood this clearly, and immediately set about to fulfil the conditions as quickly as they could manage. Moreover, Gandhi realised that he had by his fast exercised some coercion on the mill-owners, and he, therefore, accepted after three days a compromise.[6]

The Phoenix fast and the Ahmedabad fast became the two prototypes for all the subsequent public fasts of Gandhi. Those following the Phoenix model could be called 'unconditional penitential fasts'. They lasted for a specified number of days, which could not be curtailed. They were fasts of penance aimed at the spiritual purification of the subject of the fast and of a target group of people. This group could consist of the inmates of an ashram or could be much wider: Hindu orthodoxy, the Hindu and Muslim communities of Calcutta, the Congress members all over India. It was a fast that aimed at improving the spiritual quality of these groups, which was usually called by Gandhi a process of purification. The fasts did not urge anybody to do anything specific, or do it quickly; it wanted people to reflect on their actions and attitudes and eradicate from their hearts and minds feeling and thoughts of hatred or injustice.

The Ahmedabad model inaugurated what could be called the 'conditional fasts to death'. In each case Gandhi felt that a critical situation had been reached that was desperate; he had exhausted all normal means to remedy it, but without success; somehow the situation needed to be reversed quickly. This led to the conditional fast: 'I will not take any food until the following conditions are fulfilled.' The fast was thus intended to galvanise those targeted to immediate action. They had to act quickly to realise the conditions Gandhi had proclaimed, because if they did not succeed, the inevitable consequence would be the death of Gandhi. As Gandhi himself wrote: 'Fasting until death . . . can be undertaken on very rare occasions. It is a very strong measure . . . a conditional fast can be undertaken only in exceptional circumstances.'[7]

THE SERIES OF FASTS: GENERAL OBSERVATIONS

In order to facilitate this discussion of Gandhi's public fasts a list of them has been appended, which describes their basic characteristics.[8] A cursory inspection of this list gives an indication how Gandhi's public fasting developed. All fasts were closely connected with socio-political issues, and were conducted in a blaze of publicity. Only one fast, the 1925 Ashram fast, was different, as it was like the Phoenix fast confined to the Ashram environment.

The period divides itself naturally into two segments of similar length, from 1915 to 1931, and from 1932 to 1947. One immediately notices the increase of the frequency of the fasts over time: eight occurred in the second period compared with only five in the first. Secondly, whereas the first period contains only two conditional fasts to death, the second period contains no less than five out of eight. Thirdly, the three unconditional fasts in the first period were respectively for 3, 5, and 21 days, whereas the three in the second period contained one of 7 days, and two of 21 days. This clearly demonstrates that from the early 1930s there was a significant intensification in the use of fasts by Gandhi, not only in their frequency, but also in their harshness and duration. The predominance of conditional fasts in the latter period also indicates that Gandhi, as time progressed, found himself more often in situations beyond his control, and had to use more frequently the weapon of the fast to establish some resolution of the crisis, which he felt could only be achieved by galvanising a target group into frantic activity.

When we look at the issues pursued in the twelve public fasts (omitting the Allahabad and the ashram fasts) some patterns emerge. No fewer than seven fasts had as their central concern a form of violence. Three fasts (1919 Ahmedabad, 1922 Delhi, 1934 Wardha) were occasioned by violence perpetrated by followers of Gandhi in the struggle for independence or the agitation for the untouchables. Another four were caused directly by outbreaks of violence of a communal nature, primarily between the Hindus and Muslims (1921 Bombay, 1924 Delhi, 1947 Calcutta, 1948 Delhi). These fasts connected with violence span the whole period, showing the continuing strength of Gandhi's abhorrence for any form of violence.

Three fasts were connected with Gandhi's fight for the untouchables and they were bunched together in those two years when the cause of the untouchables was his main concern (1932 Yeravda, 1933 Poona, 1933 Yeravda). The fight for the abolition of untouchability was started by Gandhi immediately after his return to India, but in the early 1930s it became for a few years the cause which eclipsed all others. This was also a period during which political agitation for independence was in the doldrums.

Only three of Gandhi's fasts specifically targeted government authorities. The 1933 Yeravda jail fast was aimed at forcing the government into reinstating all the facilities for his Harijan work, which Gandhi had enjoyed in his previous jail period. The 1939 Rajkot fast targeted the Thakore Sahib of Rajkot and the British authorities to force them to temper the repressive regime of the state. The 1943 Poona fast was directed at the Government's harsh repression of the Quit India Movement, and the riots connected with it, which it blamed on the Congress leaders. All the fasts will now be analysed in the three groups mentioned above.

FASTS FOR THE UNTOUCHABLES

Gandhi's three fasts for the cause of the untouchables were very heavy ones, two were fasts to death and one an unconditional fast of 21 days; moreover, they happened within a period of 12 months. Nothing shows more eloquently the immense importance of this fight for Gandhi. He constantly analysed these fasts, because he was repeatedly challenged by the orthodox Hindu establishment, for whom this was an extremely important cause.

Gandhi had decided as early as March 1932 that he would fast against the creation of separate electorates for the untouchables; he wrote to Sir Samuel Hoare about it: 'I respectfully inform His Majesty's Government that in the event of their decision creating separate electorates for the Depressed Classes, I must fast unto Death.' On 17 August Ramsay MacDonald announced the Communal Award, which decreed that the untouchables were entitled to separate electorates. On 18 August Gandhi wrote to him that he would resist the scheme by starting 'a perpetual fast unto death' on 20 September, which would only cease 'if, during its progress, the British Government of its own motion or under pressure of the public opinion, revised their decision and withdraw their scheme'. He added a paragraph in which he justified this decision:

> It may be that my judgement is warped and I am wholly in error in regarding the separate electorate for the Depressed Classes as harmful to them or to Hinduism. If so, I am not likely to be in the right in reference to other parts of my philosophy of life. In that case, my death by fasting will be at once a penance for my error and a lifting of a weight from off the numberless men and women who have childlike faith in my wisdom. Whereas, if my judgement is right, as I have little doubt it is, the contemplated step is but due to the fulfilment of the scheme of life which I have tried for more than a quarter of a century, apparently not without considerable success.[9]

The obvious implication of this was that his survival of the fast would be a clear sign of the justness of his cause, if there were any doubt about it.

The Government's answer was also clear: 'The Government's decision stands, and only an agreement of the communities themselves can substitute other electoral arrangements for those that the Government has devised.' This statement had now fundamentally changed the condition which could release Gandhi from his fast. In his first statement the condition was, 'if the British Government revise their decision'. Now the Government had stated that its decision stood – but a revision of electoral arrangements could be achieved by an agreement of the communities themselves. The onus of fulfilling Gandhi's condition was no more on the Government, but it now rested squarely with the communities: if they could reach and agreement, the Government would accept it. There followed a week of frantic activity. Hindu leaders and leaders of the untouchables organised themselves, constantly consulted Gandhi, and by 25 September hammered out an agreement, the Yeravda Pact, that was accepted by Gandhi. All that was now needed was the acceptance of the British Government, which was expedited in London, and announced on 26 September. Gandhi broke his fast.[10]

In several statements Gandhi made it quite clear who the people were his fast was targeting:

> Impending fast is against those who have faith in me, whether Indians or foreigners, and not for those who have it not. Therefore, it is not against the English official world, but it is against those English men

and English women who . . . believe in . . . the justice of the cause I represent. Nor is it against those of my countrymen who have no faith in me . . . but it is against those countless Indians . . . who believe that I represent a just cause. Above all it is intended to sting Hindu conscience into right religious action.[11]

So, the purpose of the death-threat was not to make people act against their conviction, but to galvanise into action those who believed in Gandhi's cause. This did not mean that the agitation for the untouchables could now go on the back burner. In fact, the conclusion of the Yeravda Pact drafted by Gandhi and adopted by all, foreshadowed continuing agitation:

This conference resolves that henceforth, amongst Hindus, no one shall be regarded as an untouchable by reason of his birth, and those who have been so regarded hitherto, will have the same right as other Hindus in regard to the use of public wells, public schools, public roads and other public institutions. This right will have statutory recognition at the first opportunity and shall be one of the earliest acts of the svaraj parliament.[12]

When in early November 1932 the Government restored to Gandhi in jail the privileges that allowed him to carry on his Harijan work, he released during the next fortnight no less than six statements calling on caste Hindus to abolish untouchability. He wrote that the Government had done its part, and that the major part of the Yeravda Pact resolutions, quoted above, had to be fulfilled by the Caste Hindus. If these resolutions were not fulfilled, how could he 'possibly live to face God and man?' He would have to resume his fast.[13]

Temple-entry was at that time the most important plank of the anti-untouchability campaign. Rajagopalachari conducted a plebiscite about allowing untouchables access to the Guruvayur temple. Fifty-six per cent were in favour, 9 against; 8 per cent were neutral, and 27 per cent abstained. The Zamorin of Calicut and his orthodox followers tried to prevent the access by claiming that the Guruvayur temple was a private temple. Other complications arose and it seemed necessary to legislate in order to change the current practice. Two bills were framed by the reformers, one for the Madras Legislative Council and the other for the Central Assembly. Gandhi postponed his fast, which was supposed to start on the 2 January 1933, until the Viceroy made a decision. On 23 January the Viceroy sanctioned the introduction of the bills, and Gandhi immediately responded by widening the cause: 'The movement for temple entry now broadens from Guruvayur to Hardwar, and my fast, though it remains further postponed, depends not now on Guruvayur only, but extends automatically to all temples in general.'[14]

In the first months of 1933 the counter-agitation of the orthodox intensified to the extent that the Yeravda Pact itself seemed to be in jeopardy. On 30 April Gandhi issued a statement that he would start on 8 May an unconditional fast of 21 days. No other fast elicited from Gandhi so many detailed and extensive reflections, and none was more strenuously challenged by Hindu orthodoxy.

The first thing that captures the attention is the way Gandhi related how the decision was made. In the message he gave to his companions in the morning, he wrote that during the night, while he was fully awake, he had heard a clear voice that actually told him that he had to go on a fast in the morning and that the fast should last 21 days.[15] Although in previous fasts Gandhi had referred to a kind of inspiration that stirred him to make a decision in a state of agonised uncertainty, he had never claimed in so many words that he actually heard the 'voice of God', and had an exchange of questions and answers with it. He was seriously challenged over this claim, but he stuck to what he had said. This indicates how important he considered this fast and how critical he judged the situation to be.[16]

The dominant theme of his explanations was that this was a fast for the purification of self and associates. This would remove all bitterness in the Hindu community, produce greater vigilance among the workers, and reveal and weed out the impurities of the movement. The fast was not directed towards the opponents of the reform, and it was not taken on to oblige the Harijans and help their Association.[17]

Gandhi was convinced that 'no ordinary propaganda would convince the Hindu mind of the sense of wrong of untouchability'.[18] Converting the Hindus through the abolition of untouchability needed stronger measures:

> The work of removal of untouchability is not merely a social or economic reform. Its goal is to touch the hearts of the millions of Hindus . . . it means nothing short of a complete revolution in Hindu thought . . . Such a change can only be brought about by an appeal to the highest in man . . . which can be made effective only by self-purification, i.e. by fasting . . . I believe that the invisible effect of such fasting is far greater and far more extensive than the visible effect.[19]

Gandhi's third fast for the untouchable cause was the 1933 Yeravda Jail fast. However, it properly belongs in the section with the other fasts directed against the Government.

FASTS AGAINST THE GOVERNMENT

In July 1933 Mass Civil Disobedience had been suspended and replaced by Individual Civil Disobedience. Gandhi was first in line, and was arrested, tried and sentenced to one year's imprisonment. During his previous stay in Yeravda jail as a detainee, Gandhi had enjoyed a number of privileges allowing him to continue his Harijan work from jail. He now asked to be granted those same privileges, but the Government refused to renew them because now he was not just a detainee but a convicted prisoner. On 14 August he wrote to the Government of Bombay, 'If I cannot have permission by noon next Wednesday, I must deny myself all nourishment save salt and water.' The Government responded by granting him a number of facilities for Harijan work. Gandhi felt that they were not sufficient to let him 'do the Harijans service without let or hindrance', and commenced a conditional fast unto death on 16 August, a fast which would only come to an end if and when the Government restored his former privileges to the full.[20]

The Government reacted negatively, and their reasoning was not without merit. Gandhi, they stated, did not devote all his time to Harijan work when he was outside the prison, but was mostly engaged in political agitation. The previous time he was only a detainee, but now he was a convicted prisoner. They were prepared to let him have a lot of privileges other prisoners did not receive, but he wanted even more. In fact, if he was willing to abandon civil disobedience activities, they would set him free at once, and he could devote all his time to Harijan work. Gandhi refused the offer and started his fast. After a week he was in a very poor state, and was transported to Sassoon Hospital, still as a prisoner. He lost the will to live. On 23 August he entered the danger zone, and the Government released him unconditionally. Before leaving hospital he broke his fast.[21]

It is very difficult to understand this fast of Gandhi as a religious act. Nowhere does Gandhi mention purification. The Government really went as far as possible to respond to Gandhi's demands. This was not a cause that deserved a fast unto death. It looks more like a case of political blackmail as the Government interpreted it. When a correspondent accused him, Gandhi answered in length. He acknowledged that the fast coerced the Government into releasing him, but he insisted that was not his intention. 'I wanted the Government to take me at my word and let me die in peace, if they could not see the justice of granting me the facilities I desired.'[22] Gandhi was considerably upset by the unexpected ending, 'since my unexpected release . . . darkness has surrounded me. The path of duty has not been clear to me . . . It is a matter of shame that I took my comrades to prison and came out of it by fasting.' He even went as far to say that if it all happened again, he would not break his fast even if released by the Government.[23] To continue a conditional fast to death when it has become impossible for the conditions to be fulfilled, does not appear to be a religious act with religious aims, but rather a spiteful form of suicide. That statement shows clearly how confused Gandhi was about that failed fast.

The Rajkot fast of 1939 was a conditional fast to death. Gandhi sent the Thakore Saheb a list of seven suggestions that would alleviate the state's authoritarian rule, and added, 'If you cannot see your way to accept my suggestions before noon tomorrow, my fast will commence from that time and will continue till after acceptance.' Gandhi started his fast on 3 March, but the ruler remained adamant. Gandhi then sent a letter to the Viceroy, telling him that he felt that 'this is a case for the immediate intervention of the paramount power'. The Viceroy agreed, and offered the service of the Chief Justice of India, Sir Maurice Gwyer to arbitrate. Gandhi accepted the offer and broke his fast.[24] Later he realised that this particular fast was flawed:

> I recognise my error . . . In taking the fast I sought immediate intervention of the paramount power, so as to induce fulfilment of the promise made by the Thakore Saheb. This was not the way of ahimsa or conversion. It was the way of *himsa* or coercion.[25]

The 1943 Quit India fast was an unconditional fast for a set period of 21 days. On 8 August 1942 the All India Congress Committee had approved the Quit India Resolution, which decided to start 'a mass struggle on non-violent lines . . . under the leadership of Gandhi'.[26] The reaction of the British was immediate: next day Gandhi and all Congress leaders were arrested. Violent riots erupted, in particular across north India. The British quelled the riots with all their might and tens of thousands of agitators were arrested. By the end of September order had been restored. The British were adamant there would be no further trouble in India during this crucial period in the war for the Allies. India had to play a key role in that war and had to be kept under control at all costs. British repression did not let up.

At the end of the year Gandhi started a correspondence with the Viceroy Lord Linlithgow. He claimed he had been accused of being the instigator of violence supposed to have been perpetrated by Congressmen. He had not been given a chance to ascertain the facts or to defend himself. He wanted a chance to study the facts and to be convinced of his errors if he had committed any. The Viceroy replied that it was the Quit India Resolution that gave rise to crime and violence throughout the country, yet neither Gandhi nor the Congress Working Committee had ever condemned it. If Gandhi now dissociated himself from that Resolution the Viceroy would be prepared to further consider the matter. The correspondence went back and forth but neither gave an inch. Already in his first letter Gandhi had mentioned the possibility of undertaking a fast and this became a threat as letters travelled between the two. On 29 January 1943 Gandhi communicated to the Viceroy his decision to fast for 21 days starting on 9 February. The Viceroy regretted his decision but wrote that he looked upon it as 'a form of political blackmail for which there can be no moral justification'. The Government proposed to set Gandhi free for the purpose and duration of the fast and to take him back into detention afterwards. Gandhi did not accept this arrangement and the Government told him that in that case he did his fast totally at his own risk. It was a difficult and dangerous fast but Gandhi came through it and broke his fast on 3 March, at the end of the 21 days.[27]

Towards the end of his fast Gandhi said in a conversation with Mirabehn: 'No fast of mine has ever had such a wonderful ending as this one is having. I do not mean what is going on in the outside world, but what is going on inside me. There is heavenly peace.'[28] However, in judging the effectiveness of his fast, the peace in Gandhi's heart seems to be rather irrelevant. What then, was Gandhi's fast supposed to achieve? At this stage one should remind oneself that this was to be an unconditional fast, which never had a concrete target, but always was concerned with penance and purification for a wide group of people.

It is very difficult to see how the above characteristics of unconditional fasts could be applied to the situation of the 1943 fast. So, was the fast supposed to influence the Viceroy spiritually? It does not seem so, because Gandhi wrote to him as follows: 'Despite your description of it [my fast] as "a form of political blackmail", it is on my part meant to be an appeal to the Highest Tribunal for justice which I have failed to secure from you.[29]

This really does not clarify at all the purpose of the fast. There is another way in which Gandhi seems to have muddied the waters. In one of his later letters to the Viceroy, Gandhi wrote as follows: 'my wish is not to fast unto death, but to survive the ordeal, if God so wills. The fast can be ended sooner by the Government giving the needed relief.'[30] What we have here is in fact the introduction into a fast that is supposed to be an unconditional fast of 21 days, of conditions under which the fast may be ended or suspended. This seems to indicate that Gandhi himself was far from clear what exactly this fast was intended to achieve. Therefore, in all fairness one can say that this fast did not accomplish anything at all. The Viceroy and the Government stuck to their guns and six months later had not moved an inch from their conviction or their policy of repression.

FASTS AGAINST VIOLENCE

Half of Gandhi's fasts in India were a reaction to violence. Four of them happened in succession between 1919 and 1924, at the beginning of Gandhi's taking up of his national role. The last two happened in the last five months of Gandhi's life. Of the seven fasts four were connected with communal violence. These are the most important. We will first say a few words about the other three.

The 1919 Ahmedabad fast was unconditional and lasted three days. After Gandhi's arrest in connection with the Rowlatt Bills agitation, some violence was perpetrated in various places. Gandhi decided to fast for three days as penance for himself as the leader most responsible. He also asked the people involved to fast for one day as penance for the degradation of satyagraha.[31] The 1922 Delhi fast was quite similar, but lasted for five days. The occasion was the brutal killing of policemen in Chauri-Chaura during satyagraha. Gandhi suspended the movement and announced his fast, which was a penance, an atonement for himself, and also a punishment for the people of Chauri-Chaura, 'for those whom I try to serve for whom I love to live, and would equally love to die . . . the only way love punishes is by suffering.' The penance would also purify Gandhi so that he may become 'a fitter instrument'.[32] The same theme of penance and purification dominated the 1934 Wardha fast. During the agitation for the untouchables Pandit Lalnath, leader of the sanatanist counter-agitation, was hit on the head during an altercation with collaborators of Gandhi. Gandhi declared that at the end of his Harijan tour he would engage in a seven-day penitential fast. Again the theme of purification of himself and the workers was stressed.[33] These three fasts were clear in their purpose, all unconditional and of short duration. None of them had a dramatic starting point or a spectacular unfolding.

The four fasts connected with communal disturbances (1921, Bombay; 1924, Delhi; 1947, Calcutta; 1948, Delhi) were very different from the previous three in their intensity. First of all, they all were very drastic fasts; three of them were conditional fasts to death and the fourth was an unconditional fast for 21 days. All four were preceded by days of intense agony on the part of Gandhi, and nights of prayer.[34] Another way in which the intensity and the drama of these fasts manifests itself is in the conditions Gandhi set for breaking the three conditional fasts. Because they had to do with communal disturbances, they required difficult, extensive and intensive communication between the leaders of the communities.

The 1921 Bombay fast had as condition that it would not cease 'till the Hindus and Musulmans of Bombay have made peace with the Parsis, the Christians and the Jews, and till the non-cooperators have made peace with the co-operators'.[35] It is close to a miracle that they managed to accomplish that within four days. The 1924 Delhi fast of 21 days about the Kohat killings was not a conditional fast, but it did lead to a Unity Conference of 300 delegates to sort out communal problems. The 1947 Calcutta fast would 'end only if and when sanity returns to Calcutta'.[36] It took four days for the leaders of the communities to get together and hammer out an agreement which took the form of a pledge signed by forty Hindu and Muslim leaders. The last fast, 1948 in Delhi, would 'end when and if I am satisfied that there is a reunion of hearts of all communities brought about without any outside pressure but from an awakened sense of duty'.[37] This time it took seven days for the community leaders to arrive at an agreement. Their Central Peace Committee of 130 members signed a solemn pledge, and Gandhi broke his fast. It is clear that from every point of view this set of four fasts for communal peace were the most agonizing, stringent, demanding, and galvanising undertaken by Gandhi. Every time he put his life on the line by setting conditions that seemed impossible of fulfilment. In each case his fast stirred the leaders responsible into frantic activity in order to fulfil Gandhi's impossible demands in record time.

WERE THE FASTS SUCCESSFUL?

The question arises whether Gandhi's fasts were successful, and how one can judge their success. As for the conditional fasts, the obvious measure of success is the fulfilment of the conditions set by the Mahatma. By that criterion one can easily conclude that of the seven conditional fasts five were successful. Although the 1939 Rajkot fast did lead to the fulfilment of Gandhi's conditions, he himself soon realised that that fast was not pure, but tainted by violence, because he had asked the Viceroy to put pressure on the Thakore Saheb. The 1933 Yeravda Jail fast which was intended to make the British restore all jail privileges to Gandhi for pursuing Harijan work, cannot be called successful. It was thwarted by the British after eight days by simply releasing Gandhi from jail and thus making his condition unfulfillable.

It is much more difficult to gauge the success of the unconditional fasts. Their aim was usually a combination of penance and purification. The penance was atonement for various violations of the moral code. The two ashram fasts were the prototypes, presenting the simple basic structure: ashram rules had been seriously violated, and as head of the ashram Gandhi shared the guilt with the perpetrators. His fast was an atonement for the sins. It was also a means of purification, of freeing oneself from the tyranny of flesh and selfishness. The ashram surroundings were ideal for the fast, because Gandhi's fast was a constant sermon that could not be ignored. The 1934 Wardha fast was very similar in its setting, and also in the fact that the targets of penance was not very large: they consisted of those who were actively collaborating with Gandhi at the time. One can imagine that in these three fasts the targeted people, who in each case were gathered around Gandhi, must have been deeply influenced by the fast.

Gandhi's 1919 Ahmedabad fast was the first one in the context of a national agitation. It was occasioned by violent communal riots. This was fast purely for penance: Gandhi was guilty as leader. The penance was extended to the people who participated in the riots by Gandhi's request that they observe a one-day fast. This request focused the attention of the people on their own misdeeds. The fast seems to have made a profound impact. The disturbances came to an end overnight, and the military proclamation was withdrawn.[38]

The 1922 Delhi fast for five days over the Chauri-Chaura killings also remained fairly restricted in its lengths and aims: 'My fast is an atonement for me, but for the people of Chauri-Chaura it is a punishment. The punishment inflicted by love is always of this nature.'[39] The 1924 Delhi fast of 21 days, occasioned by the Kohat communal killings was the first of such length. Gandhi clearly announced what it was about:

It is both a penance and a prayer. As a penance I need not to have taken the public into my confidence, but I publish this fast as, let me hope, an effective prayer both to Hindus and the Musulmans, who have hitherto worked in unison, not to commit suicide. I respectfully invite the heads of all the communities including Englishmen, to meet and end this quarrel which is a disgrace to religion and to humanity.[40]

The second part of the aim was splendidly fulfilled by the Unity Conference in Delhi of 200 Delegates. But, besides his personal aim of penance, another new aim was now coming to the fore. Gandhi reflected on his 'powerlessness', 'I must recover the power to react on them . . . This fast is but to purify myself, to strengthen myself . . . Have I erred, have I been impatient, have I compromised with evil?'[41] What Gandhi was saying here was that because of some imperfection within himself the power he had to control violence had waned, and he was stating that this fast was a means of increasing that mental power.

The 21-day 1933 Poona fast for the untouchables was commented on by Gandhi more than any other and it gave him great satisfaction: 'I have enjoyed peace during all my fasts but never so much as in this. Perhaps, the reason was that there was nothing tangible to expect.'[42] What was the aim of this fast? 'The fast . . . will be intended to sting into action those who have been my comrades . . . to strengthen the weak, to energise the sluggards, and give faith to the sceptics.' Since 'no ordinary propaganda would convince the Hindu mind of the sense of wrong of untouchability', it required 'the extraordinary propaganda of penance'.[43] This would be accomplished, as Gandhi repeated endlessly, 'by purification of self and associates'. 'I believe,' he wrote, 'that the invisible effect of such fasting is far greater and far more extensive than the visible effect.'[44] Gandhi here again referred to his belief in the spiritual power of fasting, a power generated by self-purification. This was clearly a fast the success of which could not possibly be assessed because its primary purpose was to empower Gandhi and through him his Hindu collaborators.

The 1943 Poona fast for 21 days was the last of the unconditional fasts. It was analysed earlier in detail, and we concluded that Gandhi was very unclear about its purpose, that the fast exerted no influence whatsoever on the Viceroy and the Imperial administration, although Gandhi claimed that it gave him 'heavenly peace'.[45]

The foregoing survey helps to face the question: what exactly is it that makes a fast successful; how does it work? The very first observation to make is that the fasts did not work when directed at the British authorities. As we saw, the 1933 Yeravda Jail fast and the 1943 Poona fast did not affect the British, and the 1939 Rajkot fast was by Gandhi himself viewed as 'flawed'. All other fasts were meant to influence Indians, and all had a significant measure of success. This clearly indicates that there was an important cultural element that influenced reaction to the fasts. The British saw them as political blackmail that should be ignored, or made ineffectual by administrative intervention. They were not acts with deep religious or moral significance. To them the death of Gandhi in a fast against them would have been a supreme embarrassment, which had to be avoided because of its possible riotous consequences.

Hindus, on the other hand, accepted fasting as a religious act that was used in order to achieve an end and that involved influencing certain people in a particular way. The saintlier the person, the more persuasive the fast. The British refused all blame for the consequences of a fast because the responsibility was totally Gandhi's, and therefore also the blame. Many Hindus could not think that way, and would have considered themselves somehow guilty if Gandhi had died. Gandhi himself was very much aware of the tradition of fasting in Hinduism:

> Although the sanatanists swear at me for the fast, and Hindu co-workers may deplore it, they know that fasting is an integral part of even the present-day Hinduism. They cannot long affect to be horrified at it. Hindu religious literature is replete with instances of fasting, and thousands of Hindus fast even today on the slightest pretext. It is the one thing that does the least harm.[46]

Elsewhere he wrote, 'Ramachandra fasted for the sea to give way for his army of monkeys. Parvati fasted to secure Mahadev Himself as her Lord and Master. In my fasts I have but followed these great examples no doubt for ends much nobler than theirs.'[47] Hindus, therefore, did not accuse Gandhi of blackmail, but some did accuse him of coercion.[48] Gandhi answered that accusation as follows:

> Coercion means some harmful force used *against* a person who is expected to do something desired by the user of the force. In the fasts in question, the force used was against myself. Surely, force of self-suffering can not be put in the same category as the force of suffering caused to the party sought to be influenced. If I fast in order to awaken the conscience of an erring friend whose error is beyond question, I am not coercing him in the ordinary sense of the word.[49]

THE POWER OF FASTING

The British only saw political blackmail in Gandhi's fasts, and some Hindus accused him of coercion. What did Gandhi himself think about the way in which his fasts influenced people? He seems to have given this little thought in his early fasts. The first three fasts were conducted in close proximity with a limited target group, and their impact could be expected to be profound. The 1921 Bombay fast was still limited, and besides penance and reparation, was also meant as a warning to Congress workers.[50] The 1922 Delhi fast occasioned by the Chauri-Chaura murders was punishment for Gandhi and the perpetrators.[51] The 1924 Delhi fast after the Kohat killings was also a fast of prayer, and an invitation to the quarrelling parties to meet and make peace.[52] In all these fasts, including also the 1925 Ashram fast, the aims were modest and achievable without superhuman effort; the realisation of the sacrifice and suffering of Gandhi was sufficient to stir the witnesses into action. Gandhi never spoke of extraordinary powers or spectacular results in the process of these fasts.

The three fasts for the untouchables in 1932 and 1933 were a watershed with new ideas coming to the fore. This time was the most intense high point of Gandhi's passionate struggle for the untouchables, a struggle which often looked hopeless. Within the span of one year Gandhi was engaged in three fasts of great seriousness. There was a note of desperation in this fight with orthodoxy. He considered untouchability as the greatest curse of Hinduism, and the more he agitated against it, the more he discovered how deeply and irrevocably many sanatanists were attached to it. This situation required much more from him than any of his previous agitations. It is no wonder that in this period Gandhi wrote much more than ever before about fasting, and that we see new ideas emerge.

The 1932 Poona Pact fast to death set, for the first time, a condition so difficult to fulfil that it must have looked to many impossible to achieve. It required serious consultation, collaboration and agreement between three very opposite and entrenched groups, the Hindu orthodox leadership, the untouchables, and the British. It was the first time that his fast targeted such a diverse and numerous group of people. The remarkable thing was that the fast succeeded in galvanising a host of people who went into frenzied action and fulfilled Gandhi's seemingly impossible condition within six days.[53]

In a letter to C. F. Andrews about that fast, he brought out two aspects that strike a new note. First of all, this fast was clearly God's will, and he did 'count my will as nothing before God's will when I see it clearly before me . . . when I am clear about it, I rejoice in obeying that will, rather than mine, although it may have no human companion to endorse it'. In other words, Gandhi's fast was a response to a clear divine command. This made it into a super-human divine activity. He went on to say 'this kind of fasting has a definite place in Hinduism, and properly so . . . but it is a privilege that comes only to a few, and when it comes in obedience to a call from above, it has a mighty force.'[54]

These reflections, six months after the fast, were the *post factum* explanations Gandhi gave to the remarkable result of that impossible fast. The fast was undertaken under a clear and strict divine command. Later he compared it to the fast the people of Nineveh described in chapter 3 of the Book of Jonah:

> Thus this was a fast unto death. But every fast unto death is not suicide. This fast of the king and the people of Nineveh was a great and humble prayer to God for deliverance. It was to be either deliverance or death. Even so was my fast, if I may compare it to the Biblical fast. This chapter from the Book of Jonah reads like an incident in the *Ramayana*.[55]

The claim of the divine character of his fasts reached its climax in the next (1933 Poona) fast. We have already commented on his account of the 'Voice of God' ordering him to undertake it. He did not repeat that claim again in such detail, but he claimed that subsequent fasts were directly commanded by God.[56] He even projected this idea on all his previous fasts when he wrote 'All my fast have come to me on the spur of the moment, gifts from God as I have called them.'[57] This, however, was not confirmed by our close study of the individual fasts.

The second new idea emerging during these fasts connected with untouchability, was that fasting constituted 'a mighty force'. At the end of 1933 he came back to that idea in passing:

> The fact is that all spiritual fasts always influence those who come within the zone of their influence. That is why spiritual fasting is described as *tapas*. And all *tapas* invariably exerts purifying influence on those on whose behalf it is undertaken.[58]

The use of the word *tapas* is significant. It refers to the 'heat', the spiritual power that is gathered and concentrated by asceticism. This theme receded into the background. It was referred to in a dissertation entitled 'Fasting' in *Harijan* of 18 March 1939 in the following way: 'Fasting is a potent weapon in the satyagraha armoury.'[59] That was a formula Gandhi would frequently use thereafter. In another article, 'Fasting in Satyagraha,' he wrote, 'Fasting is a fiery weapon. It has its own science. No one, as far as I am aware, has a perfect knowledge of it. Unscientific experimentation with it is bound to be harmful to the one who fasts, and it may harm even other people.'[60] The implication here is that fasting has a certain inherent power, which can be used to great advantage by the one who knows it, but that may explode in the face of him who ignorantly meddles with it. That idea was regularly repeated.[61]

In his last two fasts amid the conflagration of Hindu–Muslim riots and killings in Calcutta and in Delhi, Gandhi faced a problem as severe, all-encompassing, and as intractable as the problem of untouchability. Desperate conditions required desperate remedies, and Gandhi conducted two fasts to death in the last five months of his life. He needed to muster all the power he could, and that power was available in divinely inspired fasts. As he started his Calcutta fast he wrote:

If the riots continue what will I do by merely being alive? What is the use of my living? If I lack even the power to pacify the people, what else is left for me to do? If God wants to make use of me, He will enter the people's heart and calm them down and preserve my body. I have started the fast only in His name. May God keep all of you safe. In this holocaust no one else can do anything.[62]

During the fast he felt 'the presence of God within me this time as never before'. In a discussion with a deputation of fifty people who controlled the turbulent elements in Calcutta, he declared:

The function of my fast is to purify, to release our energies by overcoming our inertia and mental sluggishness, not to paralyse us or render us inactive. My fast isolates the forces of evil; the moment they are isolated they die, for evil by itself has no legs to stand upon.[63]

When somebody asked why Gandhi fasted when faced with extreme difficulties he answered:

The answer is easy, it [fasting] is the last weapon in the armoury in the votary of ahimsa. When human ingenuity fails, the votary fasts. This fasting quickens the spirit of prayer, that is to say, the fasting is a spiritual act and, therefore, addressed to God. The effect of such action on the life of the people is that when the person fasting is at all known to them, their sleeping consciousness is awakened.[64]

The decision to go on his last fast in Delhi on 13 January 1948 did not come easily to Gandhi.

Though the voice within has been beckoning for a long time, I have
been shutting my ears to it, lest it may be the voice of Satan, otherwise called my weakness. I never like to feel resourceless, a satyagrahi never should . . . My impotence has been gnawing at me of
late. It will go immediately the fast is undertaken.[65]

Clearly Gandhi here stated his conviction that the fast as such would
cause a surge of spiritual power. This was to him no ordinary fast: 'I
have undertaken it after much reflection. Yet it is not reflection that has
impelled me; it is God who rules over reason.'[66] At the start of it he
wrote in *Harijan*:

My fast is against no one party, group or individual exclusively and
yet excludes nobody. It is addressed to the conscience of all, even the
majority community in the other Dominion. If all or any of the groups
responds fully, I know the miracle will be achieved.[67]

Devdas Gandhi wrote to him that he thought he had taken his decision in
haste, and had given in to impatience. On the second day of his fast
Gandhi wrote him a long letter explaining his actions:

It was only when in terms of human effort I had exhausted all resources and realised my utter helplessness that I laid my head on
God's lap. That is the meaning of the fast . . . Rama who has
prompted me to go on fast will bid me give it up if He wants me to do
so.[68]

Gandhi considered this his 'greatest fast'. Never did he have higher
expectations. 'When there is perfect peace in Delhi there will be peace
all over India. I have no wish to live if I cannot see peace established all
around me in India as well as in Pakistan. This is the meaning of this
yajna.'[69]

CONCLUSION

The fifteen fasts that dotted Gandhi's public life played a large part in it,
and they were also a very important part of his developing personal
religion. We have seen how the 1932-3 fasts for the untouchables
constituted a turning point, because of Gandhi's intense conviction about
the evil of untouchability and the stubborn intransigence of many ortho-

dox. Gandhi's own understanding of the fasts changed too. The earlier ones were very much exercises in atonement, penance, and purification. Their effect on the target people came from their proximity to Gandhi, and from the way he made them participate in his own feelings. After the incredible success of the Poona Pact fast, Gandhi looked increasingly at his fasts as exercises of concentrating spiritual power. Their effect did not depend on the malleability of the subjects and their acceptance of Gandhi's example and attitudes; their effect was caused by an emanation of spiritual power inherent in them. This consciousness of Gandhi was most apparent in his last two fasts, at a time when he felt hopeless and powerless in the midst of the Hindu–Muslim conflagration of hatred and murder. He stressed his powerlessness, he stressed that this was God's inspired fast more than any before, and that its effects would constitute 'a miracle', because never before had he set such high expectations as this last time.[70] To put it in a nutshell: fasts used to be exercises in atonement and purification with a certain influence of moral persuasion on a close public; they had become methods of unleashing spiritual power that could move masses, because they were dictated by God and they activated divine power.

13

Never Enough Non-violence

SOUTH AFRICA

The doctrine of *ahimsa*, non-violence, was often at the very centre of Gandhi's attention all through his Indian period. It is therefore surprising how very little it featured during his South African period. A perusal of the first eleven volumes of the *Collected Works* shows that there is in the indices of these volumes not one single reference under *ahimsa* or non-violence. A careful study of these volumes strongly confirms that first impression. In Gandhi's Lectures on Hinduism of 1905, the term *ahimsa* does not feature, but he does affirm that the three means of achieving *moksha* included compassion for all living beings.[1] In a letter to Jamnadas in 1913, he wrote that if one wanted to compare religions one should compare them on the basis of morality, and that 'compassion was the root of morality'.[2] It is noteworthy that in neither case did Gandhi use the term *ahimsa*, but the word *daya*, compassion. In his free paraphrase of William Mackintire Salter's *Ethical Religion*, which he published in 1907, and wherein he did interpolate some of his own convictions, there is no mention of non-violence.[3]

It is in the context of *satyagraha* as a method of political protest related to 'passive resistance', that one expects the concept of non-violence to be prominent. *Indian Opinion* reported in June 1909 a lecture by Gandhi on 'The Ethics of Passive Resistance', wherein he was reported as saying that:

> Jesus Christ, Daniel and Socrates represented the purest form of passive resistance or soul force [*atmabal*]. Resist not evil meant that evil was not to be repelled by evil but by good; in other words, physical force was to be opposed not by its like but by soul force. The same idea was expressed in Indian philosophy by the expression 'freedom from injury to every living thing'.[4]

That final expression obviously was an English description of the term *ahimsa*. The interesting thing here is that Gandhi spoke in English terms about passive resistance, and that he mentioned the term non-violence only in an aside. In his work *Hind Svaraj*, which he wrote towards the end of that same year, 1909, he devoted a whole chapter to 'passive resistance'. He wrote, 'After a great deal of experience it seems to me that those who want to become passive resisters for the service of the country have to observe perfect chastity, adopt poverty, follow truth and cultivate fearlessness.'[5] One cannot but notice the absence of non-violence from this list. In November 1911 Gandhi wrote to Raojibhai Patel, who wanted to come and work at Phoenix. He listed his obligations if he came: chastity, truth, manual labour, oppose caste injustice, and embrace absolute poverty. Here too there is no mention at all of *ahimsa*.[6] In contrast, the constitution of the Satyagraha Ashram written in 1915 in India, would require from the inmates the vow of non-violence in conjunction with those of truth, celibacy, control of the palate, non-stealing, and non-possession.[7]

It is obvious that the concept, the principle of *ahimsa* did not loom large in Gandhi's mind during the South African period. He acknowledged this in his autobiography. He described how he discovered corrupt behaviour against Asiatics by officers of the state, and succeeded in having the two worst offenders who were acquitted by the court, cashiered by the Government. Nevertheless, he later abstained from objecting when they had a chance of being employed by the Johannesburg Municipality. Many years later, he reminisced as follows:

> This attitude of mine put the officials with whom I came in contact perfectly at ease, and though I had often to fight with their department and use strong language, they remained quite friendly with me. I was not then quite conscious that such behaviour was part of my nature. I learnt later that it was an essential part of Satyagraha, and an attribute of *ahimsa*.[8]

The other context in which one expects non-violence to appear is that of cruelty to animals. In fact, the concrete application of the principle of non-violence in the life of the inmates was one of the major problem areas for the later Sabarmati Ashram, where, according to Gandhi, 'the greatest difficulties perhaps were encountered as regards the observance of ahimsa'.[9] Not surprisingly, it is the topic of snakes that generated the very rare occasion that Gandhi wrote about *ahimsa* and the treatment of animals in the South African period. His serial publication 'General Knowledge about Health', contained a chapter entitled: 'Accidents: Snake-bite', which consisted of a random and weird amalgamation of facts, figures, superstitions, and old wives' tales about snakes and snake-bites. In the midst of all this he related the stories that thousands of 'jogis and fakirs' lived in the forests of India and moved 'fearlessly among tigers, wolves, snakes, etc., and one never hears of their coming to any harm on that account'. This led Gandhi to comment as follows:

> This proves that some dreaded beasts are friendly to, or at any rate, do not touch some jogis and fakirs. I personally feel that when we did rid ourselves of all enmity towards any living creatures, the latter also cease to regard us with hate. Compassion or love is man's greatest excellence. Without this he cannot cultivate love of God. We come to realise in all the religions, more or less clearly, that compassion is the root of the higher life.[10]

However, the chapter does not anywhere explicitly condemn the killing of snakes. In his *Satyagraha in South Africa* Gandhi recalled his frequent talks about religion with Kallenbach at Tolstoy Farm. When he told his friend 'that it was a sin to kill snakes and such other animals, he was shocked to hear it, as my numerous other European friends had been.'[11] This story clearly shows that *ahimsa* was not a vow at Tolstoy farm, although the students did ask Gandhi permission to kill a snake that had ensconced itself in Kallenbach's room and refused to be removed. Such problems were quite different in their impact in Sabarmati Ashram, where all inmates took a compulsory vow of *ahimsa*.

THE VOW OF NON-VIOLENCE

It was during his first half-year in India, when the draft constitution of the Ashram was being composed, that Gandhi came to the decision that the vow of non-violence should be included among the Ashram vows. In a letter to Maganlal, his prime collaborator in establishing the Ashram, he stated:

> You are right in what you think about non-violence. Its essentials are *daya, akrodha, aman,* etc. [compassion, non-anger, absence of a desire for fame]. Satyagraha is based on non-violence. We saw this clearly in Calcutta and came to the conclusion that we should include it among our vows . . . In my talks with hundreds of men here I place the various *yamas* above everything else.[12]

Gandhi had referred to the five *yamas* in an earlier letter to Mathuradas Trikamji: 'Truth, brahmacharya, ahimsa, non-stealing, and non-possession, to cultivate those five *yamas* is necessary for anyone striving after *moksha*.'[13] The above does not mean that Gandhi discovered *ahimsa* at this time; he had always believed in it and lived by it. What he discovered was the ancient Hindu scheme of the five *yamas*; by making them into essential ashram vows, he strongly affirmed his connection with the ancient kernel of the Hindu tradition. In fact, the list of the five *yamas*, dates back to one of the most ancient and influential texts of Hinduism, the *Yoga Sutras* of Patanjali. Verse 30 of the second book states that their observance is necessary for one who strives after *moksha*. Kane, in his *History of Dharmashastra*, confirms that central position of the *yamas*, and also their vital connection with the practice of vow-taking:

> The observance of yamas would be called *vrata* [vow], but the rigorous observance of yamas without allowing exceptions is called by the Yoga Sutras *Mahavrata* [the great vow], which has to be observed by yogins without exceptions at all stages.[14]

From now on *ahimsa*, which previously was as it were taken for granted and 'unconscious', became a central focus in Gandhi's theory and practice of religion.

Swan has argued that the main reason why non-violence was largely absent from Gandhi's religious discourse and from his discussion of satyagraha in South Africa was that 'he took non-violence so much for granted in the first decade of the century that there was little need for elaboration'.[15] The economic, political, and social suppression of Indians in South Africa was not so severe as to breed rage and frustration erupting into violence, and police action against the agitators only rarely became violent. In contrast, the situation Gandhi found himself in during his first half-year in India, was one that continually led to the discussion of violence. The First World War was in full swing, and in India the discussion of violent resistance to British rule by sabotage and assassination was rampant. Violence being in the air, talk of non-violence became equally frequent.

NON-VIOLENCE AND WAR SUPPORT

One of the very first pressing questions Gandhi had to face during this early period was how he, a believer in non-violence, justified his support for the British war effort in 1914, by organising an Ambulance Corps of Indians in England during the time he was there, between leaving South Africa and arriving in India. In a letter to Maganlal Gandhi he tried to explain and justify his action. 'Recently, I used to say, in South Africa, that, as satyagrahis we cannot help in this way either [i.e., by nursing], for such help also amounted to supporting a war. One who would not help in a slaughter-house should not help in cleaning the butcher's house either.' He then went on to explain his decision by saying that he was, simply by living in London, 'in a way participating in the war'; he was protected by the British and his food was available because of the protection of the Navy. If he wanted to adhere to the strict *ahimsa* principle of not participating in war in any way, he would have 'to go away to live in some mountain or cave in England itself and subsist on whatever food or shelter Nature might provide'. However, he did not yet 'possess the spiritual strength necessary', and therefore, as he accepted 'food tainted by war' he had in some way to earn his food by participating in the war; this he would do not by firing a rifle, but by nursing the wounded. It is not surprising that, having given such a strange and weak-sounding argument, he added 'I cannot say for certain that the step I have taken is the right one'.[16] He repeated in detail the same argument in a letter to Pragji Desai, adding just one new touch: he referred to the text of the *Gita* which says that he who eats his food without performing *yajna* is a thief.[17]

Four years later, in April 1918, Gandhi took a further step that mystified his best friends: he actually became a recruiting agent travelling around India to urge young Indians to join the Indian Army and fight for the allies at a time when the long war was not going well for them. In his support of the British Gandhi was completely out of step with most contemporary Indian politicians, who wanted to exploit the war for the furtherance of Indian freedom; Gandhi stood practically alone on his recruiting platform.[18] In a series of letters he tried to explain his stand to some of his horrified followers and admirers like Ester Fearing, Hanumantrao, Maganlal Gandhi, S. K. Rudra, and, most importantly, C. F. Andrews,[19] who commented as follows on their disagreement in his biography of Gandhi: 'I am obliged to leave his argument about war without discussion. It does not convince or satisfy me.'[20] In fact, it appears from these very letters that Gandhi himself, even in the midst of his recruiting journey, was not quite clear about his own justification. He wrote to C. F. Andrews:

I know that I have put the argument most clumsily. I am passing through new experiences. I am struggling to express myself. Some things are still obscure to me. I am praying for light and guidance and acting with the greatest deliberation . . . My difficulties are deeper than you have put them . . . I have not yet reached the bottom of my difficulties, much less have I solved them.[21]

Gandhi's argument as culled from that series of letters, ran as follows. He still mentioned the argument he used in 1914, 'Either we must renounce the benefits of the State or help it to the best of our ability to prosecute the war. We are not ready to renounce.'[22] This argument, however, was no more the main argument he put forward. In fact, though one could accept that it could justify some form of help to the British, one cannot see how it could possibly justify participating in the war as soldiers. Gandhi's new fundamental argument tackled the 'soldier' topic head on. In his letter to Hanumantrao he put it most succinctly:

It is my practice of ahimsa and failure to get our people even to understand the first principles of ahimsa that have led to the discovery that all killing is not *himsa*, that, sometimes, practice of ahimsa may even necessitate killing and that we as a nation have lost the true power of killing. It is clear that he who has lost the power to kill cannot practice non-killing . . . A weak and effeminate nation cannot perform this grand act of renunciation even as a mouse cannot be properly said to renounce the power of killing a cat. It may look terrible but it is true that we must, by a well-sustained, conscious effort, regain this power.[23]

That was why he felt that he was 'absolutely right as things are in calling upon every Indian to join the army, always telling him at the same time that he is doing so not for the lust of blood, but for the sake of learning not to fear death'. Indians should join the army because, 'We must have the ability in the fullest measure to strike and then perceive the inability of brute force and renounce the power.' 'It is personal courage that is an absolute necessity, and some will acquire that courage only after they have been trained to fight.'[24] It is not surprising that many people were not convinced by this reasoning. Gandhi himself seems to have been confused. Twice in later life he returned to the question of recruiting; in neither of these instances did Gandhi refer to the above argument.[25]

However, there was another argument in favour of recruiting for the Army which Gandhi never mentioned in his letters to Indian friends. It appeared right at the beginning, after taking the decision to recruit, in his letter to the Viceroy, which was published. The text was very explicit:

> I recognise that in the hour of its danger we must give, as we have decided to give, ungrudging and unequivocal support to the empire of which we aspire in the near future to be partners in the same sense as the dominions overseas. But it is the simple truth that our response is due to the expectation that our goal will be reached all the more speedily . . . We must perceive that if we serve to save the empire, we have in that very act secured Home Rule.[26]

It is only in his letter to C. F. Andrews that he referred to this very pragmatic political argument as follows:

> My refrain is, 'Let us go and die for the sake of India and the Empire', and I feel that, supposing the response to my call is overwhelming and we all go to France and turn the scales against the Germans, India will then have a claim to be heard and she may then dictate a peace that will last.[27]

THE DILEMMAS OF NON-VIOLENCE

We have seen how Gandhi early included *ahimsa* among the new ashram vows. In his address on 'Ashram Vows' at the YMCA in Madras in February 1916, he tried for the first time to clarify his ideas. First he described the reach of non-violence: it was much more than just a prohibition of physical violence and killing. It also forbad all violence of speech and even of thought. Moreover, it should be practised not only with friends, but also with enemies: enemies, in fact, did not exist for the person practising non-violence; it required that he love his enemies. Secondly, he stressed that this was a very high ideal, a goal which it was difficult to achieve. Thirdly, he assured his audience that the high level practice of the virtue would exert a very great moral persuasive power over all, even one's enemies.[28]

During the following years, these themes were reiterated, and Gandhi had to come to grips with a number of moral dilemmas pertaining to the use of violence. He came to see that there can be 'non-violence in violence', in situations such as physically restraining a drunkard from evil, or killing a dog in agony. He recognised that in some cases, for instance of a man overcome by lust, or of a woman about to be dishonoured, the violence of suicide was acceptable. He admitted that there could be real non-violence in defending one's wife and children even at the risk of striking down the assailant.[29] This acceptance that there could be real *ahimsa* in certain violent acts did not lead him to water down the uncompromising ideal. He held on to the tenet that '*ahimsa paramo dharma*', non-violence is the highest duty, and that therefore all acts of violence constituted a violation of the ideal. Instead of watering down the ideal, Gandhi started to realise more and more that as an ideal state non-violence was an ever distant goal towards which one progressed, and one not completely achievable in this world. In fact, the full practice of non-violence, he wrote, 'is inconsistent with possession of wealth, land, or rearing of children'. In final instance, 'the fullest application of ahimsa does make life impossible'.[30]

Thus Gandhi stumbled along in his elaboration of his concept of non-violence. There was a constant trickle of case law that forced him to think his position through. In October/November 1926 Gandhi wrote eight essays in eight weeks, entitled 'Is This Humanity?' These essays constituted his matured concept. They were occasioned by the very heated controversy that arose over the destruction by an Ahmedabad mill-owner of 60 rabid dogs on his mill premises, an action condoned by Gandhi. Right at the beginning of these articles he clearly put forward the principle that the killing of a living being was sinful. This was a fundamental truth of Hinduism, and he thought that all religions were in agreement with that principle which expressed 'perfection'. However, this principle, this counsel of perfection, was put into practice by imperfect beings, and necessarily led to compromises in practice. The ideal was, by definition, not attainable in the body.[31]

After stating clearly the principle, practically the whole text concentrated on the way the imperfection of human beings led to compromises. First of all, they were imperfect for the simple reason that they were embodied. The body needs food, air, and warmth, to subsist. The accommodation of these needs, however non-violently done, would always entail a certain amount of unavoidable violence.[32] There was another condition of man consequent on being embodied: life frequently generated pain, an unavoidable part of living. However, when pain intensified to the point that some being was living under continuous torture from which there was no liberation possible, then killing, executed purely for giving peace to the creature, could be an act of mercy.[33] In fact, Gandhi made it clear that he was not just referring to suffering

animals: 'Should my child be attacked by rabies and there was no
hopeful remedy to relieve his agony, I should consider it my duty to take
his life.' Later on, he approved of the mercy-killing of a calf and called
it 'an expression of purest ahimsa', and stated that he would 'do the
same for his own child'.[34]

But Gandhi realised that man was not only a bodily creature, but also
a social being. Belonging to a family and a society created certain
responsibilities, which placed people in situations when, even if killing
was a sin, abstaining from killing would be an even greater evil. This
responsibility of householders for their family, of teachers for their
pupils, of employers for their staff, may demand from them, for instance, the killing of roaming rabid dogs, or of a threatening poisonous
snake. It may even require them to kill a man who had become a vicious
killer.[35] In 1938 Gandhi stuck to his idea of responsibility, writing about
a hypothetical case of a Minister ordering the army to shoot people:

> I wish to work through non-violence while yet solving the problems
> of everyday life. If while I am a Minister Hindus and Muslims start
> fighting amongst themselves, and if I realise that I can stop this
> violence and bloodshed by calling in the army and having a handful of
> men shot, I would have to resort to this course for the sake of restor-
> ing order. I will have to give orders to stop the massacre with the
> least violence.[36]

Gandhi thus gathered all allowable breaches of the law of *ahimsa*
under three headings: the necessities of the body for staying alive, the
relief from excruciating pain and agony, and the duties of giving protection to those who are under one's care. He was also quite clear in his
judgement which of these unavoidable breaches really did constitute
himsa. To make this judgement he used the following moral principle:
'The sin of *himsa* consists not in merely taking life, but in taking life for
the sake of one's perishable body.' He then applied this principle in the
following way:

> All destruction therefore involved in the process of eating, drinking
> etc., is selfish and, therefore *himsa*, but man regards it to be unavoid-
> able and puts up with it. But the destruction of bodies of tortured
> creatures, being for their own peace cannot be regarded as *himsa*, or
> the unavoidable destruction caused for the purpose of protecting one's
> wards cannot be regarded as *himsa*.[37]

JAIN *AHIMSA*

In that way Gandhi clearly distanced himself in his understanding and application of non-violence from the Jain doctrine, which tends to regard all forms of violence to life, even when committed by accident or in ignorance, as sinful. In 1928 he wrote in *Young India* an article entitled 'Jain Ahimsa?', which was a response to a long letter of a Jain friend who was very versed in the study of Jain philosophy.[38]

First Gandhi reminded his readers that with changing times, religious terms have to constantly adapt themselves; therefore definitions of what is violence, and what is non-violence are not dogmatic. Then he tackled the most important problem, where the Jain scholar presented three principles 'on which the Jain view of ahimsa rests'. His first principle was that the taking of life cannot in any circumstances be morally justified. Gandhi firmly argued against this. He was convinced 'that the principle of clinging to life in all circumstances betrays cowardice and is the cause of much violence . . . , and is a hindrance to the attainment of salvation'. The absolute condition for salvation is the total annihilation of all desire, and to hang on to life at all costs is the very height of selfishness. A second principle proposed by the Jain was that there were two kinds of *himsa*: direct, such as in agriculture, and indirect, such as in the eating of agricultural produce; a votary of *ahimsa* should avoid direct *himsa*. Gandhi clearly showed his abhorrence for this principle; which seemed to condemn millions of peasants to commit violence so that 'a few elect could practice *ahimsa*'. This was to him the ultimate cowardice. He found it difficult to believe that was really a principle of Jainism. But even if it were, he could never reconcile himself to it.

Thirdly, the Jain scholar felt that there was a vital difference between Gandhi's view and the Jain view in that the latter was based on a philosophy of renunciation of action, whereas Gandhi's was based on a philosophy of action. Gandhi's answer was exactly the one given in the *Gita*: action is unavoidable in our bodily existence, and the Wheel of Life cannot turn even for one second without some action. Renunciation of action is, therefore, an impossibility. Renunciation can only mean total detachment and freedom of the spirit while the body is engaged in unavoidable action; that is selfless service without egoism. Gandhi was throughout his life active in that flexible and morally sensitive application of the *ahimsa* principle to the various realities of life.

COW-PROTECTION

It is significant that Gandhi's first statement about cow-protection was part of a chapter in *Hind Svaraj* entitled 'The Condition of India: The Hindus and the Mahomedans'. Gandhi's references to cow-protection throughout his life were nearly always connected with Hindu–Muslim relations. The reason for this was simple: the custom of Muslims to ritually slaughter cattle at particular religious feasts incensed a number of Hindus, and the event frequently led to Hindu–Muslim riots.

Gandhi's cow-protection statement in *Hind Svaraj* mentioned in a few paragraphs the basic principles of his attitude. First of all, he chose the cow for special attention because he had 'respect and affectionate reverence' for that animal, which was the protector of India, an agricultural country that depended on the cow for hundreds of uses. Secondly, because of his respect for all his fellow men, he considered attacking or killing Muslims in order to save a cow, to be morally unacceptable. Thirdly, whenever Hindus became militant in this matter, and fostered cow-protection societies, the killing of cows increased, showing not only the immorality but also the futility of the exercise. And lastly, he accused the Hindus of ill-treating the cow in a most callous manner.[39]

In April 1947, towards the end of his life, Gandhi heard of whispers among some Hindus that the beef-eating Muslims were the natural enemies of Hinduism, and deserved to be destroyed. He brought the matter up in his next prayer meeting. He recalled that he had written about cow-protection forty years earlier in *Hind Svaraj*, and he stated that his views had not changed. He reiterated his basic accusation that the cow was ill-treated in India more than elsewhere, and that cow-protection societies were counter-productive: they were an excuse to attack the Muslims.[40] There was a remarkable consistency of Gandhi's attitudes in this matter throughout his public life. All we want to do here is to indicate in what way the basic principles stated in *Hind Svaraj* were enlarged and refined without change in the essentials.

The 'affectionate reverence' that Gandhi expressed for the cow in *Hind Svaraj* grew over the years. He explained to Asaf Ali that 'the Rishis of old regarded the cow as sacred'.[41] In his very important article entitled 'Hinduism' published in 1921, he waxed lyrical about cow-protection and attempted to explain its deeper meaning and its profound symbolism:

The central fact of Hinduism however is cow-protection. Cow-protection to me is one of the most wonderful phenomena in human evolution. It takes the human beyond his species. The cow to me means the entire sub-human world. Man through the cow is enjoined to realise his identity with all that lives. Why the cow was selected for apotheosis is obvious to me. The cow was in India the best companion. She was the giver of plenty . . . Protection of the cow means protection of the whole dumb creation of God.[42]

In a personal letter to Jawaharlal Nehru he wrote that 'Cow-protection means protection of the weak, the helpless, the dumb and the deaf . . . The cow to me is a sermon in pity.'[43] Gandhi did not follow the ancient sages in exalting the 'sacredness' of the cow. That exaltation was often a cover for cruel treatment, and it was intended to magnify the killing of cows by the Muslims into being an act of deliberate desecration. Gandhi removed that artificial halo of sanctity, and replaced it with a powerful moral symbolism: the cow became the symbol of all living beings, but especially of the weak, the helpless, the downtrodden.

His exposure of the hypocrisy of much of Hindu cow-protection was savage and relentless: the treatment of cows, calves, and bullocks by their Hindu owners was utterly cruel and totally exploitative; the Hindu owners tended to pour all their milk into the lucrative manufacture of butter and cheese while the children missed out on their necessary milk; the pinjrapoles, supposed to be retirement havens for aged and sick cattle, were an absolute disgrace. Fanatical Hindus used every opportunity for attacking the Muslims because of their ritual slaughter of cows. But they remained silent about the enormously greater slaughter perpetrated in slaughter-houses all over India that provided meat for the British. They did nothing to try to expose and prevent that slaughter, and they willingly sold their cattle for that purpose.[44]

Gandhi's savage condemnation of the treatment of the cow by Hindus, and of their hypocrisy in linking cow-protection with attacks on the Muslims, was accompanied by many practical efforts to improve the care for cattle. He tried to implement those in his ashrams, and in the All-India Cow-Protection Sabha he founded. These plans and these activities fall outside the immediate concern of this study.[45]

NON-VIOLENCE AND POLITICS

Discussion of this topic should not lead us too far from the centre of our concern, Gandhi's personal religion. The importance he attached to non-violence in political agitations is well-known, as is his drastic and uncompromising reaction of suspending the agitation when violence did occur. It is interesting to listen to Gandhi's reflections in an article entitled 'How Non-Violence Works', published in *Harijan* in the middle of 1938, in which he considered the role of non-violence in the Congress movement. His article was a response to the following question that had been raised to him by a Congress leader: 'How is it that in quality the Congress is now not what it used to be in 1920–5?'

Gandhi wrote that Congress started with an initial handicap in 1920, because very few members believed in non-violence as a creed, while most accepted it as a policy. There came a profound change over the leaders, and their enthusiasm infected the rank-and-file. However, that phenomenal change was due to Gandhi's promise of 'Svaraj in one year'. Yet, the experiment of non-violence on a mass scale did not succeed, because the people did not adhere to Gandhi's conditions. Gradually enthusiasm waned, and confidence was shaken in non-violence even as a policy. Things did not improve, 'The evil has continued to grow'.

Gandhi went on the conclude that he had in some way failed, because he had not yet 'the power that there must be in the word of a satyagraha general'. 'If my non-violence is to be contagious and infectious, I must acquire greater control over my thoughts. There is perhaps a flaw somewhere which accounts for the apparent failure of leadership.' His faith in non-violence had remained as strong as ever and 'it should, if properly applied, prevent the bloodshed that is going on outside India and is threatening to overwhelm the western world'. He ended the article with a passionate declaration of hope:

> My aspiration is limited. God has not given me the power to guide the world on the path of non-violence. But I have imagined that he has chosen me as His instrument for presenting non-violence to India for dealing with her many ills. The progress already made is great. But much more remains to be done. And yet I seem to have lost the power to evoke the needed response from Congressmen in general . . . But I do entertain the hope that there is yet work for me to do, that the darkness that seems to have enveloped me will disappear, and that, whether with another battle more brilliant than the Dandi March or without, India will come to her own demonstrably through non-violent means. I am praying for the light that will dispel the darkness. Let those who have a living faith in non-violence join me in the prayer.[46]

TRUTH AND NON-VIOLENCE

A very special relationship between *satya* and *ahimsa*, truth and non-violence, has often been commented upon as a very typical and fundamental Gandhian doctrine. It became such, but it was not so from early days. In 1919 he mentioned a special relationship between the two in a letter to a Burmese friend: 'I made the early discovery that if I was to reach God as Truth and Truth alone, I could not do so except through non-violence.'[47] This, however, seems to have been only a passing remark, and was at the time not further elaborated. The first attempt at describing the relationship between truth and non-violence is found on the very last page of Gandhi's autobiography written in 1929. In his introduction, Gandhi wrote, 'I have given the chapters I propose to write the title of *The Story of My Experiments With Truth*. These will of course include experiments with non-violence, celibacy and other principles of conduct.' Here he did not make a special connection between truth and non-violence. In the body of the autobiography he occasionally mentioned them together, but only once did he suggest a special connection: 'This *ahimsa* is the basis of the search for truth.'[48]

The following are the key sentences in Gandhi's conclusion of his autobiography:

> My uniform experience has convinced me that there is no other God than Truth. And if every page of these chapters does not proclaim to the reader that the only means for the realisation of Truth is *ahimsa*, I shall deem all my labour in writing these chapters to have been in vain . . . The little fleeting glimpses therefore that I have been able to have of Truth can hardly convey an idea of the indescribable lustre of Truth . . . But this much I can say with assurance, as a result of all my experiments, that a perfect vision of Truth can only follow a complete realisation of Ahimsa. To see the universal and all-pervading Spirit of Truth face to face one must be able to love the meanest of creation as oneself . . . Ahimsa is the farthest limit of humility.[49]

The basic doctrine of the relation of truth and non-violence became clear to Gandhi during the writing of his autobiography, as a direct result of his meditation on his own life and endeavours. Five years later he clarified the relation between truth and non-violence as follows in a letter to Narandas Gandhi:

> It is perhaps clear from the foregoing that without ahimsa it is not possible to seek and find Truth. Ahimsa and Truth are so intertwined

that it is practically impossible to disentangle and separate them . . .
Nevertheless, ahimsa is the means and Truth is the end. Means to be
means must always be within our reach, and so ahimsa becomes our
supreme duty and Truth becomes God for us. . . . We . . . should
ever repeat one *mantra*: 'Truth exists, it alone exists. It is the only
God and there is but one way of realising it.'[50]

Thus Gandhi ended up by putting *ahimsa* at the very core of religious
endeavour, recognising it as the fundamental means by which Truth can
be realised, that is, *moksha* can be achieved. In this process *ahimsa* had
developed into an all-encompassing principle which, besides nonviolence
in thought, feeling, and action, also came to mean total self-abnegation,
total humility, compassion, love, and service.

THE POWER OF NON-VIOLENCE

It is from that latter broad perspective that we can attempt to understand
a final development in Gandhi's conception of *ahimsa* in the last years of
his life. From the early days back in India Gandhi occasionally referred
to the moral power that resulted from the practice of non-violent action.
In his speech on the Ashram Vows in Madras in 1916, he said: 'If you
express your love – ahimsa – in such a manner that it impresses itself
indelibly upon your so-called enemy, he must return that love.'[51] In a
reply to Lala Lajpat Rai, that same year, he wrote:

Our shastras seem to teach that a man who really practises ahimsa in
its fullest has the world at his feet, he so affects his surroundings that
even snakes and other venomous reptiles do him no harm. This is said
to have been the experience of St Francis of Assisi.[52]

In a letter to C. F. Andrews two years later, he clearly described this
influence of non-violence as a 'moral force'.[53] And in 1930, in a letter to
the Viceroy Lord Irwin, he wrote that 'non-violence can be an intensely
active force'. He wanted to use this force against the organised violence
of British rule 'through civil disobedience'. It was his ambition 'no less
than to convert the British people through non-violence, and thus to make
them see the wrong they have done to India'. It is quite clear that Gandhi
conceived the influence, the power of non-violence as a 'moral' force,
one that worked through persuasion and 'conversion'.[54]

On rare occasions Gandhi got carried away by his subject, and
described the power of non-violence in different terms. He did so in the

last of his famous eight articles about non-violence entitled 'Is This Humanity?'

> What torments me is the impotence of the votary of ahimsa. Ahimsa is not impotence. Ahimsa is not powerlessness. Ahimsa is unconquerable power. We shrink from it as we are dazed by its overpowering lustre. Only very few of us can catch a glimpse of it.[55]

We noticed a similar reference to the great power that there needs to be in the 'satyagraha general' in order to be an effective leader, and that power had to spring from the intensification of *ahimsa*.[56] This description of the power of non-violence is quite different from the earlier references to the moral power of persuasion. The preoccupation with this power pervaded Gandhi's last years. What was the catalyst that switched Gandhi's attention? The unleashing of the violence of the atom bomb at the end of the Second World War did affect Gandhi very deeply, but his article in *Harijan* of 1 July 1946, entitled 'Atom Bomb and Ahimsa', does not give any indication of a switch. Gandhi argued that it was wrong to expect that the destructive power of the atom bomb 'would so disgust the world that it would turn away from violence for the time being'. He held that once the disgust was worn out, 'the world would return to violence with renewed zeal'. He concluded:

> The moral to be legitimately drawn from the supreme tragedy of the bomb is that it will not be destroyed by counter-bombs even as violence cannot be by counter-violence. Mankind has to get out of violence only through non-violence. Hatred can be overcome only by love.[57]

It was, in fact, a different kind of violence that caused Gandhi to give a dramatically new slant to his concept of non-violence: the eruption of communal violence of unprecedented scale and savagery between Hindus and Muslims in Bengal. It was after his arrival in the Bengal town of Noakholi in November 1946, on his mission to stop the killings, that *ahimsa* suddenly appeared in a new dramatic context, which would dominate his thoughts on non-violence until the end of his life.

The first element of this context was the 'darkness', the bewilderment, the uncertainty that enveloped his mind and disoriented him. Surrounded by falsity, in order to 'find his bearings', he felt he should isolate himself even from his companions. He felt that the 'reason for the present darkness lies within me', 'was due to his own limitations'. He was indecisive, and perplexed where he should be going as the violence spread to Bihar, Punjab, and Delhi. Even right at the end of his life, he said that he had lost the wish to 'live the full span of life, in view of the prevailing darkness'.[58]

Certain things had become clear to him as regards non-violence. The non-cooperation campaigns he had fought for forty years had been an imperfect form of non-violence 'the weapon of the weak'. Gandhi had been aware of this *'ahimsa of the weak'* even in 1918 before he engaged in his nation-wide satyagrahas. In the small campaigns in Champaran and Kaira, 'with the majority it was purely passive resistance that they resorted to, because they were too weak to undertake methods of violence'.[59] He now looked upon the larger campaigns of the past too as not real satyagraha, but only passive resistance, the weapon of the weak. Again and again Gandhi came back to this theme because he wanted to make abundantly clear that the non-violence he was striving for was very different.[60]

He knew that this *ahimsa* was to be 'the *ahimsa* of the brave', and he had recognised examples of it in the 1946 Ahmedabad carnage, when two Congress workers waded into the killings to stop them, and were themselves killed in the process. Their non-violence required more courage than violence itself, and therefore it was the 'non-violence of the brave'. Gandhi commented as follows:

> It will be disgraceful on my part to sit at home and tell others to go and lay down their lives. Such a thing cannot be an indication of non-violence. I have never had the chance to test my non-violence in the face of communal riots. It might be argued that it was my cowardice which prevented me from seeking such a chance. Be that as it may, God willing, the chance will still come to me, and by throwing me in the fire, He will purify me and make the path of non-violence clear.[61]

That was the non-violence that was required, the one that leads to a pure sacrifice, and, he added, 'There is nothing that such sacrifice cannot achieve.'[62] When he was asked by a correspondent what on earth his non-violence could possibly achieve in a world where violence was rampant everywhere, he gave the following answer which in a nutshell presented his new concept of the power of non-violence:

> For me ahimsa is not disabled; it is not weak; it is supreme. Where there is ahimsa there is Truth, and Truth is God. How that God manifests Himself I do not know. All I know is that He is all-pervad-

ing and where He is all is well. There is therefore one law for all. Wherever in the world truth and ahimsa reign there is perfect peace and perfect happiness.[63]

In other words, the true non-violence of the brave is supremely powerful simply because wherever it is, 'there is God'.[64]

This idea of the absolute power of perfect non-violence was quite different from the earlier conviction of Gandhi that non-violence had a 'moral power' of persuasion and conversion. This new theme pervaded the consciousness of Gandhi in the last two years of his life, while he was trying to quell the communal riots and the killing sprees that preceded and followed independence and partition. That divine character of the power of *ahimsa* was repeatedly stressed: it was a power 'immense and incomparable', 'a moral and spiritual force, motivated by infinite soul-force', and it possessed 'miraculous strength'.[65] In order to emphasise its superhuman power Gandhi frequently compared it to the weapons of man, including the atom bomb: it is a 'wonderful and unrivalled weapon', a force 'mightier than the force of arms however powerful', 'even a weapon like the atom bomb will prove ineffective against it, because it is a mightier weapon by far than the atom bomb'.[66] No wonder that its power was effective: it would 'completely liquidate the forces of enmity and evil', 'cure all our ills', and 'drive out the poison of hatred'.[67] In fact, 'if our non-violence were genuine and of the brave, the shameful things which are happening in India today would not have happened', as 'where ahimsa is perfect, there can be no failure'.[68]

There is another way in which the focus of this new non-violence had shifted. Previously, the effectiveness of non-violence, the non-violence of the weak, its moral power, depended upon its adoption by groups of people, the inmates of an ashram, the satyagrahis trained for a particular action, or the crowds engaged in mass agitation. On the other hand, the non-violence of the brave, that formidable 'infinite spiritual force', was 'inherent in every human being'. Therefore, a single individual could activate the immense power of non-violence, provided it was perfect.[69] It is very striking how much Gandhi's concern with non-violence during this period was not focused on teaching disciples or masses, but on upon his own non-violence. He stated it clearly that 'today he was seeking for a non-violent solution for his own sake alone. For the time being, he had given up searching for a non-violent remedy applicable to the masses.'[70] Very early in this stay in Noakholi, Gandhi clearly enunciated where he stood in relation to non-violence, and how this connected with his presence there:

I know positively that ahimsa is a perfect instrument. If it did not answer in my hands, the imperfection was in me. My technique was at fault. I could not discover the error from a distance. Hence I came here trying to make the discovery. I must, therefore, own myself in darkness till I see the light. God only knows when it will come.[71]

Gandhi was convinced that 'when *ahimsa* had been fully established it would completely liquidate the forces of enmity and evil' around him, and that as long as hatred was still rampant, the inference had to be that his own *ahimsa* was still defective. Again and again he came back to this conclusion that there still was something wanting in his non-violence, that there was 'a flaw,' 'a shortcoming', 'an ineptitude', an imperfection in the method of his own non-violence. 'Whenever *ahimsa* is found to have failed, that *ahimsa* cannot be perfect.'[72]

That is why he went to Noakholi, to find the flaw and eliminate it: 'To test myself, I am going to a village called Srirampur.' 'I am being tested. My truth and non-violence are being weighed in a balance which is much more accurate than any pearl merchant ever used.' He was there because non-violence 'could be tested only in such conditions [of violence and heinous crime]'. Although Noakholi 'offered an almost ideal situation for testing ahimsa',[73] months later in Delhi the test was still continuing: 'God has chastised me severely. I have not known a test more severe than this'.[74] The gruelling test continued. At the end of October 1947, he said to Congress leaders from Sind who had fled the killing and deserted their people:

God is really testing me, and if I am sincere in my effort to live up to my slogan of 'do or die' and if I am firm in my faith in Rama-nama, I will, if I can do nothing else, cheerfully sacrifice myself in this *yajna* of unity with the name of the Faultless and Formless Rama on my lips and not run away from its flames however fierce they may be.[75]

The test did not come to a conclusion, and on 11 November 1947, two months before his death, he wrote prophetically:

Who knows, my ahimsa might be tested at the fag end of my life. A proverb says that 'a dying flame burns the brighter before it burns itself out'. Maybe my end is approaching. I am fully prepared.[76]

CONCLUSION

Gandhi travelled a long journey of non-violence from his days in South Africa to his death. In South Africa, his practice of non-violence mostly remained below the threshold of clear consciousness, until it started to raise its head timidly towards the end. As soon as he was back in India, the many issues of *ahimsa* grabbed his attention, and never let him go again. It was an important decision to give the vow of *ahimsa* a prominent place in his ashrams, where it always successfully occupied a central spot. His application of non-violence to the struggle for independence did not have such a happy history. Initially he succeeded in training an elite group of satyagrahis steeped in non-violence. They performed at their best at the time of the Salt March. But the Congress movement could not as a whole adopt non-violence as a creed. Even when it was adopted as a policy, many only paid lip-service to it. Gandhi realised only too well that he had not succeeded in converting the masses to his belief.

Over the years he clarified his doctrine of non-violence by deciding on a great number of cases that were referred to him. He moved consciously away from the severely ascetic and uncompromising doctrines of Jain *ahimsa*. His own decisions stand out by the clarity and soundness of their reasoning, and by the deep humanity of their directives. He never forgot that people are embodied, have special bodily needs and weaknesses, and that they are part of a family and a society to which they are tightly bound by bonds of service and responsibility. He accepted that the human condition set limits to the morally acceptable application of non-violence.

As time went on, his concept of non-violence seemed to grow wider, as a result of the fact that various aspects of his spirituality such as renunciation, chastity, self-purification, and service coalesced more and more in his mind into one basic religiosity.

In the last years of his life, Gandhi's conception of non-violence underwent a striking change. During the years of his leadership of the Congress movement he preached non-violence to the Congress workers, and exalted it as a strong moral force which, if used by many people in concert, could have a decided influence on the British, and accelerate the liberation of India. In the last years of his life, he looked upon *ahimsa*, perfect *ahimsa*, as a potential spiritual force of great magnitude. It was a force that was latently present in all human beings, and could be activated by the person who allowed it to dominate all thought and action. Lost and despairing in the midst of the communal carnage that raged about him, Gandhi saw in perfect non-violence a sure way of mustering in his own person that divine spiritual force that could still stop the killings.

14

The Passion to Serve

We have seen how the importance of service in Gandhi's religion grew during his South African period. The idea sprang from his childhood under the influence of his mother, and was fostered by Vaishnavite stories and songs. The reading of Tolstoy and Salter strengthened the development, as did the various service practices he engaged in. As a consequence, he connected service with *moksha* for the first time in his letter to Jamnadas Gandhi in 1910. He repeated it more clearly in his first letter to him written in India, where he stated that in the final instance they are the same goal, looked at from different perspectives: 'The end [*sadhya*, what has to be achieved] is, from the lower point of view service of the people and, from the higher point of view *moksha*.'[1]

It took another three years before Gandhi brought this idea forward in a more public way, in his Foreword to a collection of Gokhale's speeches. There he presented it as an argument used by Gokhale to justify his Servants of India Society. Gokhale had proposed that 'every age had its predominant mode of spiritual effort best suited for the attainment of *moksha*.' He thought that in the contemporary age of colonial oppression 'popular awakening could be brought about only through political activity. If such activity was spiritualised, it could show the path to *moksha*'. He put it even more strongly: 'One who aspires to a truly religious life cannot fail to undertake public service as his mission, and . . . that service of the people is impossible without taking part in politics.'[2]

It was only in 1924, six years later, that Gandhi declared publicly his own conviction in an article in *Young India* entitled 'My Mission', which was his personal manifesto linking service with *moksha*:

> I am impatient to realise myself, to attain *moksha* in this very exis-
> tence. My national service is part of my training for freeing my soul
> from the bondage of flesh. Thus considered, my service may be
> regarded as purely selfish. I have no desire for the perishable king-
> dom of earth. I am striving for the Kingdom of Heaven which is
> *moksha* . . . For me the road to salvation lies through incessant toil in

the service of my country and therethrough of humanity. I want to identify myself with everything that lives . . . so my patriotism is for me a stage in my journey to the land of eternal freedom and peace.[3]

This connection of service with *moksha* having been made, was thereafter regularly repeated by Gandhi:

When I am a perfect being, I have simply to say the word, and the nation will listen. I want to attain that perfection by service . . . What is the aim of life? It is to know the self. In the words of Narasinh Mehta, 'so long as the essence of the Self is not realised, all our efforts are in vain'. This realisation of the Self, or Self-knowledge is not possible until one has achieved unity with all living beings – has become one with God. To accomplish such a unity implies deliberate sharing of the suffering of others and the eradication of such suffering [which in the article is described as service]. . . . No one has ever attained *moksha* by means of learning whereas many a soul did and does attain its salvation through service . . . Self-realisation I hold to be impossible without service of and identification with the poorest.[4]

This reiteration goes right though Gandhi's career, constantly linking service with *moksha*, which sometimes he called self-realisation or the realisation of God.[5]

Once Gandhi had clearly established the basic connection of service and *moksha*, he continued to enrich the concept in various ways. His study of the *Bhagavadgita* in the late 1920s led him to a re-interpretation of the concept of *yajna*, sacrifice, in that work. The ancient concept signified in the Vedas a sacrifice to the gods, which was a means of appeasing them and getting favours from them. In the *Brahmanas* this had been transformed into an exercise in sacrificial power, where the sacrificial formulas themselves, independently from the gods, were considered sources of cosmic power. Gandhi proceeded to reinterpret *yajna* in the following manner: it signified the offering, the dedication of an action in devotion to Lord Krishna. In his *Discourses on the Gita* he explained this new interpretation in great detail:

But a person may be eating with proper attention and yet we may say of him that he is, nevertheless, not eating. Of whom can we say this? Of one who eats as though he was performing a *yajna*, who offers up his action of eating to Shri Krishna, who eats with the feeling that he does so in obedience to the Lord's command. Or, such a person may also tell himself that it is not he, but his body, that is eating – the *atman* does not eat, or drink or sleep; he will then eat to serve others, to serve the lame, the crippled and the afflicted. That will be service of God, for God who dwells in the afflicted is also like them. That person's karma of eating will be in truth *akarma*, and will not bind him. If we aspire to be good, we must ceaselessly work to serve others, serve them in a perfectly disinterested spirit. We should not serve anyone with the hope that he, too, will serve us one day, but we may serve him because the Lord dwells in him and we serve that Lord.[6]

Service is a *yajna*, a sacrifice, because the action is not performed for selfish purposes, but for the sake of others. Because the Lord dwells in them, the act of offering becomes a sacred act, a liberating act consecrated to the divine. This presentation of service linked with the concept of *yajna* of the *Gita*, was repeated by Gandhi several times.[7]

This idea that the service of mankind and of every living being, was the real service of God, who dwells in all that lives, became from the late 1920s the theme that dominated Gandhi's concept of service. He called it the service of 'the others', of 'the lame and the afflicted', of 'all people in the world'. It was service of the country, universal service, service of all fellow beings.[8] He never grew tired of singing its praises:

Realisation means nothing but pure and selfless service of all living creatures . . . Realisation of Truth is impossible without a complete merging of oneself in and identification with this limitless ocean of life . . . Hence, for me, there is no escape from social service; there is no happiness on earth beyond or apart from it.[9]

The practice of service was not only one possible way among others to achieve *moksha*; for Gandhi it became the only way to liberation. When Maurice Frydman asked Gandhi if his aim was just humanitarian, sitting down in the village serving the villagers, Gandhi answered:

I am here to serve no one but myself, to find myself self-realisation through the service of these village folk. Man's ultimate aim is the realisation of God, and all his activities, social, political, religious, have to be guided by the ultimate aim of the vision of God. The immediate service of all human beings becomes a necessary part of the endeavour simply because the only way to find God is to see Him in His creation and be one with it. This can only be done by service of all . . . I am part and parcel of the whole, and I cannot find Him apart from the rest of humanity . . . If I could persuade myself that I should find Him in a Himalayan cave, I would proceed there immediately. But I know that I cannot find Him apart from humanity.[10]

To his close friend and relative Narandas Gandhi he wrote:

We thus arrive at the ideal of total renunciation and learn the use of the body for the purposes of service so long as it exists, so much that service and not bread, becomes for us the staff of life. We eat and drink, sleep and wake, for service alone. Such an attitude of mind brings us real happiness and the beatic vision in the fulness of time.[11]

Towards the end of his life, a new concern of Gandhi, his desire to live till age 125, became closely connected with his idea of service. This desire was first expressed by Gandhi rather as a throw-away line in his speech of 8 August 1942 to the All India Congress Committee, when he launched the Quit India Movement. Calling everyone to the impending struggle, he pointed out that it was not without danger, and continued: 'Believe me, friends, I am not anxious to die. I want to live my full span of life. According to me, it is 120 years at least.' He reiterated that desire in a similar off-hand way a month later on the occasion of his seventy-fifth birthday.[12]

Three years later, in March 1945, Gandhi finally explained his desire in Sevagram to a meeting of the All India Spinners Association. He excused, as follows, his decision not to be present throughout the proceedings. 'The reason is that I wish to live for 125 years so that I can serve the country longer . . . I earnestly endeavour to fulfil this wish of mine and to this end I try to conserve as much of my energy as I can.'[13] A couple of months later he explained himself further in an article published in *The Hindu*. There he stated that the idea came to him from the study of the *Ishopanishad*, which says at the start that 'Only doing works of service on this earth, you should wish to live 120 or 125 years.' Being a convinced naturopath, Gandhi believed in the feasibility of living the full span of life:

I have come to the conclusion, based on observation and scriptural reading, that when a man comes to that complete living faith in the Unseen Power, and has become free from passion, the body undergoes internal transformation. This does not come about by mere wish. It needs constant vigilance and practice. In spite of both, unless God's grace descends upon one, human effort comes to naught.[14]

Gandhi used his desire to live 125 years to urge people not to put too many unreasonable demands on him.[15] In an article in *Harijan* of February 1946, entitled 'Living up to 125', he reiterated the basic meaning of his wish: 'service in a spirit of detachment', stressing again and again that service must be accompanied by a spirit of total renunciation.[16] In a talk with a friend he expressed this with a sense of agony:

> I am filled with agitation; why could I not suffer this inner anguish with unruffled calmness of spirit? I am afraid I have not the detachment required for living up to 125 years . . . A burning passion coupled with absolute detachment is the key to all success.[17]

In fact, a few weeks later, pressure of work made him hurry and make a small mistake. This hit him hard, and 'he seemed, for the moment, to have lost confidence in himself and the belief that he would live for 125 years'. He felt it would take a long time to regain his lost confidence.[18] A few months later he was still doubting his capacity: 'If, however, I cannot overcome my passion and anger, I cannot live to be 125. In that case I ought to give up such an aspiration.'[19]

Gandhi's desire to live 'a full span' was fuelled by his desire for service. But in that last year of his life the Hindu–Muslim killings erupted continuously and he felt increasingly powerless. When his grand-niece Manu had to be operated on for appendicitis, he felt that it showed his own spiritual shortcoming: 'If Ramanama is firmly rooted in my heart, this girl should be free from her ailments.' After the operation he told Manu, 'Though I have no longer the desire to live for 125 years, as I have said again and again of late, my striving to meet death unafraid with Ramanama on my lips continues.'[20]

When on 2 October 1947 many people came to congratulate him on his seventy-eighth birthday, he felt he actually needed condolences instead, in view of the continuing communal slaughter:

> Many friends had hoped he would live to be 125, but he had lost all desire to live long, let alone 125 years. He was utterly unable to appropriate any of the congratulations showered on him. He could not live while hatred and killing marred the atmosphere.[21]

He told his friends that this was not done 'in a spirit of depression', but rather of helplessness: 'In that state I invoke the aid of the all-embracing power to take me away from this 'vale of tears' rather than make me a helpless witness of the butchery by man become savage.' He felt that 'today his words had ceased to carry weight, and if he was not able to render more service, it would be best that God took him away'.[22]

During his very last fast to death, just before his death, Gandhi felt that his wish for a long life may be revived. This fast was one more try to stop communal slaughter.

> Before I ever knew anything about politics in my early youth, I dreamt the dream of communal unity of the heart. I shall jump in the evening of my life like a child, to feel that the dream has been realised in this life. The wish for living the full span of life portrayed by the seers of old and which the seers permit us to set down at 125 years, will then revive. Who would not risk sacrificing his life of the realisation of such a dream?[23]

Gandhi went on to describe his dream of Ramraj, of Paradise on earth. When the leaders of the communities came across with a full promise of peace, Gandhi broke his fast, and he was ecstatic:

> How I wish that God will keep me fit enough and sane enough to render the service of humanity, that lies in front of me! If the solemn pledge made today is fulfilled, I assure you all that it will revive with redoubled force my intense wish and prayer before God that I should be enabled to live the full span of life, doing service of humanity, till the last moment.[24]

Gandhi's wish of longevity had sprung from the desire to serve humanity for a long time. It languished and withered away during that last year, when increasingly he felt that his efforts were ineffective, and his service was flawed because of his spiritual imperfections. The wish had a last flare-up in these final days after his last successful fast, because he felt that he had effectively served, and could go on serving his people for a long time to come. But his assassin was already waiting in the wings.

Conclusion:
A Homespun Shawl

The time has now come to pull together all the strands of Gandhi's religious endeavours, and uncover the basic design of his inner life, and the main passions and convictions that drove his relentless activity. His infancy and youth imprinted on his young mind a lasting image of his parents. His father's generosity, his love for his family, and his dedication to his public service were extraordinary. His mother's total surrender of her life to her family and to the poor and afflicted around her, with a total disregard of self, was to Gandhi the very ideal of religiosity. The external paraphernalia of Hinduism in temples and rituals rather repulsed him.

In South Africa, within a year after his arrival, pressed by the zealous Christian apologia of his friends, he was assailed by humiliating uncertainties and crippling doubts about religion, and deliberately set out to find lasting principles and sustaining certainties. With the help of Raychand and some serious reading, he distilled four fundamental principles of religion, that would remain the supporting pillars of his religious edifice throughout his life. First of all, the only real and permanent centre of religion is the spirit within man, not a god, or a book, or an organisation without. Secondly, the drama of religion is the fight between spirit and matter, between good and evil, not the clashes of sects, the disputes of theologians, or the frantic exertions of ritual. Thirdly, this fight for freedom can only be fought and won by personal moral action, not by ritual, the telling of beads, sentimental devotion, or mystical endeavours. Fourthly, the final and only purpose of religion is freeing the spirit from all the shackles of body, mind, and passions, so that it may find total freedom, and merge with the Absolute Spirit residing in man. About mid-way in his stay in South Africa, Gandhi started to seriously engage himself in that drama of religion. Gradually, but in final instance ruthlessly, he renounced sex and the intimacy of family life, all personal and family property, and his own personal ambition and security.

247

This determination to become a renouncer did not, however, lead him towards the social isolation and the spiritual solipsism of the *sannyasi*. There were other very strong forces that influenced his development. The most important living religious legacy from his parents, and in particular from the mother he adored, was an extraordinary spirit and life of service. Gandhi, who was at first overwhelmingly engaged in the defence of the rich Indian merchants, became more and more involved in protecting and serving the most lowly of the local Indians, with whom he increasingly identified himself. His desire for the liberation of his soul became more and more enmeshed with his desire for the liberation of his oppressed compatriots. This intense interaction was most fruitful. It produced the beginnings of a concept of political action that was startlingly original; the combination of service, non-violent action and soulforce as an all-encompassing ethic that was meant to achieve both personal *moksha*, and the political liberation of the downtrodden.

When Gandhi left South Africa for good, he had become totally different from the young man who arrived there twenty years earlier. Then he was a rather superficial youth with the great ambition of becoming a successful lawyer, who would be a worthy successor of his father and grandfather, and lead his family towards a new prosperity. That dream had been brutally shattered by his professional frustrations and humiliations in India. He then had practically no interest in religion, and he saw his exile in South Africa as a last chance to recover some of his dignity and revive his professional hopes and ambitions. But as his stay dragged on, his life and his horizons changed. He finally left the continent as a religious and political figure, famous in South Africa, in Britain, and in India. He had become a remarkably original and effective political leader who had successfully fought the South African Government with his new weapon of satyagraha. But he had developed at the same time into a startling renouncer with very firm convictions about religion and the meaning of life, whose philosophy and achievements had laid the solid foundations of the personality who would in the coming years be given the title of Mahatma.

Back in India, the first task he took up was to give concrete form to the ideals and the spiritual and political methodology he had created in South Africa. He founded the Satyagraha Ashram, which was to become the sacred place where his new Indian *sannyasis* would be trained, who would also be *satyagrahis*, combining the strictest vows of chastity, poverty, and non-violence with a total dedication to the service of the people. He started his political career with localised satyagraha agitations, which were successful and, five years later, brought him to national leadership. During this period of political growth, he increasingly experienced a confrontation with the forces of orthodox Hinduism. His jail terms gave him the leisure to study the scriptures and to think deeply about the gritty reality of Hinduism which surrounded him on all sides. By the mid-1920s he had rounded out his concept of Hinduism, and decided on the areas of confrontation with orthodoxy: he published two important articles on the essence of Hinduism, and two on the caste system.[1]

Two issues became dominant in his confrontation with orthodoxy: the system of untouchability and the question of the seat of religious authority, which were often intimately linked. Gandhi was always convinced that the practice of untouchability was totally immoral, and was the greatest shame of Hinduism. He never wavered in that conviction, and in the early 1930s he devoted his complete energy to campaigning for the abolition of untouchability and the opening of Hindu temples to the untouchables. In a period of twelve months he mounted no fewer than three dangerous fasts for that cause. In 1934 he declared that the devastation brought by the Bihar earthquake was 'due to the sin of untouchability'.[2] Gandhi's conviction about the moral horror of untouchability never changed, but after the early 1930s he did not again engage in a full-scale lengthy agitation.

From very early days many orthodox resented Gandhi's statements on religious matters, because they felt that he did not have the knowledge nor the authority to pronounce on questions relating to Hinduism. From his South African days Gandhi had come to the conclusion that all scriptures, even if inspired from above, were, as concrete texts, the only form in which they were available, human productions, and therefore by nature imperfect and fallible. He denied that those pandits and Shankaracharyas who claimed the right to interpret scripture and pronounce on matters of morality, had any such right on the basis of their titles only. He held that only he who faithfully and forcefully implemented the counsels of scripture in his own life, had the qualification and the right to interpret the texts. He claimed that right for himself because he had for many years put into practice the teachings of the *Gita*. It was in connection with untouchability that he put that right above everything. He was convinced that the regime of untouchability was so grossly immoral that it was impossible that it could have been promoted by divine scripture. Therefore, if anybody could conclusively prove that the Vedas or any scripture approved of the custom, then that scripture had to be rejected 'like a rotten apple'.[3] Gandhi not only claimed the right to interpretation; he amply exercised it by his lengthy commentaries on the *Gita*.

Besides those two main causes of friction with orthodoxy, Gandhi was not deeply concerned with other major facets of Hinduism. He did make his ideas on ritual, idol-worship, and the function of temples quite clear, but they did not take much of his attention, were generally moderate, and did not constitute a challenge to orthodoxy. Although he proclaimed the importance of the protection of the cow as a symbol of love for the downtrodden, he had his doubts about cow-protection organisations, because he knew that historically they were intimately connected with anti-Muslim agitations on the part of fanatical Hindus.

Our survey of Gandhi's religious thought and practice has shown that there is a fundamental and strong thread of asceticism that runs right through the whole fabric. The basis of this asceticism was his conviction that the essence of religion consists in the conflict of good and evil, spirit and matter. This ascetical trend had strong roots in the Jain dualism of soul and body, which deeply influenced Gandhi through the writings of Raychand. When Gandhi discovered the *Gita* as the best of scriptures, he declared that the subject of that text was none other than the epic fight between good and evil, matter and spirit, which was also the topic of the *Mahabharata*. Many of his religious ideas were rooted in that conception. The function of vows was the subjection of the body by the spirit. Chastity, *brahmacharya*, was the royal road to *Brahman* because it stood for the total control of all desires and passions. The liberation of the spirit from the shackles of matter was according to Gandhi the common ideal that inspired all religions, and the very basis of the doctrine of the equality of religions, and of the one common trunk of which all religions were but branches. That harsh ascetic approach was also evident in his reaction to the devastating Bihar earthquake of 1934, which he proclaimed to be a punishment by God for the sinfulness of the people of Bihar. Similarly, when he became a fervent apostle of Nature Cure Treatment, as the only remedy for illness, he justified his approach by claiming that all illness was in fact a consequence of sin.[4]

This thread of asceticism as a necessary aspect of the meaning of religion did not only run through Gandhi's religious conceptions, but it also deeply influenced his way of life. It lent radicalism and harshness to the demands he put on himself and also to his expectations from his close collaborators.

Gandhi ruled his personal life with the iron rods of abnegation and strict self-control, in order to achieve that great ideal of the *Gita*: the *sthitaprajna*, whose body and mind are totally controlled. He was not satisfied with denying himself all sexual enjoyment, but he also banished from his life all possibility of sensual savouring of food and all forms of bodily luxury. He totally abdicated any personal property, any right to private time, any pampering of the body, even in illness. It was this passion to renounce, and to be in total command of mind and body, that made him very distressed when he once suffered an involuntary emission of semen, and when he once made a small mistake by absentmindedness.[5] His relentless practice of subjecting his frail body to the torture of public fasts was probably the most glaring proclamation of his personal belief in extreme asceticism. He did three gruelling fasts within the span of one year for the cause of the untouchables. As a very frail old man, exhausted emotionally and physically by his arduous pilgrimages to the fields of Hindu–Muslim slaughter, he still subjected himself in the last five months of his life to two fasts to death, either of which could easily have claimed his life. It was that same passion for total renunciation that drove him into his solitary exile in Sevagram, probably one of the harshest, most miserable and most desperate little villages in India, where he wanted to share the life of the wretched.

Gandhi also tended to demand a similar harsh asceticism from his closest collaborators. This is evidenced in the constitution of the Satyagraha Ashram, with its strict vows and its demanding rules. At the beginning he banished all wedding celebrations from the Ashram precincts, because he thought that marriage itself was a denial of ashram ideals. His extreme asceticism drove him to consider the sensual attraction between husband and wife as 'unnatural' and their intercourse as 'extremely ugly'. Even the sex act engaged in specifically for procreation was 'contaminated with lust, and a violation of ahimsa'.[6] Total suppression of all sexual activity was necessary for spiritual growth. It distressed Gandhi greatly that after years some ashramites still longed for small luxuries, or spent some money on private needs. When he found that Kasturbai had kept a little money given to her for her personal use, he called it 'theft'.[7] His faithful secretary Mahadev Desai considered that Gandhi's spiritual ambition for his ashramites drove him constantly to reform, and that he was putting on them a strain that was becoming unbearable. In the earlier years Gandhi also tended to approve of the severe caste restrictions on interdining and intermarriage; they deserved his approval because they were agents of self-control, putting strict boundaries on human appetites.

But there was besides the harsh and demanding ascetic, another Gandhi, full of tenderness and mercy, who was surrounded and loved by many who clustered within the warmth of his presence. He delighted in playing with children and in nursing the sick and the desperate. This was the Gandhi who throughout his life fostered his memory and admiration for his mother, who remained for him the greatest exemplar of dedicated, selfless service. This tenderness and service progressively influenced the development of his ideas and actions, and thus wove themselves into the very fabric of his life.

In the matter of *brahmacharya* his harsh negativity towards marriage softened over the years. He was delighted by his discovery that sex for the purpose of procreation was in fact, according to the scriptures, compatible with being an avowed *brahmachari*. He now referred to marriage as 'a natural thing in life, a sacrament', and called the sex urge 'a fine and noble thing', which was only intended for the act of creation.[8] That more positive view of marriage was also evident in his total reversal of his earlier advice that among a married couple mutual consent was necessary for intercourse, but no such consent was necessary for abstention by one partner. He now recognised the lasting value of the marriage vows, which prevented either of the partners from taking a vow of abstinence without the consent of the other partner.

From early days Gandhi held that child-widows should have the right to marry again because their marriage was never valid. But this compassion for the plight of child widows led him to widen that right as much as he could. Although Hindu law permitted the widower to remarry, in early days Gandhi's moral view was that neither husband nor wife should marry again after the death of their partner. His compassion for the plight of many Hindu widows made him reverse that opinion. He now proclaimed that 'the rights or latitude allowed to widowers' by Hindu law, namely the right to re-marry, should be extended to widows too. The reason he gave was that 'otherwise widows become victims of coercion'.[9]

Initially Gandhi supported the very strict caste taboos on interdining and intermarriage as aids to self-control. But as time went on, and he became more and more familiar with the harsh reality, absurdity and tyrannical abuse of those caste laws, he withdrew his approval. Actually he ended up by declaring that the choice of dining or marriage partner was purely a matter of personal preference and decision, and he actively promoted intercaste marriages. Although he continued to believe in the ideal Hindu *varna* system, he ended up by totally rejecting the caste system. He felt that the division of society in a hierarchical ladder of many castes offended justice and non-violence. One should accept the fact that caste had to be eliminated, and that the *varna* system was in such decay that in reality only one single *varna* remained operative: that of Shudra, servant. His compassion for the untouchables and the lower castes brought Gandhi to that radical conclusion.

When he founded the Sabarmati Ashram for the training of satyagrahi monks who would be dedicated to the liberation of their own spirit and that of India, he wrote a constitution the harsh demands of which vied with those of the strictest of monastic orders. At first he was rather impatient with the imperfection of the inmates, but gradually he learned the humane acceptance of human weakness. His second foundation, the Sevagram Ashram, was much more relaxed by not imposing too many rules and regulations. Gandhi was much more inclined to accept human frailty, and one even hears a hint of gentle irony when he called it a *'pinjrapole'* – a retirement village for old and dying cattle.[10]

Non-violence was a basic imperative in Gandhi's life, both in the smaller circle of the Ashram and in the wider circle of political action. He abhorred any form of violence, and half of his public fasts were staged in response to acts of violence. In the application of the ideal of non-violence to the realities of life, Jainism tended to adhere to the harsh rule of mechanical literalness: every form of violence, whether intentional or accidental, unavoidable or deliberate, was evil. Gandhi rejected that dogma, but that did not prevent him from espousing a radical and wide-ranging definition of *ahimsa*. From his very first public speech on the subject he accepted that non-violence was a high and demanding ideal that comprehended not only a prohibition of physical violence, but also of all violence of speech and thought, and that it should embrace not only friends but also enemies. In political agitation, after initial high expectations, he came to accept that most members of the Indian National Congress were not able or inclined to adopt non-violence as a creed, but supported it only as a policy appropriate in certain circumstances.

It was in the application of case-law of violence and non-violence in human behaviour that Gandhi developed his balanced and humane guidelines. By 1926 he acknowledged that there were allowable breaches of non-violence under three headings: the necessities of the body for staying alive, the relief of excruciating and unremediable pain, and the duty of the protection of those under one's care. The third circumstance could sometimes actually allow the killing of attackers, and the second did provide for a form of mercy-killing, not only of animals but also of humans.[11] The driving force of his definition of the limits of *ahimsa* was compassion. As time went by, non-violence became increasingly identified with the positive attitude of love. He expressed this most eloquently in the conclusion of his autobiography:

> This much I can say with assurance . . . that a perfect vision of Truth can only follow a complete realisation of Ahimsa. To see the univer-

sal and all-pervading Spirit of Truth face to face one must be able to love the meanest of creation as oneself.[12]

If the Jain dualism of matter and spirit remained throughout his life an important basis of Gandhi's asceticism, what was the root of his tenderness and love? From the very start Gandhi distanced himself from rigid Jain dualism by his belief in the Absolute Spirit, *Brahman*, undefinable, impersonal and without qualities. That great Spirit underlay all reality, and was present within all human spirits as their essential centre. Gandhi became increasingly consumed by love for that Spirit. But how can one love an impersonal Absolute? There was a strong popular Hindu tradition that had answered that question: the Sants of *nirguna bhakti*, whose songs were Gandhi's favourites. Like Gandhi they were not interested in the confusion, complexity, and often sensuality of the Hindu pantheon and its avatars, neither were they interested in the metaphysical subtleties of Advaita Vedanta. But they chose the pure Spirit inherent in everything as the focus of their fervent devotion.

Gandhi added his own special variation to that *nirguna bhakti*. He combined it both with his own interpretation of the concept of *yajna* in the *Gita*, his most favourite scripture, and with his basic ideal of service. The *yajna* of the *Gita* is the loving dedication of all actions to Lord Krishna; thus it becomes the *bhakti* that leads to *moksha*.[13] Gandhi transformed that *yajna* into the dedication of all actions to the Spirit abiding in all. This Spirit can primarily be seen in the living beings of our world, especially in mankind. Dedicating all actions to the Universal Spirit meant to Gandhi making all actions into a service of mankind, of the people around us. Gandhi had thus created a *bhakti* that was not only free from all connection with superficial emotionalism or mythological sentimentality, but also rooted in moral action. This was a new and profound combination of three of the most important ingredients of Gandhi's religion: service, the *yajna* of the *Gita*, and the idea of the all-pervading *Brahman*. Gandhi's religion was thus totally centred on moral action of the highest order, the service of mankind. This total service would not only bring the servant to *moksha*, but it would at the same time advance the liberation of India, and eventually the establishment of *Ramrajya*, the perfect kingdom of God in this world.

When looking at the overall development of Gandhi's religion, it is necessary to set apart the last two years of his life. Although what was said in the preceding paragraphs remains applicable to those last years, a startling new element came to the fore. On account of the explosion of massive violence in India between Hindus and Muslims at the time of independence and partition, Gandhi had to witness the destruction of two ideals dearest to his heart: the unity of India and the peace between the communities. These were years of darkness and despair such as he had never experienced. Gandhi remained convinced that he could stop the violence, provided he could muster enough spiritual power. He felt sure that an enormous reservoir of spiritual divine power was available to him as long as he strove hard enough to conquer it. We have seen how in these years he repeatedly asserted that the divine power was accessible to whoever could bring to perfection the practice of *Ramanama*, of *brahmacharya*, of *ahimsa*, or of fasting. He convinced himself that if he did not succeed in his mission of pacification, it was because his practice of religion was imperfect and did not activate the fullness of that power. The assassin's bullet put a merciful end to that agony at a time just after his second successful fast, when he thought he may be achieving some success in stopping the carnage.

As we were pulling together the principal threads of Gandhi's religiosity, it soon became clear that the final result would not be similar to the one we get when we do the same with the teachings of the great philosopher Shankara, for instance. In Shankara's case we would end up with a beautifully woven tapestry, extremely complex, where every colour and every thread takes its proper place in a symphonic whole, that is yet simple as a *mandala*, a masterpiece of intellectual delight. With Gandhi it is totally different. Once, when Swami Yogananda interviewed him, and asked him very profound metaphysical questions, Gandhi prefaced his response with the following observation: 'I can only give what I may call a villager's answer.'[14] It is not surprising then, that the result of the synthesis in his case is more like a large, bulky homespun woollen shawl. At first it looks very plain to the eye, but we can detect the beauty of the strong patterns and the contrasting shades of folk art. With its knots and unevenness, it feels at first rough to the touch; but soon we can experience how effective it is in warming cold and hungry limbs. Gandhi combined in his frail body the ideals of total renunciation and of total dedication; the ideal of Shiva, Lord of ascetics in the harsh Himalayas, and the ideal of the Bodhisattva, who postponed his own liberation in order to devote himself to the removal of all suffering in the world.

Although we feel at the end of this long quest that we understand Gandhi better, we must admit that the paradoxes remain. Gandhi, Hindu to the core, was rejected by orthodoxy; believer in tolerant relativism, he was stubbornly dogmatic in his personal view of religion; fanatically non-violent, he accepted that sometimes violence may be a sacred duty; mercilessly ascetic, he was overflowing with tenderness. It was in his life and his actions that these paradoxes resolved themselves as on the loom of his life he doggedly criss-crossed the warp of asceticism with the weft of love. It was by looking at his actions that we discovered under the homespun shawl a giant who in our age gave active witness to the reality of the divine.

Appendix 1:
Gandhi's Questions to Raychand

[This translation is taken from G 1: 90-1, 'Questions on Religion'. The numbers are those used in Appendix 1 of G 32: 593-602, 'Gandhiji's Questions to Rajchandra and His Replies'.]

1. What is the soul? Does it perform actions? Do past actions impede its progress or not?
2. What is God? Is He the creator of the universe?
3. What is *moksha* [salvation]?
4. Is it possible for a person to know for certain, while he is still living, whether or not he will attain *moksha*?
5-7. It is said that after his death, a man may, according to his actions, be reborn as an animal, a tree, or an even a stone. Is that so?
8. What is *Arya Dharma*? Do all Indian religions originate from the Vedas?
9. Who composed the Vedas? Are they *anadi* [without origin]? If so, what does *anadi* mean?
10. Who is the author of the *Gita*? Is God its author? Is there any evidence that He is?
11. Does any merit accrue from the sacrifice of animals and other things?
12. If a claim is put forward that a particular religion is the best, may we not ask the claimant for proof?
13. Do you know anything about Christianity? If so, what do you think of it?
14. The Christians hold that the Bible is divinely inspired and that Christ was an incarnation of God, being His Son. Was He?
15-16. Were all the Old Testament prophecies fulfilled in Christ?
17. Can anyone remember his past lives or have an idea of his future lives?
18. If yes, who can?

19. You have given the names of some who have attained *moksha*. What is the authority for this statement?

20. What makes you say that even Buddha did not attain *moksha*?

21. What will finally happen to this world?

22. Will the world be morally better off in the future?

23. Is there anything like a total destruction of the world?

24. Can an illiterate person attain *moksha* by *bhakti* [devotion] alone?

25. Rama and Krishna are described as incarnations of God. What does that mean? Were they God Himself or only a part of Him? Can we attain salvation through faith in them?

26. Who were Brahma, Vishnu, and Shiva?

27. If a snake is about to bite me, should I allow myself to be bitten or should I kill it, supposing that that is the only way in which I can save myself?

Appendix 2:
Schedule of Gandhi's Fasts

DATE	PLACE	CAUSE	KIND OF FAST	TARGET, ISSUE
1913	Phoenix S. Africa	Misbehaviour of young ashram dwellers	Unconditional, 7 days	Reformed behaviour
1918	Ahmedabad	Mill-strikers' resolve collapsing	Conditional, lasted 3 days	Resolution of mill strike
1919	Ahmedabad	Riots during Rowlatt Satyagraha	Unconditional, 3 days	Penance for violence
1921	Bombay	Prince of Wales strike, communal violence	Conditional, lasted 4 days	Stop violence
1922	Delhi	Chauri-Chaura murder of policeman	Unconditional, 5 days	Penance for violence
1924	Delhi	Hindu–Muslim riots, Kohat killings	Unconditional, 21 days	Penance for violence
1925	Sabarmati Ashram	Misbehaviour of young ashram dwellers	Unconditional, 7 days	Reformed behaviour
1932	Yeravda Jail	Special electorates for untouchables	Conditional, lasted 6 days	Stop separate electorates
1933	Poona	Opposition to temple entry by untouchables	Unconditional, 21 days	Convert the orthodox
1933	Yeravda Jail	British restrictions on Gandhi's Harijan work	Conditional, ceased after 8 days	Force British to relent

259

1934	Wardha	Pandit Lalnath hit by Gandhi followers	Unconditional, 7 days	Penance for violence
1939	Rajkot	Civil resisters brutally repressed by Raja	Conditional, lasted 5 days	Raja to ease conditions
1943	Poona	British repression of Quit India riots	Unconditional, 21 days	British repression
1947	Calcutta	Hindu–Muslim riots and killings	Conditional, lasted 4 days	Stop violence
1948	Delhi	Hindu–Muslim riots and killings	Conditional, lasted 6 days	Stop violence

Notes

Introduction

1. M. K. Gandhi, *The Collected Works of Mahatma Gandhi*, 90 vols, Publication Division, Government of India. They were published between 1958 and 1982. (Hereafter all references to the *Collected Works* will be indicated as 'G', followed by the volume in bold type, followed by a colon and the page numbers.) This note refers to G **87**: 522. Jawaharlal Nehru, *The Discovery of India*, Meridian Books, London, 1960, p. 366.
2. G **25**: 202 and 514.
3. G **26**: 58; **25**: 86; **41**: 98.

Preamble: Infancy and Youth

1. Gandhi's autobiography, entitled 'The Story of My Experiments with Truth', appeared as a series of articles in *Navajivan* from 29 November 1925 to 3 February 1929. An English translation of these chapters was simultaneously published in *Young India*. The autobiography was frequently republished in one volume. We refer to this work as published in vol. 39 of the *Collected Works* of Gandhi in the following way: Auto., G **39**, followed by the page number. The reference for this note is Auto., G **39**: 165.
2. Auto., G **39**: 31.
3. Auto., G **39**: 33.
4. Auto., G **39**: 33.
5. S. N. Hay, 'Gandhi's First Five Years', in *Encounter with Erikson*, eds D. Capps, W. H. Capps, and M. G. Bradford, Santa Barbara, Calif., 1977, p. 71.
6. Joseph J. Doke, *M. K. Gandhi, An Indian Patriot in South Africa*, Government of India, 1967, p. 22.
7. Pyarelal, *Mahatma Gandhi: The Early Phase*, Ahmedabad, 1965, vol. 1, p. 201; quoted by S. Hay, 'Digging up Gandhi's Psychological Roots', *Biography*, (Honolulu), 6/3 (Summer 1983), p. 210.
8. Prabudhas Gandhi, *Jivannum parodh*, Ahmedabad, 1948, p.18; quoted by S. Hay in 'Gandhi's First Five Years', p. 87.
9. Mahadev H. Desai, *Day-to-Day with Gandhi: Secretary's Diary*, N. D. Parikh (ed.), Rajghat, 1968, vol. 1, p. 61; quoted by S. Hay, 'Digging up Gandhi's Psychological Roots', p. 214.
10. Auto., G **39**: 10–11.
11. Auto., G **39**: 24.
12. Auto., G **39**: 27.
13. Auto., G **39**: 11.
14. Auto., G **39**: 30.

15. Auto., G **39**: 33.
16. G **1**: 53–4.
17. Auto., G **39**: 37.
18. Auto., G **39**: 38–9.
19. Auto., G **39**: 47.
20. Auto., G **39**: 61.
21. Doke, pp. 50–1.
22. Auto., G **39**: 61.
23. See S. Hay, 'The Making of a Late-Victorian Hindu: M. K. Gandhi in London, 1888–1891', *Victorian Studies*, Autumn 1989, pp. 84–5.
24. Annie Besant, *Why I Became a Theosophist,* The Theosophist Office, Adyar, 1912, pp. 26–7 and p. 32. H. P. Blavatsky,*The Key to Theosophy*, 3rd rev. edn, London, 1920, pp. 2, 20, 42–5.
25. Besant, p. 35. Blavatsky, pp. 133ff.
26. Besant, p. 33. Blavatsky, pp. 8,10, 28, 47, 57.
27. Blavatsky, pp. 3 and 11.
28. Auto., G **39**: 61. *This Was Bapu,* compiled by R. K. Prabhu, Ahmedabad, 1954, p. 11; quoted by Hay, 'The Making of a Late-Victorian Hindu', p. 87.
29. Hay, 'The Making of a Late-Victorian Hindu', pp. 80–1.
30. Hay, 'The Making of a Late-Victorian Hindu', pp. 87–95.
31. Quoted in Hay, 'The Making of a Late-Victorian Hindu', p. 91.
32. Quoted in Hay, 'The Making of a Late-Victorian Hindu', p.94.
33. G **37**: 261.
34. See Gandhi's 'Preface to Shrimad Rajchandra,' G **32**: 1–13. See also Pyarelal, *Mahatma Gandhi: The Early Phase*, Ahmedabad, 1965, vol. 1, pp. 273–6.

Chapter 1: The Making of the Mahatma

1. Auto., G **39**: 173. Pyarelal, *Mahatma Gandhi, The Early Phase*, vol. 1, Ahmedabad, 1965, pp. 645ff.
2. Auto., G **39**: 139, 143.
3. Auto., G **39**: 164.
4. Auto., G **39**: 179.
5. Pyarelal, *Mahatma Gandhi, The Early Phase*, vol. 2, *The Discovery of Satyagraha – On the Threshold*, Bombay, 1980, p. xi.
6. Auto., G **39**: 193ff, 202.
7. D. G. Tendulkar, *Mahatma, Life of Mohandas Karamchand Gandhi*, Publication Division, Government of India, in 8 volumes, new edition, October 1969, vol. 1, p. 63. Henceforth we will refer to these volumes as Tendulkar, followed by vol. and page numbers.
8. Auto., G **39**: 229.
9. M. Swan, *Gandhi, The South African Experience*, Johannesburg, 1985, pp. 112–15.
10. Auto., G **39**: 252.
11. Auto., G **39**: 253.
12. Auto., G **39**: 253–4.
13. Auto., G **39**: 247; Tendulkar, vol. 1, p. 71.
14. G **12**: 45–52.
15. G **12**: 46, 48–9.

16. G 12: 46, 51.
17. G 12: 47.
18. Auto., G 39: 211.
19. *The Complete Works of Swami Vivekananda*, Almora, 1946, vol. 1, p. 263.
20. *The Complete Works of Swami Vivekananda*, p. 170.
21. M. G. Polak, *Mr Gandhi: The Man*, foreword by C. F. Andrews, Bombay, 1949, pp. 78-9.
22. G 9: 374.
23. G 10: 52.
24. Auto., G 39: 212.
25. Auto., G 39: 212.
26. Tendulkar, vol. 1, pp. 70-1, 66, 69.
27. Tendulkar, vol. 1, pp. 70-1, 77-8.
28. G 6: 430.
29. G 6: 433.
30. G 6: 434.
31. G 10: 32, 33, 34, 63.
32. Tendulkar, vol. 1, pp. 120, 128.
33. Auto., G 39: 238-9.
34. Joseph J. Doke, *M. K. Gandhi, An Indian Patriot in South Africa*, Publication Division, Government of India, 1967, p. 82. Swan, pp. 59-60.
35. Auto., G 39: 247.
36. Prabhudas Gandhi, *My Childhood with Gandhiji*, Ahmedabad, 1957, p. 43.
37. 'History of the Satyagraha Ashram', G 50: 189.
38. Prabhudas Gandhi, p 45.
39. G 50: 189. Tendulkar, vol. 1, p 128.
40. G 50: 190.
41. M. G. Polak, p. 127.
42. Auto., G 39: 255-7, 260-6.
43. Auto., G 39: 274.
44. G 10: 350.
45. See Chapter 2, pp. 50-62.
46. G 35: 172.
47. Leo Tolstoy, *The Kingdom of God is Within You, Or, Christianity Not as a Mystical Teaching but as a New Concept of Life*, trans. Leo Wiener, Noonday Press, 1961 (first published 1905), p. 380.
48. Tolstoy, pp. 105, 373.
49. Tolstoy, *A Confession, The Gospel in Brief*, and *What I Believe*, trans. Aylmer Maude, London, 1958, pp. 373, 283, 298.
50. William Mackintire Salter, *Ethical Religion*, London, 1905. The paraphrase by Gandhi was published in eight consecutive issues of *Indian Opinion* in January and February 1907. See G 6: between pp. 273 and 342.
51. Salter, p. 26.
52. G 6: 281.
53. G 6: 331.
54. Tendulkar, vol. 1, p. 46. Auto., G 39: 139, 143, 164, 232-6, 250-2.
55. Doke, p. 22.
56. Doke, p. 22.
57. Prabhudas Gandhi, pp. 72-9.

58. M. Chatterjee, *Gandhi's Religious Thought*, London, 1983, p. 15.
59. C. D. S. Devanesan, *The Making of the Mahatma*, London, 1969, p. 265.
60. See Gandhi's articles on 'Ethical Religion'. These poems are reproduced in the Hindi edition of the *Complete Works*, vol. 6, pp. 298, 304, 318, 322, 360.
61. See G **19**: 72. Auto., G **39**: 34, 61.
62. Doke, p. 99. Auto., G **39**: 34. For Indian methods such as *dharna*, see H. Spodek, 'On the Origins of Gandhi's Political Methodology: The Heritage of Kathiawad and Gujarat', *Journal of Asian Studies*, vol. 30 (1971), pp. 361–73; A. L. Basham, 'Traditional Influences on the Thought of Mahatma Gandhi', in R. Kumar (ed.), *Essays on Gandhian Politics*, Oxford, 1971, pp. 33–9.
63. G **5**: 461.
64. G **12**: 423.
65. G **6**: 293, 475, 448, 457.
66. G **7**: 67.
67. G **7**: 121–2.
68. Henry David Thoreau, 'Resistance to Civil Government', 1849. Gandhi's articles can be found in G **7**: 217–18 and 228–30. See G **7**: 252, 399, 401, 471.
69. G **8**: 35.
70. G **9**: 224–7.
71. G **10**: 52.
72. G **9**: 118.
73. G **9**: 243.
74. G **9**: 392.
75. G **9**: 474.
76. G **9**: 483. See also G **10**: 370.
77. G **9**: 507.
78. G **10**: 20–1.
79. G **10**: 37.
80. Devanesan, pp. 356–7.
81. G **8**: 244.
82. G **9**: 389, 423–4, 476, 477–82.
83. G **9**: 396.
84. James D. Hunt, *Gandhi in London*, New Delhi, 1978, pp. 143–72.
85. G **10**: 47–53.

Chapter 2: Bewildering Doubts, Convincing Answers, 1894–5

1. Auto., G **39**: 101.
2. J. D. Hunt, *Gandhi and the Nonconformists, Encounters in South Africa*, New Delhi, 1986, p. 29.
3. Auto., G **39**: 102.
4. Auto., G **39**: 112–13.
5. G **43**: 98.
6. Appendix 1 reproduces the list of questions as they are recorded in G **1**: 90–1. G **32**: Appendix 1, pp. 593–602, contains the questions and the English translation of Raychand's first letter. The Gujarati version of all three letters of Raychand is available in *Mahatma Gandhiji ane Shrimad-Raychandra*, published by Bhogilal Nagindas Shah, 1935.
7. H. B. Blavatsky, *The Key to Theosophy*, London, 1920, pp. 42 ff; Annie

Besant, *Why I Became a Theosophist,* Madras, 1912, p. 26.
8. Blavatsky and Besant *passim.*
9. Blavatsky, p. 28.
10. See Appendix 1, above.
11. Besant, p. 25.
12. Blavatsky, p. 135; Besant, p. 35.
13. Blavatsky, p. 57.
14. The full Gujarati text of Raychand's letters is available in *Mahatma Gandhiji ane Shrimad-Raychandra.* There is also a translation into English of the first letter in *Mahatma Gandhi and Kavi Rajchandraji, Questions Answered,* trans. Brahmachari Sri Goverdhandas, Srimad Rajchandra Gyan Pracharak Trust, Ahmedabad, n.d.
15. The Sanskrit text and English translation of this work is available in *Saddarshana Samuccaya, A Compendium of Six Philosophies by Haribhadra,* trans. K. Satchidananda Murti, Eastern Book Linkers, Delhi, 2nd rev. edn, 1986.
16. See G 32: p. 594 for the English translation. My translation is direct from the Gujarati version.
17. For a description of the *Guna* theory, see any work on the Samkhya system or any general work on Hindu philosophy.
18. Blavatsky, p. 57.
19. This third letter is available in the Gujarati volume referred to above in note 6.
20. We used the following edition of the text: *The Yogavasishtha of Valmiki,* ed. Wasudera Laxmana Shastri Pansikar, Munshiram Manoharlal, 3rd edn, 181. The two chapters we are concerned with are in vol. 1. We also consulted the following translation, to which we will refer under the abbreviation YV. *The Yoga-Vasishtha-Maharamayana of Vamiki,* trans. Vihari-Lal Mitra, vol. 1, Bharatiya Publishing House, Varanasi, 1976.
21. Auto., G 39: 114.
22. YV, p. 2.
23. YV, see esp. chs 4 and 8.
24. YV, Mumuksha Kanda, x, 22 and xi, 36.
25. YV, Mumuksha Kanda, xi, 72; xiv, 1–5, 42, 53.
26. YV, Mumuksha Kanda, xviii, 3; xix, 35.
27. *Panchikarana,* text and the Vartika with word-for-word translation, English Rendering, Comments and Glossary, 1962, Advaita Ashrama, Calcutta.
28. *Maniratnamala,* ed. Pandit Ramratna Sharma, Nemavar, 1914.
29. *Maniratnamala,* verses 10, 13, and 30.
30. Auto., G 39: 114.
31. Auto., G 39: 114.
32. Anna (Bonus) Kingsford and Edward Maitland, *The Perfect Way; or The Finding of Christ,* 4th edn, London, 1909.
33. Kingsford and Maitland, pp. 8, 39, 50.
34. Kingsford and Maitland, p. 38.
35. Kingsford and Maitland, pp. 43, 50, 75.
36. Kingsford and Maitland, p. 110; see also 51, 186, 212.
37. Kingsford and Maitland, pp. 219, 223–4.
38. Kingsford and Maitland, p. 21.
39. Kingsford and Maitland, pp. lxxi, 26, 29, 151.
40. Kingsford and Maitland, pp. 225, 13.
41. Kingsford and Maitland, pp. 219, 228, 248.

42. Leo Tolstoy, *The Kingdom of God is Within You, or, Christianity Not as A Mystical Teaching But as A New Concept of Life*, trans. Leo Wiener, the Noonday Press, 1961.
43. Tolstoy, pp. 100–2.
44. Tolstoy, pp. 102, 55, 319, 218.
45. Tolstoy, pp. 78–9.
46. Tolstoy, pp. 79, 366, 19.
47. Tolstoy, pp. 57–60.
48. Tolstoy, pp. 59, 61, 71–2.

Chapter 3: The First Definition of Hinduism

1. The lectures can be found in G **4**: 368–70; 375–7; 405–8; the Hindi version is available in the Hindi edition of the *Collected Works*, vol. 4.
2. Especially W. W. Hunter, *The Indian Empire, Its History, People and Products*, London, 1882.
3. G **4**: 370.
4. G **4**: 376.
5. G **4**: 376–7.
6. G **4**: 407.
7. The Hindi text, which is very similar to the original Gujarati, can be found in the *Collected Works*, Hindi edition, vol. 4.
8. G **4**: 408.
9. G **4**: 406.
10. G **4**: 408.
11. *Bhagavadgita*, ix, 26–7.
12. See G **6**: 273–342; see also the Hindi edition, vol. 6, 298–360.
13. G **12**: 126.
14. For a study of this *nirguna bhakti* see *The Sants: Studies in a Devotional Tradition of India*, eds K. Schomer and W. H. McLeod, Motilal Banarsidas, Delhi, 1987.
15. G **4**: 405, 370.
16. G **4**: 375–6.
17. G **11**: 189.
18. William Mackintire Salter, *Ethical Religion*, London, 1905. G **6**: 274.
19. G **6**: 274–5, 280, 300; G **26**: 58.
20. Salter, p. 26.
21. Salter, p. 48.
22. Salter, p. 113.
23. G **6**: 275, 285, 300.
24. G **11**: 126.
25. G **12**: 92–4, 125–7, 145–7, 154–6.
26. G **12**: 93, 126, 127.
27. G **12**: 126.
28. G **12**: 94, 155.
29. G **12**: 126.
30. See Chapter 2.
31. G **12**: 94, 155, 127.

Chapter 4: A New Definition of Hinduism: 1921

1. See Chapter 3.
2. G **19**: 327–32 and G **21**: 245–50.
3. G **19**: 327.
4. G **21**: 246.
5. G **19**: 327 and G **21**: 246.
6. G **21**: 246.
7. G **21**: 246.
8. G **19**: 329. See Chapter 2.
9. G **19**: 328.
10. G **21**: 246.
11. G **21**: 248.
12. G **10**: 30–1.
13. G **21**: 24 and G **19**: 328.
14. G **21**: 246; G **19**: 330; G **21**: 247; G **19**: 331; G **21**: 250

Chapter 5: Facing the Gritty Reality of Hinduism

1. G **16**: 161.
2. G **20**: 116.
3. G **75**: 431.
4. G **41**: 366.
5. G **35**: 37. See also G **21**: 104; G **26**: 516; G **51**: 337.
6. G **58**: 448–9. See also G **26**: 351.
7. G **21**: 249.
8. G **26**: 424–5.
9. G **26**: 424–5.
10. G **27**: 21.
11. G **31**: 102; G **41**: 292, 339.
12. G **41**: 339. About avatars, see Chapter 6.
13. G **51**: 10.
14. G **90**: 143–4.
15. Auto., G **39**: 31.
16. G **28**: 432.
17. G **54**: 50.
18. G **54**: 51, 129.
19. G **35**: 37.
20. G **21**: 233.
21. G **48**: 482–3.
22. G **48**: 482–3.
23. G **54**: 129.
24. G **54**: 51, 127.
25. G **35**: 37, 203.
26. G **54**: 129.
27. G **55**: 62–3.
28. G **54**: 129, 127.
29. G **54**: 128.
30. Tendulkar, vol. 4, 123.

31. Tendulkar, vol. 4, 131.
32. G **51**: 109.
33. G **16**: 276; G **18**: 385, 391; G **42**: 75-7.
34. G **8**: 10-13, about the Ganapati festival and Dussehra.
35. G **30**: 321; G **29**: 286; G **47**: 226.
36. G **50**: 269.
37. Auto., G **39**: 221-2; G **9**: 181.
38. G **13**: 69.
39. G **13**: 277-9.
40. G **13**: 301-3. Hindi edition of *Collected Works,* vol. 13, pp. 303-5.
41. G **13**: 94; G **14**: 73; G **17**: 471.
42. G **19**: 83-5, 174-6.
43. G **32**: 199.
44. G **14**: 73-7.
45. G **14**: 73-7.
46. G **14**: 73-7.
47. G **59**: 62. See also G **80**: 224.
48. Answers to letters, see G **24**: 400-3; **26**: 64-7, 538-41, 568-71; **28**: 60-3; **31**: 404-5; **35**: 258-63; **46**: 302-3; **51**: 350-1; **54**: 25, 130-4, 326-9, 348-50, 458-73; **56**: 46-9; **59**: 89-92; **62**: 142-3; **69**: 219-23. Public speeches and articles, see G **26**: 322-5; **34**: 510-13; **35**: 1-3, 80-2, 104-7, 259-63; **62**: 120-3.
49. G **59**: 60-7; G **80**: 222-4.
50. For reaffirmations of his basic doctrine see G **26**: 540; G **32**:199; G **34**: 511; G **35**: 81, 259-63, 517-25.
51. G **24**: 223-4.
52. G **24**: 400.
53. G **24**: 401-24.
54. G **24**: 402.
55. G **21**: 447.
56. G **26**: 540.
57. G **35**: 1.
58. G **26**: 132; G **364**: 110; G **57**: 23.
59. G **17**: 45. See also G **19**: 85, 151.
60. G **46**: 303.
61. G **51**: 351.
62. G **54**: 327.
63. G **14**: 74; G **26**: 65; G **35**: 1-3, 80-3, 104-6; G **35**: 261.
64. G **46**: 303; G **51**: 350; G **54**: 131, 327; G **59**: 63; G **62**: 121; G **69**: 220; G **80**: 222.
65. G **25**: 566.
66. Responses to letters: G **15**: 44-5; G **28**: 344-51, 376-81; G **31**: 212-15; G **41**: 494-7; G **54**: 238-41, 416-17; G **57**: 88-93, 250-1, 414-16; G **58**: 46-7; G **59**: 308-9. Speeches: G **14**: 73-7; G **18**: 438-9, 448-9; G **19**:148-55, 546-8, 569-75; G **20**: 269; G **21**: 132-5, 135-7; G **22**: 382-4; G **25**: 510-17, 566-9; G **26**: 260-3, 264-7, 348-51, 251-2, 477-82; G **27**: 102-3; G **28**: 178-9; G **34**: 416-17; G **35**: 94-6; G **48**: 296-8; G **56**: 408-9, 410-11, 467-8, 471-2; G **57**:169-70, 171; G **58**: 49-50, 132-7, 241. Articles: G **17**: 470-1; G **19**: 519-21; G **20**: 318-20; G **21**: 213-14, 232-3, 398-9; G **26**: 330-1; G **27**: 272-

5; G **29**: 292-3; G **52**: 346-51, 358-61; G **55**: 170-1; G **56**: 428-9; G **58**: 238-40; G **62**: 290-3; G **65**: 296-9.
67. G **19**: 149; G **21**: 213; G **26**: 330; G **29**: 292; G **41**: 495; G **56**: 411.
68. G **28**: 179.
69. G **19**: 547; G **34**: 416; G **48**: 298.
70. G **26**: 46. See also G **25**: 566.
71. G **19**: 547.
72. G **21**: 137; G **25**: 511; G **26**: 265; G **41**: 495; G **52**: 347; G **57**: 169; G **58**: 132, 238; G **59**: 308.
73. G **56**: 468.
74. G **57**: 7.
75. G **19**: 573.
76. G **25**: 511; G **26**: 480.
77. G **20**: 319; G **55**: 170.
78. G **26**: 265.
79. G **14**: 73-74.
80. G **26**: 64.
81. G **35**: 262.
82. G **35**: 263.
83. G **46**: 302-3; G **51**: 350-1; G **54**: 130-4, 327; G **56**: 46-8; G **59**: 60-7; G **69**: 220; G **80**: 222-4.
84. G **26**: 322; G **35**: 106.
85. G **50**: 225; G **59**: 63.
86. G **24**: 85-7; G **27**: 61-5; G **35**: 343-7, 310-13.
87. G **24**: 85; G **35**: 312.
88. Auto., G **39**: 22.
89. G **34**: 23. For a lengthy paper by Gandhi on Raychand, see 'Preface to Shrimad Rajchandra', G **32**: 1-13.
90. G **24**: 105; G **34**: 24; G **67**: 59.
91. G **24**: 105; G **49**: 327-8.
92. G **19**: 522; G **23**: 20; G **31**: 126; G **34**: 23. See Chapter 8.
93. G **28**: 263; G **24**: 105.
94. G **27**: 273.
95. G **27**: 274.
96. G **5**: 48.
97. G **13**: 187.
98. G **24**: 228-31, 264-6.
99. G **32**: 451, 459-62, 473-5.
100. G **32**: 515-6, 566-7; G **33**: 8-9, 90-91, 100-01.

Chapter 6: The Persistence of Advaita

1. See Chapter 3.
2. G **14**: 97; G **30**: 388, 510; G **32**: 162; G **34**: 92-3; G **41**: 125; G **54**: 165, 195; G **80**: 432; G **88**: 148.
3. G **32**: 162, 189, 226, 263, 273, 300, 308.
4. G **36**: 110. See also G **26**: 132; G **42**: 77; G **57**: 23.
5. G **45**: 13.

6. G **34**: 289; G **42**: 77. See also G **30**: 510; G **51**: 40; G **54**: 471; G **60**: 164.
7. G **32**: 228.
8. See D. M. Datta, *The Philosophy of Mahatma Gandhi*, Calcutta, 1968.
9. G **39**: 411–12 .
10. Quoted by T. M. P. Mahadevan in his excellent article 'The Advaita of Mahatma Gandhi', in *Gandhi Marg*, 13/4, October 1969, p. 167.
11. G **26**: 224; G **49**: 136. For the conversation with Fabri, see G **70**: 26–8, and the commentary in Chapter 10.
12. G **32**: 154–5.
13. G **32**: 162.
14. G **14**: 385; G **22**: 209, 271; G **26**: 224.
15. Auto., G **39**: 4.
16. Auto., G **39**: 4.
17. G **48**: 404.
18. G **48**: 405.
19. T. K. Mahadevan, *Gandhi My Refrain: Controversial Essays 1950–72*, Bombay, Popular Prakashan, 1973, p. 117.
20. G **50**: 36; G **59**: 43–4; G **61**: 81; G **71**: 321; G **78**: 7.
21. G **32**: 196.
22. G **37**: 349; G **71**: 321.
23. G **83**: 141. See also G **85**: 12.
24. G **89**: 273; G **84**: 236. See Chapter 13.
25. G **26**: 224; G **30**: 388.
26. G **37**: 348–9.
27. G **50**: 37, 238; G **76**: 334.
28. G **85**: 136–7.
29. G **88**: 148–9. See also G **88**: 324–5.
30. See Chapter 12.
31. G **12**: 126. See Chapter 3.
32. G **12**: 93–4.
33. G **32**: 188–9.
34. G **88**: 148.
35. G **41**: 94.
36. G **28**: 264; G **36**: 163; G **40**: 405; G **54**: 471; G **84**: 212; G **88**: 148.
37. G **32**: 189; G **36**: 163; G **41**: 94; G **54**: 471; G **88**: 148.
38. G **70**: 27; G **32**: 146; G **28**: 316.
39. G **32**: 289; G **41**: 95; G **32**: 351, 372.
40. G **49**: 327; G **32**: 305.
41. G **41**: 96; G **49**: 1375; G **12**: 126; G **41**: 97.
42. G **32**: 601.

Chapter 7: Scriptural Authority and 'the Voice Within'

1. See Chapter 3.
2. G **15**: 288.
3. G **28**: 314–21.
4. G **20**: 7–8.
5. G **24**: 70.

6. G **21**: 246.
7. G **28**: 316–17.
8. G **15**: 312–13.
9. Tendulkar, vol. 2, p. 111.
10. G **33**: 384; G **34**: 89; G **35**: 367; G **41**: 92; G **43**: 85; G **56**: 341.
11. G **24**: 320.
12. G **35**: 98. See also G **26**: 290; G **35**: 156; G **19**: 63.
13. G **32**: 228.
14. Tendulkar, vol. 4, p. 75.
15. G **52**: 9.
16. G **57**: 7.
17. G **52**: 9; G **64**: 397; G **31**: 156.
18. G **28**: 316.
19. G **28**: 316; G **51**: 344; G **56**: 341; G **53**: 396; G **51**: 344.
20. G **62**: 334. See also G **52**: 9; G **53**: 370; G **58**: 271; G **62**: 334; G **63**: 310; G **64**: 258.
21. Gandhi's works on the *Gita* are the following. *Discourses on the Gita*: G **32**: 94ff; *Anasaktiyoga*: (trans. with introduction and commentary), G **41**: 90ff; *Letters on the Gita*: G **49**: 111ff.
22. See J. T. F. Jordens, *Dayananda Sarasvati, His Life and Ideas*, Delhi, 1978.
23. G **34**: 395.
24. G **71**: 30; G **51**: 244.
25. G **64**: 75; G **34**: 395. Tendulkar, vol. 7, p. 77; G **56**: 341.
26. G **28**: 316.
27. G **71**: 29; G **32**: 146, 31.
28. G **51**: 324–5. For the place Gandhi gives to *bhakti*, see Chapter 6.
29. G **58**: 17.
30. G **64**: 259–60, 263–4, 289–90, 304–5.
31. G **64**: 258–9.
32. G **64**: 263, 264, 290.
33. G **54**: 273.
34. G **26**: 289; G **28**: 218; G **58**: 141; G **32**: 100, 154.
35. G **63**: 339.
36. G **32**: 154.
37. G **34**: 89.
38. G **15**: 288.
39. See G **18**: 125, 195; G **21**: 515; G **27**: 316; G **28**: 320.
40. For Gandhi's conception of Krishna and of *bhakti* see Chapter 6.
41. G **31**: 156–7.
42. G **41**: 92, 100.
43. G **45**: 96.
44. G **26**: 140.
45. G **50**: 326.
46. G **18**: 112.
47. G **49**: 85.
48. G **49**: 311.
49. G **48**: 405; G **51**: 316. See also G **52**: 10.
50. Tendulkar, vol. 3, p. 198.
51. G **55**: 254.

52. G **55**: 255-65.
53. See Appendix 2 for a schedule of Gandhi's fasts, and Chapter 10 for a detailed treatment of them.
54. Auto., G **39**: 342.
55. Tendulkar, vol. 2, pp. 68, 148. Pyarelal, *The Epic Fast*, Ahmedabad, 1932, p. 11.
56. G **55**: 256.
57. G **56**: 182, 468; G **57**: 227; G **63**: 58; G **65**: 98.
58. G **67**: 75; G **68**: 172.
59. G **90**: 408-9.
60. T. K. Mahadevan, 'Gandhi – A Modernist Heresy', in Donald H. Bishop (ed.), *Indian Thought, An Introduction*, New York, Toronto, 1975, p. 360.

Chapter 8: Religious Pluralism

1. Pyarelal, *Mahatma Gandhi*, vol.1, *The Early Phase*, Ahmedabad, 1965, pp. 213ff. Besides Gandhi's autobiography, Pyarelal's work and C. D. S. Devanesan, *The Making of the Mahatma*, London, 1969, are the best sources for the details of this paragraph. See Introduction.
2. See Chapter 2 for details.
3. G **32**: 598.
4. See Mallishena Suri's *Syadvadamamjari*, ed. J. C. Jain, vol. 12 of the *Shrimad Rajchandra Jain Shastamala*, Anand, 1970: Biographical Sketch of Rajchandra, p. 9.
5. G **32**: 4, 11, 13.
6. G **7**: 338.
7. See Chapter 5.
8. G **21**: 250; G **23**: 530; G **27**: 61; G **28**: 194; G **35**: 166, 254.
9. G **4**: 370; G **23**: 20; G **34**: 24.
10. *Young India*, 21 January 1926, p. 30. Quoted in Pyarelal, p. 277.
11. G **26**: 324; G **23**: 485. See also G **26**: 131; G **23**: 485.
12. G **44**: 398. See also G **12**: 127; G **23**: 196; G **24**: 139; G **32**: 11; G **44**: 167; G **45**: 223; G **72**: 254.
13. G **13**: 220; G **35**: 166, 254; G **36**: 164; G **23**: 485.
14. G **28**: 194; G **37**: 224.
15. G **35**: 166.
16. G **44**: 166.
17. G **64**: 204.
18. G **86**: 155.
19. G **44**: 166.
20. G **57**: 17; G **64**: 203, 420; G **72**: 254; G **85**: 31 ; G **86**: 155.
21. G **44**: 190.
22. G **45**: 223.
23. G **72**: 253.
24. G **25**: 86 ; G **64**: 75 ; G **44**: 167.
25. G **23**: 196, 485.
26. G **24**: 139; G **25**: 202.
27. G **41**: 98. See also G **15**: 317; G **29**: 444 ; G **32**: 228.

28. G **28**: 316; G **51**: 344; G **56**: 341; G **28**: 316; G **32**: 31, 146; G **71**: 29.

Chapter 9: The Ashram-dweller

1. See Chapter 3.
2. G **50**: 190.
3. B. R. Nanda, *Mahatma Gandhi, A Biography*, London, 1958, p. 134.
4. Auto., G **39**: 134.
5. G **13**: 91, 94. See also G **19**: 151, 331; G **25**: 512, 567.
6. G **13**: 229.
7. G **13**: 91–2, 231.
8. G **13**: 93, 95.
9. G **50**: 197, 199. See also G **34**: 418; G **36**: 305; G **42**: 411; G **50**: 68, 245; G **59**: 17.
10. J. M. Brown, *Prisoner of Hope*, New Haven and London, 1989, p. 199.
11. G **55**: 302. See Nanda, p. 293; Tendulkar, vol. 3, p. 20.
12. G **36**: 410; G **50**: 232.
13. G **36**: 398–410.
14. G **50**: 222. See Brown, p. 101, and Nanda, p. 136.
15. G **50**: 198.
16. G **50**: 209. See Chapter 10 for fasts. G **40**: 211; Brown, p. 200; G **40**: 209, 210; G **55**: 104.
17. Brown, pp. 200, 264.
18. R. M. Thomson, 'Gandhi at Sevagram: "India in a Village"', *Gandhi Marg*, vol. 2, 1980, p. 435.
19. G **40**: 212.
20. G **55**: 288.
21. G **55**: 294, 303.
22. G **55**: 310.
23. Nanda, p. 364.
24. Nanda, pp. 364–5.
25. B. R. Nanda, 'Gandhi Goes to Sevagram', *Gandhi Marg*, 9/2, May 1987, pp. 101–2.
26. Thomson, pp. 433–4.
27. Pyarelal, 'Gandi's Last Experiment: Sevagram Ashram', *The Illustrated Weekly of India*, 2 December 1962, p. 21.
28. Thomson, p. 436.
29. Nanda, 'Gandhi Goes to Sevagram', p. 103.
30. Mahadev Desai, 'At Sevagram', in *Gandhiji, His Life and Work*, eds D. G. Tendulkar et al., Bombay, 1944, p. 248.
31. Thomson, p. 437.
32. Desai, pp. 256–8, 248; Nanda, 'Gandhi Goes to Sevagram', p. 105.
33. Nanda, 'Gandhi Goes to Sevagram', p. 108.
34. G **75**: 139–41; G **75**: 232.
35. Pyarelal, p. 23.
36. See G **74**: 189; G **81**: 139; G **84**: 304. See also G **80**: *passim*,containing a great number of letters trying to deal with these problems, and G **83**: 193, about half-yearly absences. See also Martin Green, *Gandhi, Voice of a New Age Revolu-*

tion, New York, 1993, pp. 339–41, for the brooding intensity of the relationships between Gandhi, his secretary Pyarelal, and Pyarelal's sister Dr Sushila Nayar.

37. G **90**: 349, 383.
38. Thomson, p. 439.
39. G **63**: 417.
40. G **74**: 310.
41. Pyarelal, p. 32; Nanda, 'Gandhi Goes to Sevagram', p. 108. For attempts at assessing the results, see Thomson, pp. 444–6; Pyarelal, p. 23, and Desai, p. 259.
42. G **63**: 240; G **80**: 397.

Chapter 10: Calling on the Divine Power

1. Auto., G **39**: 37, 44, 52.
2. G **12**: 238.
3. G **13**: 325–35.
4. B. R. Nanda, *Mahatma Gandhi, A Biography*, London, 1958, p, 133.
5. G **15**: 76–7.
6. G **30**: 111, 149; G **31**: 140; G **40**: 355.
7. G **41**: 272–4.
8. M. Chatterjee, *Gandhi's Religious Thought*, London, 1983, p. 69.
9. G **44**: 219–21.
10. For details and discussion, see Raghavan Iyer, *The Moral and Political Thought of Mahatma Gandhi*, 2nd edn, London, New York, 1983, pp. 75–80. Chatterjee, pp. 68–70.
11. G **44**: 264–5.
12. See Padmanabh S. Jain, *The Jaina Path of Purification*, Delhi, 1979, pp. 157–87.
13. G **50**: 21; Tendulkar, vol. 7, p. 28; G **86**: 169; see also Chapter 9.
14. G **85**: 420. See G **31**: 225; G **34**: 418; G **36**: 305; G **50**: 68; G **86**: 201. See also Tendulkar, vol. 6, pp. 307–8.
15. G **34**: 418.
16. G **64**: 307.
17. G **42**: 411–12.
18. G **50**: 245–6.
19. G **70**: 26–28.
20. G **50**: 246.
21. Auto., G **39**: 24, 63, 88. *Navajivan*, G **27**: 108–13. Auto., G **39**: 274.
22. G **12**: 375.
23. G **23**: 302.
24. G **24**: 117–19; G **27**: 108–13.
25. G **23**: 303; G **25**: 112; G **26**: 44, 504; G **32**: 170; G **34**: 162; G **51**: 249; G **54**: 112; G **57**: 197; etc.
26. G **24**: 119; G **25**: 134; G **26**: 7, 504; G **32**: 265; G **50**: 326; G **83**: 407; G **84**: 91.
27. G **29**: 434. See also G **26**: 63; G **52**: 223.
28. G **26**: 28, 43.

29. G **28**: 447; G **84**: 202.
30. G **31**: 511; G **36**: 296; G **44**: 302–3; G **84**: 190.
31. G **34**: 163; G **58**: 290.
32. Tendulkar, vol. 7, pp. 81ff.
33. G **83**: 176.
34. G **83**: 234, 413; G **84**: 203, 456; G **88**: 185.
35. G **88**: 272.
36. G **87**: 468; G **90**: 343.
37. G **87**: 401. See also G **87**: 468.
38. G **87**: 521–2.
39. G **84**: 24; G **85**: 421; See also G **84**: 236.
40. G **83**: 235, 263, 413; G **84**: 202; G **89**: 373.
41. G **89**: 273.
42. G **84**: 180.
43. G **84**: 24, 236.
44. G **84**: 237, 91; G **85**: 187; G **88**: 185.
45. G **89**: 272.
46. G **85**: 421; G **89**: 500.
47. G **90**: 520.

Chapter 11: The Potency of Perfect Chastity

1. G **12**: 45–52.
2. G **10**: 52.
3. G **13**: 229; G **30**: 572; G **73**: 69. See also G **17**: 539.
4. G **17**: 54.
5. G **23**: 102; G **29**: 415; G **30**: 235–6.
6. G **30**: 143. See also G **17**: 347; G **18**: 347; G **30**: 143; G **36**: 389.
7. G **44**: 69; G **32**: 359; G **62**: 159.
8. G **26**: 194.
9. G **26**: 196. See also G **30**: 84–8.
10. G **38**: 88–9.
11. Tendulkar, vol. 4, pp. 45–63.
12. G **62**: 247.
13. G **62**: 261, 348; G **65**: 316; G **67**: 156.
14. G **75**: 380; G **62**: 297.
15. G **30**: 143.
16. G **66**: 70. See also G **82**: 19–20.
17. G **14**: 449.
18. G **17**: 423.
19. G **23**: 523–4.
20. G **23**: 527.
21. See also G **30**: 35, 216, 258.
22. G **23**: 524.
23. G **41**: 69.
24. G **41**: 179.
25. G **87**: 241.
26. G **17**: 534.

27. G **80**: 78. See also G **79**: 36.
28. G **82**: 86. See also G **82**: 162, 433; G **84**: 388-9.
29. G **17**: 327; G **24**: 116.
30. G **30**: 235; G **31**: 180. See also G **33**: 414, 429; G **44**: 70.
31. G **26**: 144. See also G **24**: 117; G **23**: 102.
32. G **31**: 180.
33. G **33**: 415; G **34**: 197; G **55**: 41; G **67**: 196; G **70**: 288; G **73**: 70.
34. G **88**: 148-9.
35. G **70**: 313.
36. N. K. Bose, *My Days With Gandhi*, Calcutta, 1953, p. 204.
37. G **79**: 213.
38. See Erik H. Erikson, *Gandhi's Truth, On the Origins of Militant Nonviolence*, New York, 1969.
39. G **67**: 194-8.
40. G **79**: 193, 222.
41. G **79**: 159.
42. G **79**: 193.
43. G **79**: 212, 216, 192, 220.
44. Bose, p. 43.
45. Pyarelal, *Mahatma Gandhi, The Last Phase*, vol. 1, Ahmedabad, 1956, pp. 575-6.
46. Bose, p. 113; Pyarelal, p. 177.
47. G **87**: 16; Pyarelal, p. 798.
48. Pyarelal, p. 470; G **86**: 335; Bose, p. 96.
49. G **86**: 415, 453, 466, 467, 476; G **87**: 13. Pyarelal, pp. 431, 577, 585, 586.
50. Pyarelal, p. 431; G **86**: 466, 476; G **87**: 14, 104.
51. G **86**: 414; G **88**: 348; G **90**: 376, on 7 January 1948.
52. G **87**: 14, 15, 384, 462.

Chapter 12: The Power of Fasting

1. G **16**: 207, 230; G **17**: 104, 110.
2. Tendulkar, vol. 2, p. 218; G **26**: 294-5; G **50**: 194.
3. Tendulkar, vol. 1, p. 219.
4. Tendulkar, vol. 1, p. 220.
5. Auto., G **39**: 342. It is instructive to compare this account in the autobiography with another one based on Mahadev Desai's notes, as told by B. R. Nanda, *Mahatma Gandhi, A Biography*, London, 1958, p. 164: 'One of Gandhi's colleagues overheard a worker remark: "After all Gandhiji and Anasuyabehn have nothing to lose. They move about in cars and have enough to eat." When this remark was conveyed to Gandhi he was filled not with anger but with anguish. The meeting under the bulbul tree that afternoon was sparsely attended and despair was writ large upon the audience. It was at this moment that Gandhi announced that he would undertake a fast. Had he not declared at the beginning of the strike that if it led to starvation he would be the first to starve? The object of the fast was to rally the workers. Nevertheless, it could not but affect the mill owners some of whom respected and even loved Gandhi. The result was an unintended but definite pressure on the mill owners.'

6. See note 5. See also Auto., G **39**: 343.
7. G **55**: 396.
8. See Appendix 2.
9. Tendulkar, vol. 3, pp. 160-3.
10. Tendulkar, vol. 3, pp. 161, 163.
11. Tendulkar, vol. 3, p. 164, 168; see also G **55**: 411.
12. Tendulkar, vol. 3, p. 174.
13. Tendulkar, vol. 3, p. 180.
14. Tendulkar, vol. 3, p. 191.
15. Tendulkar, vol. 3, p. 189.
16. See Chapter 8, where this claim is discussed.
17. G **55**: 74, 135, 156-7, 257-8; Tendulkar, vol. 3, pp. 180, 185.
18. Tendulkar, vol. 3, p. 191.
19. G **55**: 258.
20. G **55**: 258.
21. Tendulkar, vol. 3, p. 215.
22. G **55**: 411
23. Tendulkar, vol. 3, pp. 216-17.
24. Tendulkar, vol. 5, pp. 52, 57.
25. Tendulkar, vol. 5, p. 106.
26. Tendulkar, vol. 6, p. 151.
27. Tendulkar, vol. 6, pp. 185-8, 193, 195.
28. G **77**: 69.
29. Tendulkar, vol. 6, p. 195.
30. Tendulkar, vol. 6, pp. 191, 195.
31. Tendulkar, vol. 1, pp. 253-5.
32. Tendulkar, vol. 2, pp. 85-6; G **22**: 425.
33. Tendulkar, vol. 3, pp. 281-2; G **58**: 301.
34. Tendulkar, vol. 2, pp. 68, 148; Tendulkar, vol. 8, pp. 105, 246.
35. Tendulkar, vol. 2, p. 69.
36. Tendulkar, vol. 8, p. 104.
37. Tendulkar, vol. 8, p. 247.
38. Tendulkar, vol. 1, p. 256.
39. G **22**: 425.
40. Tendulkar, vol. 2, p. 148.
41. Tendulkar, vol. 2, p. 152. G **25**: 183, 200.
42. G **55**: 257.
43. Tendulkar, vol. 3, pp. 180, 185, 191.
44. G **55**: 74, 135, 156, 157, 257, 258.
45. G **77**: 69.
46. G **54**: 414.
47. G **69**: 51.
48. G **25**: 259; G **53**: 259; G **55**: 157, 410.
49. G **55**: 412.
50. G **21**: 481.
51. G **22**: 425.
52. Tendulkar, vol. 2, p. 148.
53. Tendulkar, vol. 3, p. 164.
54. G **54**: 328.

55. G **54**: 415.
56. G **69**: 51. Tendulkar, vol. 8, p. 246.
57. G **73**: 91
58. G **55**: 412.
59. G **69**: 51.
60. G **73**: 91, and note 1.
61. G **73**: 151; G **76**: 318–19; G **78**: 225; G **83**: 401.
62. G **89**: 134.
63. G **89**: 141, 150.
64. G **90**: 202.
65. Tendulkar, vol. 8, p. 247.
66. G **90**: 419.
67. G **90**: 413.
68. G **90**: 421.
69. G **90**: 435.
70. G **89**: 141; G **90**: 413, 435.

Chapter 13: Never Enough Non-violence

1. G **4**: 408.
2. G **12**: 127.
3. G **4**: between 272 and 342.
4. G **9**: 243 and note 1.
5. G **10**: 52.
6. G **11**: 101.
7. G **13**: 91–3.
8. Auto., G **39**: 220.
9. G **50**: 205.
10. G **12**: 158.
11. G **29**: 201.
12. G **13**: 37–8.
13. G **13**: 17.
14. P. V. Kane, *History of Dharmashastra*, vol. 5, part 2, p. 420, Poona, 1962.
15. M. Swan, *Gandhi: The South African Experience*, Johannesburg, 1985, p. 169.
16. G **12**: 531–2.
17. G **12**: 554–5.
18. J. M. Brown, *Gandhi, Prisoner of Hope*, New Haven and London, 1989, p. 125.
19. G **14**: 462–3, 484–5, 504–5, 474–7, 509–10.
20. C. F. Andrews, *Mahatma Gandhi, His Life and Ideas*, Delhi, 1987, p. 145.
21. G **14**: 463, 474, 510.
22. G **14**: 462.
23. G **14**: 485.
24. G **14**: 477, 511, 463.
25. Auto., G **39**: 278–80, 352–7.
26. Tendulkar, vol. 1, pp. 227–8.
27. G **14**: 477.
28. G **13**: 228–9.

29. G **14**: 505; G **22**: 186-7; G **14**: 509.
30. G **26**: 334; G **23**: 24-5; G **14**: 509; G **26**: 334.
31. G **31**: 487; G **38**: 68-9.
32. G **31**: 488, 545.
33. G **31**: 545.
34. G **32**: 42; G **49**: 430; G **50**: 207.
35. G **31**: 488, 506; G **32**: 72; G **31**: 544.
36. G **66**: 438.
37. G **31**: 545.
38. G **37**: 381-6.
39. G **10**: 30-1.
40. G **87**: 357-9.
41. G **16**: 508.
42. G **21**: 248.
43. G **26**: 545, See also G **34**: 125 and 55, 407.
44. G **14**: 3, 58, 80; G **18**: 117, 128; G **23**: 473-4; G **27**: 18-19. See also Tendulkar, vol. 2, pp. 378-9 and vol. 6, pp. 55-6.
45. See G **26**: 35-6; G **28**: 404-5; G **50**: 229-32; Tendulkar, vol.2, pp. 267-8.
46. G **67**: 194-8.
47. Raghavan Iyer, *The Moral and Political Thought of Mahatma Gandhi*, 2nd edn, London, 1983, p. 226.
48. Auto., G **39**: 4, 330, 363, 220.
49. Auto., G **39**: 401-2.
50. G **44**: 59.
51. G **13**: 229.
52. G **13**: 295.
53. G **14**: 476.
54. Tendulkar, vol. 3, p. 17.
55. G **32**: 380.
56. G **67**: 194-8.
57. G **84**: 393-4.
58. G **86**: 134, 138, 183, 196, 197, 278, 335; G **88**: 209, 298; G **90**: 522.
59. G **14**: 475.
60. See G **85**: 55; G **86**: 416; G **88**: 116, 160, 163, 213, 300, 305, 397; G **89**: 63; G **90**: 130, 337, 502.
61. G **85**: 55.
62. G **85**: 203.
63. G **85**: 342-3.
64. G **88**: 331.
65. G **87**: 250, 295; G **89**: 443, 452.
66. G **87**: 371, 440; G **88**: 160; G **89**: 493; G **90**: 165, 522.
67. G **87**: 279; G **88**: 48, 116.
68. G **88**: 212; G **90**: 34.
69. G **87**: 295, 300, 331.
70. G **86**: 211-12.
71. G **86**: 183.
72. G **86**: 279, 262, 196, 335; G **88**: 117; G **89**: 121, 397, 384; G **90**: 34.
73. G **86**: 138, 263, 264, 416.
74. G **88**: 289; G **89**: 121.
75. G **89**: 437.

76. G **90**: 5.

Chapter 14: The Passion to Serve

1. G **13**: 43.
2. G **14**: 201.
3. G **23**: 349.
4. G **27**: 449; G **28**: 385; G **30**: 66; G **31**: 511.
5. See G **41**: 291; G **44**: 104; G **60**: 2, 106, 159; G **63**: 240; G **80**: 438.
6. G **32**: 222.
7. G **32**: 356; G **34**: 410; G **44**: 240, 259-60.
8. G **32**: 322; G **34**: 90; G **35**: 173; G **36**: 296; G **41**: 291; G **44**: 260; G **46**: 255; G **48**: 52; G **51**: 372.
9. G **60**: 2, 106, 159.
10. G **63**: 240.
11. G **44**: 104.
12. Tendulkar, vol. 6, pp. 166, 286.
13. G **79**: 296.
14. G **80**: 299-300.
15. G **83**: 291; 384, 385; G **84**: 20; G **85**: 347.
16. G **83**: 118. See also G **83**: 318.
17. G **85**: 370. See also G **85**: 382.
18. G **85**: 455.
19. G **87**: 497.
20. G **87**: 468, 522.
21. Tendulkar, vol. 8, p. 142.
22. Tendulkar, vol. 8, p. 146.
23. Tendulkar, vol. 8, p. 256.
24. Tendulkar, vol. 8, p. 270.

Conclusion: A Homespun Shawl

1. 'Who is a Sanatani Hindu?', G **19**: 327-32. 'Hinduism', G **21**: 240-50. 'The Caste System', G **19**: 83-5. 'Caste Versus Class', G **19**: 174-6.
2. D. G. Tendulkar, *Mahatma*, vol. 3, p. 249.
3. G **57**: 7.
4. G **83**: 176.
5. G **62**: 212, 372, 428; G **85**: 455.
6. G **30**: 236; G **32**: 359; G **62**: 159.
7. G **40**: 210.
8. G **62**: 297.
9. G **41**: 179.
10. G **90**: 349.
11. G **31**: 488, 506, 545.
12. Auto., G **39**: 402.
13. See *Bhagavadgita*, chapter 9.
14. G **61**: 392.

Index

282 *Index*

(Gandhi *continued*)
Prabhudas, 31
Putlibai (Mohandas's mother), 5, 6, 9,
35-6, 172, 241, 247, 252
God, *see Ishvar*
Golden Age, *see Ramraj*
Government of India, 203-5, 207-10,
212-14

Harischandra, 7
Hay, Stephen N., ix, 12
Hills, Arnold F., 12
Hind Swaraj, 27, 29, 40-2, 44, 74, 75, 85,
163, 221, 230
Humanitarian League, 12-13

idol worship, 72, 89-91
Indian National Congress, 22, 41, 82, 236,
239, 253
Indian Opinion, 23, 25, 28, 30, 36, 40, 68,
73, 161, 173
interdining, 97-103
intermarriage, 97-103, 191-2
Irwin Lord (Viceroy), 234
Isha Upanishad, 136-7, 244
Ishvar (God), 48, 52, 53, 61, 68-9, 74, 75,
83, 113, 115-16
Islam, 68

jail periods, 23, 29
Jain relativism, *see anekantavada*
Jainism, 51, 52, 67, 71, 108, 229
Jati (caste), 9, 14, 56, 85, 96-107, 191-2

Kali Temple, Calcutta, 22, 87
Kallenbach, Hermann, 31, 32, 222
Kasturbai, *see* Gandhi: Kasturbai
Kheda District, 82
Koran, 46, 81, 83
Krishna, 49, 50, 53, 54, 70, 75-6, 123, 124
Kumarappa J. C., 175

Linlithgow, Lord (Viceroy), 209
longevity, 182, 244-6

Mahabharata, 75, 139
Maitland, Edward, 34, 60-2, 63, 65, 76,
149, 150
Maniratnamala, 59
Manusmriti, 5, 9, 99
marriage, 185-92
Mehta, Raj Chandra, *see* Raychand
mercy killing, *see* euthanasia
Mirabehn, 115, 169, 209
moksha (salvation), 33, 51, 53, 54, 57-9,

61, 65, 69, 104, 241-2, 248
Muslims, 32, 85

Narsinh Mehta, 36, 242
Nature Cure, 181-2, 250
Navajivan, 83
Nayar, Dr Sushila, 194
Nehru, Jawaharlal, 1, 231
nirguna bhakti, see bhakti
non-violence, *see ahimsa*

Oldfield, Josiah, 12

Panchikarana, 12, 59
Parker, Rev. Joseph, 10
passive resistance, 37, 38-9
Phoenix Settlement , 25, 28, 30, 31, 32, 176
pinjrapole, 170, 231, 253
Polak, M. G., 27, 42, 43
poverty, 27-30
power, 120- 2, 193-8, 214-19, 234-8, 244,
255
prayer, 163-4, 176-8
Puranas, 53, 83, 140
Pyarelal, 21, 274

Rama, 6, 40, 53, 54, 57, 58, 123-4
Ramanama recitation, 6, 9, 164, 176,
179-83
Ramcharitmanas, *see* Tulsidas
Ramraj, 106, 254
Raychand, 14, 33-4, 36, 47-60, 61, 63, 64,
65, 72, 75, 76, 77, 149-50, 247, 250,
257-8
revelation, 48, 54, 61, 64, 65, 67, 104, ch.
7, 149, 249
Ruskin, John, 28, 30

Sabarmati Ashram, *see* ashrams
sacraments, *see samskaras*
sacred thread, 95
sacrifice, *see yajna*
Saddarshana Samucchaya, 51, 52, 64, 67,
72
Salt, Henry, 11, 12
Salt March, 164
Salter, William Mackintire, 34-5, 73, 241
salvation, *see moksha*
samskaras, 95
Sanger, Margaret, 187
satyagraha, 37-40, 232
Satyagraha Ashram, *see* ashrams
scripture, *see* revelation
service, 5-7, 32-7, ch. 14, 248, 252, 254
Sevagram Ashram, *see* ashrams